Designing Backtest Engines

Foundations of Reproducible Quant Simulation

Thomas V. Trex

Published by NobleTrex Press

For permissions and other inquiries, write to:
P.O. Box 3132, Framingham, MA 01701, USA

Contents

Introduction

Backtests are the laboratory of systematic investing. They are where ideas meet data, assumptions are made explicit, and claims are tempered by evidence. Yet too often, the laboratory is improvised: datasets drift, environments mutate, random seeds are forgotten, and results cannot be reproduced when it matters most. This book is a remedy. It sets out the foundations for designing backtest engines that are not only fast and featureful, but also scientifically credible, auditable, and scalable. Our premise is simple: if a result cannot be reproduced on another machine, by another researcher, on another day, it is not knowledge-it is a rumor.

We begin with reproducible research as a first-class engineering goal. The opening chapter articulates a disciplined workflow that borrows from the scientific method: hypothesis pre-registration, success metrics defined in advance, and rigorous review to guard against hindsight. Determinism is treated as an invariant, not an aspiration. You will learn how to manage pseudorandom number generators as shared resources; how to seed, partition, and checkpoint stochastic components; and how to tie every run to immutable data and code identities. Environments are pinned through containers and lockfiles, numerics are made deterministic across hardware, and continuous integration validates that small changes do not silently shift results. Experiment tracking unifies these practices into a run registry where configurations, code hashes, and data fingerprints anchor each outcome to a precise provenance.

With methodological scaffolding in place, we turn to the temporal bedrock of markets. Time in finance is irregular, exchange-bound, and full of exceptions. We show how to encode sessions and calendars, normalize timestamps across timezones and daylight transitions, and preserve nanosecond-level ordering. Core market data structures-bars, trades, quotes, and depth-are standardized with explicit units, currencies, and identifiers, then stored in formats that balance compression with reproducible access. Alignment is handled through as-of joins and lagged windows that respect causality and prevent leakage, while corporate actions are represented via adjustment factors that maintain continuity without falsifying history. Robust data quality checks catch gaps, outliers, and survivorship artifacts before they contaminate inference.

The heart of the book is the architecture of a deterministic event engine. We build clocks that respect sessions, inject latency, and schedule priorities; we design feeds that replay historical events with backpressure and recovery; and we implement the core loop that guarantees causal ordering and reproducible snapshots. Because real research scales, we discuss parallelization across cores and clusters, deterministic reductions, PRNG partitioning, and fault-tolerant checkpointing. A versioned, stable strategy API allows teams to innovate within a safe sandbox: strategies can be swapped, extended, and compared without entangling engine internals.

From architecture we move to trading mechanics. Features flow through deterministic DAGs that cache and memoize without leaking future information. Signals carry units, horizons, and decay semantics that survive handoff to sizing, portfolio construction, and execution. Orders inhabit real microstructure: spreads, depth, queues, and venue behavior. Execution models make their assumptions explicit-latency, queue priority, book selection-so that slippage is not an afterthought but a reproducible consequence of a stated world. Costs are enumerated, scheduled, and applied: commissions and fees, spreads and impact, borrow and financing. Compliance, risk, and liquidity guardrails are encoded as deterministic policies enforced at simulation time.

Accounting closes the loop. We maintain an exacting portfolio state-positions, lots, cash, and financing-capable of processing corporate actions point-in-time and attributing PnL unambiguously. Return definitions are clarified to prevent subtle aggregation errors, especially in the presence of currency effects, leverage, and settlement. Shorting and borrow dynamics are modeled with the same reproducible care as longs, acknowledging operational constraints that often decide real-world viability.

Finally, we evaluate and govern results. Validation methods-purged walk-forward splits, embargoes, and disciplined tuning-estimate out-of-sample performance while minimizing bias. We quantify uncertainty with resampling methods suited to dependent returns, and we control false discovery amid the combinatorial search typical of quant research. Performance is decomposed against benchmarks and factors; scenario and Monte Carlo engines-driven by controlled PRNG streams-stress strategies under shocks. Outputs become artifacts: metrics, attribution, dashboards, logs, and hashed bundles that support review, replication, and compliance. Governance is not decoration; it is an operating stance that ensures repeatability under pressure.

This book is for practitioners who build or rely on backtests-quant researchers, data engineers, risk managers, and technologists-who believe that speed and rigor should reinforce one another. You can read it linearly, as the construction of a complete engine, or modularly, dropping into chapters when a particular subsystem becomes your bottleneck. Throughout, our aim is to replace ad hoc convention with explicit contracts, to surface assumptions as configuration rather than code paths, and to make every result something you can bet your reputation on: precise, explainable, and reproducible.

Chapter 1

Reproducible Research Foundations

Every profitable backtest tells a story-but only reproducible backtests can be trusted. In this chapter we turn "I once got this result" into "any skilled reader can independently re-create and extend this result," by treating quant research as an engineered, fully traceable process rather than a sequence of lucky scripts.

1.1 Quant Research Workflow

Most quantitative research groups write code and run backtests all day. Far fewer treat those backtests as *experiments* in the scientific sense: planned in advance, tied to explicit hypotheses, executed under controlled conditions, and followed by structured review. This section introduces a workflow that makes that mindset concrete.

Our goal is not to slow you down with bureaucracy. It is to replace an ad-hoc sequence of notebook runs with a repeatable, hypothesis-driven process that produces results you can trust, reproduce, and explain months or years later. Later chapters will show how to support this workflow with robust data, environments, and experiment tracking; here we focus on the human and logical structure of the work.

From playing with data to running experiments

A lot of quant research begins with "playing with data": you load a dataset, plot some signals, try a few features, and quickly wire up a backtest. This kind of exploratory work is essential, especially when you are new to a market or data source. The problem is not exploration itself; it is when *all* of your work lives in this mode.

Exploratory work has characteristic patterns:

- You change parameters until the curves "look good".
- You add or remove stocks from the universe when the results disappoint you.
- You try different data cleaning choices but do not record which ones went into which run.
- You rarely write down what you planned to test before running the code.

These behaviors are understandable, but they have two consequences:

- They inflate the chance of discovering patterns that are just noise.
- They make it hard or impossible to reproduce a specific result later.

A disciplined quant research workflow does not eliminate exploration, but it wraps it in a structure inspired by the scientific method:

- Formulate a precise hypothesis.
- Derive testable predictions from that hypothesis.
- Define in advance how you will decide whether the hypothesis "passed" or "failed".
- Design a backtest or set of backtests that implement this test.

- Run the experiments under controlled, reproducible conditions.
- Review the results in a structured way and decide what to do next.

Backtests are the laboratory of systematic trading. The rest of this section explains how to treat each backtest as a proper experiment: what you declare upfront, what you log, and how you iterate.

Formulating precise, falsifiable hypotheses

The starting point of a disciplined workflow is a hypothesis that is specific enough to be tested and potentially falsified. In research conversations, one often hears ideas like:

> "Momentum works better in small caps."

That is an intuition, not yet a testable hypothesis. To make it useful, you need to pin down several dimensions:

- **Universe:** What exactly do you mean by "small caps"? Which exchange, which region?
- **Signal definition:** How precisely is "momentum" measured?
- **Time frame:** Over which historical period is the statement meant to apply?
- **Portfolio formation rules:** How is the signal turned into positions?
- **Benchmark and constraints:** Compared to what? Under what risk or liquidity constraints?

A sharper version might read:

> "Between January 2010 and December 2022, a monthly-long-only strategy that buys the top 20% of U.S. common stocks by 12-month, skip-1-month momentum (measured as close-to-close total return) and holds them for one

> month, equal-weighted and rebalanced monthly, will outperform an otherwise identical strategy on the full U.S. universe by at least 1% annualized net of estimated transaction costs."

This is verbose, but now you have something concrete:

- A defined time period.
- A defined universe.
- A well-specified signal and rebalance rule.
- A clear comparison (small-cap subset vs full universe).
- A quantitative success threshold (1% annualized).

Most good hypotheses have this character: they are *falsifiable*. That is, you can run a reasonably designed backtest and obtain a result that clearly contradicts them.

In practice, you may not know enough to be that specific at the outset. You may start with a looser idea, then refine it as you learn the data. Even so, the discipline of turning vague beliefs into structured, testable statements will significantly improve the quality of your research.

From hypothesis to testable predictions

Once you have a hypothesis, you need to translate it into predictions that a backtest can check. Backtests cannot directly tell you if a story about markets is "true" in some philosophical sense; they can tell you if the data behave in ways your story implies.

There are several categories of predictions to think about:

Performance predictions.

These are the most obvious: expected ranges for performance metrics such as annualized return, volatility, Sharpe ratio, or maximum drawdown. For example:

- "If the hypothesis holds, the in-sample Sharpe ratio will be at least 0.8."
- "Under realistic transaction costs, the strategy will still have a positive net return."

Behavioral predictions.

These describe how the strategy behaves through time:

- "Drawdowns will tend to coincide with sharp market reversals rather than slow trends."
- "Turnover will stay below 20% per month on average."
- "The strategy's capacity will exceed 50 million USD under our impact model."

These are important because a strategy that looks good on aggregate metrics but behaves erratically day-to-day may be untradeable.

Robustness predictions.

Robust hypotheses generate patterns that are not overly sensitive to arbitrary choices:

- "If we vary the lookback from 9 to 15 months, the effect persists."
- "The signal works similarly on mid caps, though with lower capacity."
- "The main conclusions do not depend on including or excluding the financial crisis years."

Each prediction suggests a concrete test: a particular backtest variant, a parameter sweep, or a cross-sectional robustness check.

Pre-declaring goals and success criteria

A common failure mode in quant research is to adapt your criteria *after* you see the results. You start out wanting "a Sharpe ratio above 1," but when the backtest comes in at 0.7 you tell yourself "maybe 0.7 is good enough in this universe." Or you decide that a strategy is "acceptable" only if it beats your best idea to date, ensuring that merely solid but diversifying strategies are discarded.

To fight this drift, you should write down, *before* running a serious experiment, what would count as:

- **Success:** The hypothesis is supported strongly enough to justify further development or production testing.
- **Partial success:** The idea is not strong enough on its own but may be worth combining with other signals or modifying.
- **Failure:** The hypothesis is not supported and should be abandoned or rethought.

Success criteria should be aligned with your actual trading goals, not just a single in-sample performance number. For example:

- "In-sample Sharpe ratio above 0.8, with maximum drawdown less than 25%, and a worst calendar year better than the market by at least 5%."
- "Capacity above 100 million USD with net return positive after impact; turnover below 100% per month."
- "At least 80% of rolling 3-year windows show positive alpha relative to our benchmark."

You may not always meet every criterion. The important thing is to have them documented and to use them as a reference when interpreting results. This keeps you honest and reduces the temptation to retroactively adjust your standards until everything looks attractive.

Pre-registration for trading experiments

In some scientific fields, researchers publicly "pre-register" their experiments: they write down hypotheses, methods, and success criteria before looking at the data. The goal is to reduce "p-hacking," where analysts unconsciously search through combinations of variables and specifications until they find something that looks significant by chance.

In quant research, you rarely publish pre-registrations outside the firm, but the concept is still useful internally. A lightweight pre-registration for a trading experiment can be as simple as a short document or ticket that includes:

- The hypothesis in specific, testable form.
- The data you will use (universe, date range, data fields).
- The backtest design (entry/exit rules, position sizing, constraints).
- The metrics you will compute and your success criteria.
- Any planned robustness checks or out-of-sample tests.

You do not need to do this for every tiny exploration, but once an idea seems promising enough that you are about to run large sweeps or extended backtests, it is worth pausing to capture this information. Pre-registration:

- Clarifies your thinking before you invest significant time.
- Provides context for colleagues reviewing your results.
- Helps you avoid unconscious cherry-picking of definitions or time periods.

Later chapters on experiment tracking will show how to link these pre-registration documents directly to backtest runs in your experiment registry.

Backtests as controlled experiments

With a pre-registered plan, running a backtest becomes more than "press Run in the notebook." It becomes a controlled experiment where you manage several degrees of freedom:

Data boundaries.

You commit to a specific dataset snapshot, with a clear end date and known corrections. You decide in advance which instruments, what lookback, and which corporate-action-adjusted prices you will use.

Model boundaries.

You specify which model components are allowed to vary and which are held constant. For example, you may decide that for this sweep you will only vary the momentum lookback, leaving the volatility scaling and position constraints unchanged.

Randomness.

If your backtest involves random elements (for example, Monte Carlo scenario generation or stochastic execution models), you decide how randomness will be controlled and documented so that the experiment is repeatable. Later sections will discuss deterministic pseudorandom number generation in depth.

Evaluation protocol.

You decide how you will split data into training and testing periods, how you will avoid leaking future information, and how you will treat outliers or missing data.

Thinking in these terms forces you to separate the *experiment* from the *production system*. In an experiment, you may deliberately simplify some components to isolate the effect of the idea under test. You are not trying to build the ultimate live-trading stack; you are trying to fairly test one hypothesis.

Defining metrics aligned with production reality

Many early-stage strategy evaluations focus almost exclusively on a single number like Sharpe ratio. While this is a useful summary, it is not sufficient to decide if a strategy is production-worthy. Your workflow should encourage you to define and track metrics along several dimensions:

Return and risk.

- Annualized return and volatility.

- Maximum and average drawdown.
- Tail behavior (e.g., the distribution of worst days or weeks).

Liquidity and capacity.

- Turnover: how much of the portfolio changes each period.
- Average and peak daily traded volume as a fraction of market volume.
- Estimated impact costs and how performance changes with assumed capital.

Operational behavior.

- Number and frequency of trades.
- Concentration of positions (e.g., top-10 holdings as a fraction of capital).
- Sensitivity to data issues and corporate events.

Stability and robustness.

- Performance in different market regimes.
- Rolling-window performance metrics.
- Sensitivity to parameter choices.

Before running the experiment, decide which metrics matter for your use case and define thresholds or qualitative expectations. For a high-capacity institutional strategy, capacity and impact costs might be more important than squeezing out an incremental Sharpe improvement. For a niche relative-value strategy, stable behavior and low correlation to existing books might dominate.

Separating exploratory and confirmatory phases

A practical workflow distinguishes clearly between two modes:

- **Exploratory analysis** is where you generate ideas, inspect data, try many parameter combinations, and get a feel for how things behave.
- **Confirmatory testing** is where you commit to a specific design and evaluate it under predefined rules.

Both are necessary, but they should not be mixed. If you treat exploratory tinkering as if it were confirmatory testing, you will underestimate uncertainty and overstate your confidence. If you avoid confirmatory testing altogether, your work will remain a collection of anecdotes and eye-catching plots.

Here is a simple way to enforce the distinction:

- Use scratch notebooks or a separate directory for exploratory work. Do not rely on their results for production decisions.
- Once an idea looks promising, write a concise pre-registration (even if informal) and move to a more structured environment for confirmatory backtests.
- In your experiment tracking system, tag runs as "exploratory" or "confirmatory" and treat their results differently in reviews.

This discipline mirrors the "training vs. test set" separation in machine learning, but extended to the entire research workflow.

Reviewing results: structured post-mortems

After a backtest finishes, the temptation is to glance at the summary statistics, declare victory or defeat, and move on. This wastes much of the information the experiment generated. A better approach is to conduct a brief, structured post-mortem, even when the idea "fails."

A simple template might include:

Restate the hypothesis.

Write down in one or two sentences what you were testing. This helps later readers (including your future self) connect results to intent.

Summarize key metrics.

Record the essential metrics you defined beforehand: performance, risk, capacity, robustness checks. Resist the urge to add new metrics just because they paint a nicer picture.

Compare to success criteria.

Explicitly state whether each criterion was met, partially met, or missed. This forces you to confront the pre-declared standards.

Diagnose failure modes.

If the results were disappointing, ask why. Did the signal show up only in a narrow period? Was the performance driven by a handful of outlier trades? Did transaction costs wipe out the theoretical edge? These insights are valuable, even if the idea does not move forward.

Decide next actions.

Conclude with a clear decision:

- "Abandon the idea; no further work planned."
- "Modify the hypothesis to focus on a subset of the universe and re-test."
- "Promote to a broader research campaign, including combining with other signals."

Documenting this review—even in a few paragraphs—turns each backtest into a learning artifact that your team can revisit and build on.

Maintaining a research log

At the scale of a single project, it is easy to remember what you tried. At the scale of a year's work across several ideas, it is not. A research log is a lightweight way to preserve context and prevent you from repeating the same dead ends.

A simple log might contain, for each idea or experiment:

- A short name and description of the idea.
- Dates when you worked on it.
- Links to pre-registrations, backtest runs, and post-mortems.
- A current status: "active", "abandoned", "implemented", "waiting for more data".

Over time, the log becomes a map of your research landscape. It shows which themes you have explored heavily, where you have unexplained gaps, and which old ideas might be worth revisiting with new data or methods.

Later in this book, when we discuss experiment tracking systems, we will see how to make much of this automatic. For now, even a manually maintained document or spreadsheet can dramatically improve your ability to reason about your body of work.

Closing the loop: from experiments to production and back

The final piece of a disciplined workflow is the feedback loop between research and live trading. A strategy does not stop being an experiment when it goes into production; it moves from historical backtests to real-time testing under new conditions.

Your workflow should therefore anticipate questions like:

- Which backtests supported the decision to launch this strategy?
- How do live results compare to backtested expectations?
- When live performance deviates, how will you diagnose whether the hypothesis has broken or the environment has changed?

If you treat backtests as fully specified experiments, tied to particular data, environments, configurations, and hypotheses, you can later revisit them in light of live outcomes. Did the stress scenarios you tested materialize? Did the regime shifts you worried about actually hurt you? These are not vague reflections; they are concrete comparisons between historical experiments and realized behavior.

In the chapters that follow, we will connect this conceptual workflow to the technical machinery that makes it reproducible in practice: deterministic pseudorandomness, versioned data, controlled environments, and experiment tracking. Together, these will allow you to run backtests as real experiments—and to build trading systems on evidence you can trust.

1.2 Determinism & Pseudorandomness

In the previous section we treated backtests as scientific experiments: ideas become hypotheses, hypotheses become pre-declared experiments, and results are reviewed systematically. To make that workflow meaningful, it must rest on runs that are *reproducible*. If you cannot re-run a backtest and obtain the *same* numbers, you cannot reliably test hypotheses, debug issues, or explain results.

This section focuses on one of the most important and subtle foundations of reproducible simulation: determinism in the presence of randomness. Modern backtest engines rely heavily on random draws: for Monte Carlo scenario generation, for bootstrapping samples, for randomized cross-validation folds, and for stochastic execution or slippage models. We will see how to control these sources of randomness so that:

- A given experiment, when re-run with the same inputs, produces *bit-wise* identical outputs.
- Random behavior can be structured into well-defined, independent streams.
- Parallel hardware and numerical libraries do not silently introduce non-deterministic variation.

The goal is not to remove randomness, but to *discipline* it.

Randomness vs. pseudorandomness

It is useful to begin with a clear conceptual distinction.

True randomness.

This is randomness derived from inherently unpredictable physical processes: radioactive decay, thermal noise, hardware randomness sources, or external data such as network jitter. True random sources are difficult to reproduce exactly, because by design they are not meant to be predictable.

Pseudorandomness.

Pseudorandom number generators (PRNGs) are deterministic algorithms that produce sequences of numbers that *look* random but are fully determined by an initial state called the *seed*. If you know the algorithm and the seed, you can reproduce the same sequence exactly, as many times as you like.

For backtesting, pseudorandomness is far more useful than true randomness. We want sequences that are statistically similar to draws from some probability distribution, but we also want to re-run the same experiment with the same configuration and get the same "random" draws. PRNGs give us exactly that.

Why determinism matters in quant simulation

At first glance, it might seem sufficient that repeated runs "roughly agree." If multiple runs with different random seeds give you similar Sharpe ratios, is that not enough? In practice, approximate agreement is often *not* enough, for several reasons:

Debugging and investigation.

When a simulation produces a surprising result, you need to trace it back: which trades caused that spike in turnover, which Monte Carlo paths produced that tail loss, which orders were routed in that unexpected way? If every re-run gives you *different* trades and paths, even under the same configuration, debugging becomes guesswork.

Scientific integrity.

In a hypothesis-driven workflow, you want to separate randomness-induced variation from model changes. When you change the strategy logic or risk model, you want to attribute any change in outcomes to that change alone, not to different random draws. Bit-wise reproducibility supports this clean comparison.

Auditability and trust.

Risk managers, senior PMs, and future-you will sometimes need to revisit a historical backtest. If you can re-run the experiment years later, on a new machine, and match the original results exactly, confidence in your process goes up. If each re-run yields slightly different outcomes, trust erodes.

Regression testing.

Once you build an experiment suite that acts as a test harness for your engine and models, you will want to detect regressions: unintended changes in behavior caused by code or dependency updates. Bit-wise determinism is a powerful guardrail here: any difference in outputs indicates a real change in code, data, environment, or random structure.

For all these reasons, a rigorous backtest engine aims for deterministic simulations wherever feasible.

The life of a random number in a backtest

Before we talk about discipline and control, it helps to picture a random number's journey through your simulation:

1. Somewhere in your engine, a component requests a random draw, often from a standard distribution (uniform, normal, etc.).
2. The PRNG algorithm advances its internal state and produces a number.
3. That number feeds into a model: for example, it perturbs an execution price in a slippage model or selects a resampled path in a scenario generator.
4. The result of this model affects trades, positions, cash flows, returns, and ultimately all your summary metrics.

If you change *anything* about this flow—the PRNG algorithm, its seed, the number of draws requested before a given draw, the order of operations, or the way threads interleave requests—you will typically change the entire downstream trajectory. A deterministic engine is one that pins down all of these degrees of freedom.

Seed discipline: one seed, many streams

The foundation of reproducible randomness is seed discipline: explicit and structured management of seeds.

A seed is just a number (or sometimes a small vector of numbers) used to initialize a PRNG's internal state. But how you choose and organize these seeds across the engine matters a great deal.

A naive setup might:

- Rely on library defaults that seed from the system clock.
- Use a single global PRNG instance shared across all components.
- Let components call random draws whenever they need them without coordination.

This leads to hidden coupling. For example, if you add a new random draw in the execution model, you may inadvertently shift the sequence of draws used by the scenario generator, changing its behavior even though you did not touch that code.

A more disciplined pattern is:

Master seed.

Each experiment or backtest run is initialized with a single *master seed.* This seed is part of the experiment configuration and is logged alongside other metadata such as data snapshot and code version.

Derived stream seeds.

From the master seed, you derive separate seeds for each logical PRNG *stream* in your simulation. For example:

- One stream for the strategy's random choices (e.g., randomized tie-breaking or sampling).

- One stream for scenario generation (e.g., Monte Carlo paths or bootstrapped return blocks).
- One stream for the execution or slippage model.
- Possibly per-asset or per-instrument streams if your execution model uses randomization at that granularity.

The derivation can be a simple, deterministic transformation (for example, combining the master seed with a component identifier). The important thing is that for a given experiment ID, you always derive the *same* stream seeds.

No hidden global state.

Each component receives its own PRNG object, initialized with its own seed, and does not share it with others. Components never reach into a process-wide global PRNG. This keeps their random behavior isolated: changing one component cannot accidentally perturb another's draws.

Controlled access points.

Random draws are requested only through clearly identified methods or interfaces. This makes it easier to audit and test the random structure of your experiment.

This is what we mean by *PRNG stream discipline*: a planned, documented structure for where randomness enters the system.

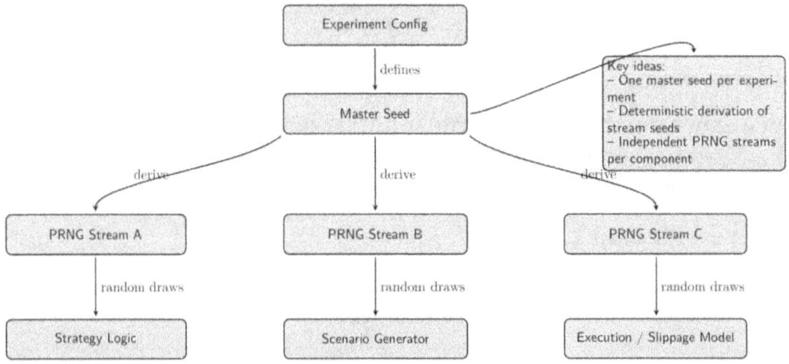

Checkpointable stochastic components

In realistic research, backtests can be long-running. You may want to pause a run, resume later, or replay a small part of it to analyze a particular episode in detail. For deterministic behavior, this implies that stochastic components should be *checkpointable*: their internal state, including PRNG state, can be saved and restored.

Checkpointability requires:

- Each component exposes a way to capture its current state, including the state of its PRNG stream(s) and any internal counters.
- The captured state can be restored later, leading the component to produce exactly the same outputs for the same sequence of inputs.

For example, if your execution model simulates fills over multiple time steps using random draws:

- You should be able to pause at the end of day 50, checkpoint the state.
- Later, restore from that checkpoint and simulate days 51–100.
- The paths of fills, slippage, and resulting trades on days 51–100 should match exactly what you would have obtained if you had run days 1–100 in one go.

This capability is valuable not only for efficiency (you can skip re-simulating earlier days) but also for debugging: you can "zoom in" on problem regions without losing consistency.

Parallelism and non-determinism

Modern research environments commonly exploit parallelism: multi-core CPUs, GPUs, distributed clusters. Unfortunately, naive parallelism often breaks determinism in subtle ways.

Race conditions and ordering.

When multiple threads request random draws from the same PRNG without coordination, the order in which they consume numbers depends on thread scheduling, which is typically non-deterministic. Even if each thread gets the "right number of draws on average," the exact sequence can change between runs.

Non-deterministic reductions.

Many numerical libraries perform operations like summation or reduction in parallel. Floating-point addition is not perfectly associative; changing the order of additions changes the rounded result at the last few bits. If a library changes how it partitions work across cores, or if thread scheduling varies, you may see small numeric differences between runs.

Hardware-specific math.

Different CPU architectures and instruction sets (for example, AVX vs. SSE, or different GPU generations) may implement math operations and approximations differently, leading to small discrepancies even for the same source code.

These effects can accumulate. A tiny change in a random draw or rounding at some early step can propagate into different trading decisions later, especially in highly path-dependent models.

To manage this, you can adopt several patterns:

Per-thread or per-task PRNG streams.

Instead of sharing a global PRNG, assign each worker its own independent PRNG stream with a carefully derived seed. Ensure that the partitioning of work across workers is deterministic: given the same configuration, the same tasks are assigned to the same worker IDs, and thus consume the same sequences of random numbers.

Deterministic scheduling.

Where feasible, structure your computation so that the order of operations does not depend on timing or hardware quirks. For example, if you parallelize over securities, always process securities in a fixed order, and ensure that each security is always handled by the same worker index for a given configuration.

Controlled numerical libraries.

Some BLAS or linear algebra libraries offer options to trade off performance for determinism, such as fixing the number of threads or turning off certain dynamic scheduling features. In a research environment, it is often worth accepting a modest speed penalty in exchange for reproducible results.

Tolerance-aware comparisons.

Even with best efforts, a few operations (especially on GPUs) may remain slightly non-deterministic at the last bit. In such cases, regression tests and comparisons should incorporate well-justified tolerances. However, for the parts of the backtest that drive decisions—like order generation and trade simulation—you should strive for exact determinism.

Testing for determinism

Determinism is not something you obtain once and forget. It is something you *test* for and enforce over time, much like you test for correctness. A few simple tests can go a long way:

Repeat-run test.

Given a fixed experiment configuration (code version, data snapshot, environment, random seeds):

- Run the backtest twice in succession.
- Compare the outputs: full time series of positions, trades, P&L, and summary metrics.

If anything differs, you have a determinism bug. Often the differences will be small at first, but if you do not address them, they can hide serious reproducibility problems.

Partial-run consistency test.

Run the backtest over the full period and save a checkpoint at some intermediate time (e.g., after one year). Then:

- Run again from the beginning to that checkpoint; save the state.

- Restore from the checkpoint and continue to the end.
- Compare the resulting outputs for the second half of the period with those from the uninterrupted full run.

Any deviation indicates that checkpointing is not fully capturing component state, often including PRNG state.

Cross-hardware test.

Run the same experiment configuration on two machines with nominally identical environments (same OS, same library versions, same code). Compare outputs. If they differ, investigate whether the cause is hardware-specific math, library behavior, or hidden dependence on machine-local state.

These tests can be integrated into your continuous integration (CI) or nightly test suite. They become part of the safety net that protects the integrity of your research platform.

Documenting the random structure of experiments

In the prior section on workflow, we emphasized pre-registration and logging of hypotheses, data, and metrics. For stochastic simulations, you should also document the *random structure* of experiments:

- The master seed used for the experiment.
- The scheme for deriving stream seeds (for example, hash of experiment ID and component name).
- The mapping from components to PRNG streams.
- Any important randomization choices (e.g., "execution model samples from normal distribution with this volatility; scenario generator uses block bootstrap with block size 20 days").

This documentation makes it possible for another researcher (or an audit process) to reconstruct not only the final outputs but the entire stochastic trajectory. It also provides a stable reference when you later decide to intentionally *change* random structure, for example to adopt a better PRNG algorithm.

Choosing and evolving PRNG algorithms

While this chapter is not about the detailed mathematics of PRNG design, a few high-level points are important for system designers:

Quality and period.

Not all PRNGs are created equal. Some have small periods (the sequence repeats quickly) or undesirable correlations. For serious simulation, use well-studied algorithms with long periods and good statistical properties, rather than legacy or ad-hoc generators.

Reproducibility vs. improvement.

Once you choose a PRNG algorithm and seeding scheme, they become part of your experiment definition. If you later upgrade to a better generator, you should treat that as a versioned change:

- Old experiments remain tied to the old PRNG version; their results remain reproducible.
- New experiments may opt into the new PRNG version; their behavior will differ, but in a controlled, documented way.

Library abstractions.

Many numerical and simulation libraries provide their own random facilities. Whenever possible, you should wrap or centralize these through your own PRNG abstraction, so that you retain control over seeds, streams, and algorithms. If different parts of your stack rely on different random systems, managing determinism becomes harder.

Putting it all together

By combining:

- Clear separation of true randomness from controllable pseudo-randomness.

- Strict seed discipline with a master seed and derived streams.
- Independent PRNG streams per component, with no hidden global state.
- Checkpointable stochastic components.
- Careful handling of parallelism, numerical libraries, and hardware.
- Regular tests for determinism and thorough documentation of random structure.

you can build a backtest engine where randomness is a first-class, controlled aspect of experiment design rather than a source of mysterious, shifting behavior.

In such an engine, when you say "run experiment X again," you mean precisely that: the same inputs, the same configuration, the same random draws, and the same outputs, bit for bit. This is the level of determinism that supports meaningful comparison of hypotheses, reliable debugging, and credible communication of results to stakeholders.

In the next sections, we will extend this foundation beyond randomness: we will see how to tie every experiment to a specific, versioned view of the data, and to a well-defined software environment. Together, determinism in randomness, data, and environment will allow your quant research workflow to be not only disciplined in concept but also reproducible in practice.

1.3 Data Versioning & Lineage

In the previous sections we treated backtests as scientific experiments, and we saw how to make their stochastic parts deterministic. We now turn to a quieter but equally fundamental question: *what exactly did we feed into the backtest?*

If you cannot say which prices, corporate actions, fundamentals, or alternative data were used for a given run, and how those raw feeds were cleaned and transformed, you do not really know what you tested.

Worse, you will struggle to reproduce or audit results, especially as vendors reissue data and your own preprocessing code evolves.

This section introduces two core ideas:

- **Immutable dataset snapshots:** frozen views of your data that never change once created.
- **Data lineage:** a traceable record of how data flowed from raw sources through transformations into those snapshots.

Together, these make it possible to rerun a five-year-old backtest and get the same answers, and to explain precisely *which* bits produced those answers.

Why “today’s database” is not a reference

Many research groups begin with a single shared database or data lake that is constantly updated. Backtests simply query “the database,” perhaps with a date filter. This seems convenient: you always get the freshest corrections, new instruments appear automatically, and storage is centralized.

However, using a live, mutable database as your only data reference has several serious problems:

Invisible corrections.

Vendors routinely correct historical data. A split factor might be fixed, stale quotes might be removed, survivorship-bias issues might be addressed. If your backtest quietly picks up these changes, results computed last year cannot be reproduced today, even with identical code and configuration.

Schema drift.

Over time, you will evolve your own data schemas: you might change field names, add new fields, or switch data types. Old backtest code written against the old schema may misbehave or silently cast values in unexpected ways.

Ambiguous provenance.

If multiple feeds are merged into a single table (for example, using mid-quote prices when available and trades otherwise), it can become unclear which vendor or source contributed what. This complicates debugging and vendor comparisons.

Regulatory and audit requirements.

If you are subject to regulatory scrutiny or internal model review, you may need to demonstrate exactly what data underpinned a strategy decision. A pointer to "whatever was in the database at the time" is often insufficient.

To avoid these pitfalls, you should treat the live database as a *staging area*, not as the final reference for experiments. Your backtests should rely on *versioned snapshots* that are deliberately created, documented, and immutable.

Immutable dataset snapshots

An immutable dataset snapshot is a self-contained, read-only collection of data files and metadata that represents a specific view of the world at a point in time. Once created, it never changes. If corrections or updates are needed, you create a *new* snapshot rather than altering the old one.

Conceptually, you can think of a snapshot as:

> "U.S. equities daily bars, corporate actions, and reference data, as of vendor files downloaded on 2024-06-30, cleaned and adjusted by pipeline version 1.3.4, stored in this directory, with this checksum."

A snapshot has several important properties:

Identity.

It has a unique identifier (for example, a version string or a hash) that you can record in experiments. This ID is stable: if you recreate the snapshot with the same inputs and transformation code, you get the same bits.

Immutability.

The underlying files are treated as read-only. Your processes may read them, index them, or derive new snapshots from them, but they do not modify them in place.

Completeness.

Everything needed to interpret the data is either contained within the snapshot or recorded as referenced metadata: schemas, calendars, and mappings.

Traceability.

The snapshot knows where it came from: which raw feeds, which transformation steps, and which code versions produced it. This is the lineage side, which we will discuss shortly.

With immutable snapshots, the phrase "backtest X used dataset Y" has precise meaning. If you keep the snapshot around, you can always reproduce the data side of the experiment.

Schema versioning and logical dataset names

In practice, you will maintain many datasets: prices, corporate actions, fundamentals, risk factors, alternative data, and internal features. Each family of data should have a *logical name* and its own versioning scheme.

For example:

- us_equities_daily_bars_v2
- global_fx_intraday_bars_v1
- corp_actions_global_v3
- fundamentals_worldscope_v1

The logical name and version speak to the *schema*: field names, units, and general structure. Within a schema version, you may have multiple *snapshots* over time, for example:

- us_equities_daily_bars_v2 / snapshot_2024_06_30

- us_equities_daily_bars_v2 / snapshot_2024_09_30

The schema version tells you that code expecting v2 fields can safely read both snapshots. The snapshot identifier tells you which particular cut of time and corrections you are using. This separation allows you to evolve schemas in a controlled way without mixing them up with time-based data updates.

Content hashing and manifests

To guarantee that a snapshot can be checked for integrity and referenced unambiguously, you should assign it a *content hash*. A content hash is a fingerprint computed from the actual bytes of the data files (and sometimes from metadata), using a cryptographic hash function. If any bit changes, the hash changes.

Practically, you can organize this as follows:

Per-file hashes.

Each physical file in the snapshot (for example, a partitioned Parquet file for a particular date or symbol) has an associated hash stored in metadata. When you read or move the snapshot, you can verify that each file matches its expected hash.

Snapshot hash.

You compute a higher-level hash that summarizes the whole snapshot, often by hashing the concatenation of per-file hashes plus some schema and configuration metadata. This gives you a single value that uniquely identifies the snapshot content.

Manifest file.

You store a manifest, typically a structured metadata file, that lists:

- Logical dataset name and schema version.
- Snapshot identifier (for example, date and hash).
- List of all included files and their hashes.
- Pointers to raw inputs and transformation steps (for lineage).

The manifest is the "ledger" of the snapshot. When an experiment says "I used snapshot us_equities_daily_bars_v2 / snapshot_2024_06_30 (hash H)," another researcher can go to that manifest, retrieve the files, verify hashes, and be certain they have exactly the same data.

What is data lineage?

If snapshots answer "what data did we use?", data lineage answers "how did that data come to be?" Lineage is the record of transformations and dependencies that connect:

- Raw vendor feeds and source files.
- Intermediate cleaned and normalized datasets.
- Final research-ready snapshots and derived features.

You can imagine a directed acyclic graph (DAG) where:

- Leaves are raw inputs: vendor price files, exchange calendars, corporate actions feeds, fundamentals, alternative data, etc.
- Interior nodes are transformation steps: parsing, validation, adjustment, alignment, feature engineering.
- Roots are final outputs: the versioned snapshots you use in backtests.

Lineage allows you to answer questions like:

- "Which raw files contributed to the price for stock X on 2018-03-15 in this snapshot?"
- "Which version of the corporate actions adjustment code produced these adjusted prices?"
- "If we discover a bug in our split-handling logic, which snapshots and experiments are affected?"

Without lineage, you may know *what* data you had, but not *why* it looks the way it does.

Capturing transformation steps

In most shops, data flows through a series of transformations before reaching the backtester. Typical steps include:

- Parsing and validating raw vendor formats.
- Standardizing field names and units.
- Handling missing or erroneous values.
- Adjusting for corporate actions (splits, dividends, mergers).
- Aligning calendars and time zones.
- Merging multiple sources (for example, combining trades and quotes, or primary and secondary vendors).
- Computing derived fields and features.

Each of these steps should be:

Explicit.

The operation is implemented in code or configuration that is under version control, not as an ad-hoc manual Excel operation or one-off script that no one remembers.

Versioned.

The version (for example, a commit hash or release tag) of the transformation code used to produce a given snapshot is recorded in the snapshot's manifest. If you later improve your corporate action handling, that becomes a new version; old snapshots remain linked to the old version.

Parameterized.

Key parameters (for example, outlier thresholds, adjustment rules, or vendor priority settings) are captured in configuration files whose versions are also recorded.

Logged.

When the pipeline runs, it logs which raw files were processed, which intermediate datasets were produced, and any warnings or anomalies encountered.

The combination of code version, configuration, and raw inputs defines a transformation step. Lineage links these steps to the resulting datasets.

Embedding provenance in data formats

Many modern columnar formats, such as Parquet, ORC, or others used in analytics systems, allow you to attach custom metadata to files or columns. You can leverage this to embed provenance information directly in the data:

- Dataset name and snapshot ID.
- Schema version.
- Transformation code version (e.g., git commit).
- Creation timestamp and pipeline run ID.
- Source vendor identifiers.

Embedding this information has several advantages:

- If a file is copied or moved, it still carries its identity and provenance.
- Tools can inspect metadata to route files correctly without external catalogs.
- Debugging becomes easier: when you inspect a random file on disk, you can see at a glance which pipeline produced it.

These embedded tags complement, but do not replace, the external manifest. Together they form a robust system for tying data to its origins.

Managing corrections and reissues

Even with the best design, your data will evolve. Vendors will send corrected histories; you will discover bugs in your own transformation logic; corporate events will be restated. The challenge is to incorporate these corrections without corrupting old experiments.

A principled approach looks like this:

Never modify old snapshots in place.

If new vendor data or new logic leads to different outputs, create a *new* snapshot with a new identifier and hash. Old snapshots remain frozen, available for reproducing past experiments.

Record change reasons.

When you create a new snapshot that supersedes a previous one, record why: for example, "vendor reissue including corrections to split factors in 2015–2017," or "bug fix in dividend handling (pipeline v1.3.5)." This context will be invaluable when you compare results.

Impact analysis via lineage.

Because you have lineage from raw feeds through transformations to snapshots, you can analyze which experiments used affected snapshots. You may decide to re-run key backtests on the updated data or to annotate existing results with caveats.

Coexistence of old and new.

It is acceptable, and often desirable, to have multiple snapshots "live" at once: one used by older experiments that you want to preserve exactly, and another used for new research that benefits from corrections. The critical part is that your experiment tracking (discussed later in the chapter) records which snapshot each run used.

Connecting experiments to data snapshots

From the perspective of the experiment workflow, every backtest configuration should explicitly reference:

- The logical dataset(s) used (for example, us_equities_daily_bars_v2 and corp_actions_global_v3).

- The specific snapshot IDs for each dataset (for example, snapshot_2024_06_30).
- Optionally, the snapshot hashes for stronger integrity guarantees.

This transforms an otherwise vague statement like:

> "We tested the strategy on U.S. equities from 2010 to 2022."

into a precise experimental condition:

> "We tested the strategy on us_equities_daily_bars_v2 / snapshot_2024_06_30 for dates 2010-01-01 to 2022-12-31, with corporate actions from corp_actions_global_v3 / snapshot_2024_06_30."

If at some later date you wish to "redo the experiment with updated data," you intentionally change the snapshot IDs in the configuration and note that this is a variant. You now have a controlled comparison between the old and new data worlds.

Lineage as a directed acyclic graph

We can now pull together the ideas of immutable snapshots and lineage into a unified visual model: a directed acyclic graph (DAG) that captures the flow from raw sources through transformations to versioned research datasets.

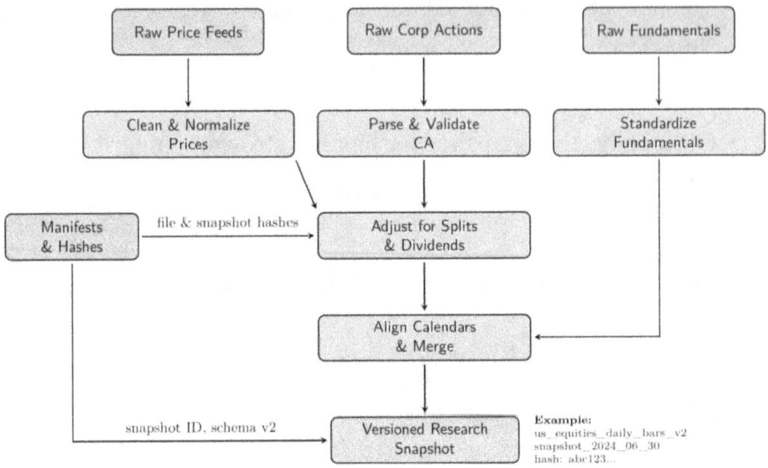

This diagram is intentionally simplified, but it captures the main ideas:

- Multiple raw sources feed into successive transformation stages.
- Intermediate datasets are produced and can be versioned if needed.
- Manifests and hashes attach to important nodes, giving each stage an identity.
- The final research snapshot is just one node in this graph, with clear ancestry.

Working with multiple derived datasets

In real research, you rarely use just one dataset. You may combine:

- Price and volume bars.
- Corporate actions.
- Fundamental factors.

- Volatility surfaces or risk model exposures.
- Alternative data (web activity, satellite data, etc.).

Each of these should follow the same discipline: versioned schemas, immutable snapshots, and recorded lineage. An experiment's configuration then becomes a structured list of dataset-snapshot pairs. This makes it clear that a change in any one of them (for example, migrating to a new vendor for fundamentals) produces a *different* experimental condition.

Practical trade-offs and storage concerns

A common worry is storage: does keeping old snapshots around not explode disk usage? In practice, several mitigations help:

Incremental storage.

If you use storage systems that support deduplication or copy-on-write semantics, multiple snapshots that differ only slightly (for example, a few corrected files) will share most of their bytes. Even simple file systems benefit from careful partitioning and reuse of unchanged files.

Selective retention.

Not every intermediate dataset needs to be kept forever. You may decide to retain only key research snapshots and the raw vendor archives, confident that you can reproduce intermediates if needed.

Compression and columnar formats.

Using compressed columnar formats can significantly reduce space while preserving performance. This is standard practice in modern analytics environments.

These trade-offs are manageable, especially when weighed against the cost of *not* being able to reproduce or understand critical backtests.

From data foundations to full experiment reproducibility

Data versioning and lineage complete the picture started earlier in the chapter:

- Hypothesis-driven workflow defines *what* you are testing.
- Deterministic pseudorandomness controls the stochastic aspects of *how* you test.
- Versioned data with clear lineage defines *what world* you tested in.

When every experiment records not just its code version and random seeds, but also explicit dataset snapshot IDs and hashes, you achieve a powerful guarantee: a future researcher can recreate the exact conditions of the test — code, data, randomness — and either replicate or thoughtfully extend your work.

In the next sections, we will see how to lock down the remaining moving parts — software environments, dependencies, and run configurations — and how to connect all of these pieces in an experiment tracking system. At that point, your backtest engine will no longer be a black box taking in "whatever the current data is," but a carefully instrumented laboratory where every result can be traced back to its precise inputs.

1.4 Environment & Dependency Management

By this point in the chapter, we have treated backtests as scientific experiments, controlled their randomness, and tied them to precise, immutable data snapshots. There is one major moving part left: the *software and hardware environment* in which your code runs.

Two researchers can use the same strategy code, the same random seeds, and the same dataset snapshot, yet still get different results if their environments differ. One may have a newer numerical library, a different BLAS backend, a GPU with a different driver, or a subtly different compiler flag. These differences can change floating-point behavior, algorithm choices, and even default parameters inside dependencies.

This section explains how to reason about environments, how to lock them down so that code executes identically across machines and over time, and how to document them so they can be recreated years later.

What is a research environment?

A research environment is more than a programming language version. It is the full stack on which your backtest engine depends. At a minimum, this includes:

- **Operating system and kernel:** for example, a specific Linux distribution and kernel version, or a particular version of macOS or Windows.
- **Language runtimes:** versions of Python, Java, C#, or any other language you use, plus their standard libraries.
- **Numerical and math libraries:** BLAS, LAPACK, FFT libraries, linear algebra packages, and any GPU-accelerated libraries such as CUDA-based stacks.
- **Third-party libraries:** data processing frameworks, backtesting frameworks, optimization packages, machine-learning libraries, database drivers, etc.
- **Compilers and toolchains:** C/C++ compilers, Java virtual machines, Just-In-Time compilers, and any configuration flags used when building native extensions.
- **Hardware characteristics:** CPU architecture and instruction sets, GPU model and driver versions, and sometimes even microcode versions.
- **Configuration and environment variables:** settings that influence threading, vectorization, floating-point behavior, default seeds, and logging.

Each layer can influence numerical results. For example:

- Changing the BLAS library may switch from a deterministic algorithm to one that reorders operations for speed, altering rounding in matrix multiplications.
- Upgrading a machine-learning library may change default regularization strength or optimizer settings, leading to different fitted models for the same training data.
- A new GPU driver may change kernel scheduling or math approximations.

For reproducible backtests, you must treat this environment as a first-class object: something that is specified, versioned, and, as far as practical, frozen.

Why "it worked on my machine" is not acceptable

In small ad-hoc projects, it is common to install dependencies as needed on a personal laptop, perhaps upgrading them over time. This leads to familiar situations:

- Code that runs on one machine fails or produces different numbers on another.
- Bug reports that cannot be reproduced because the reporter and the investigator have different environments.
- Subtle performance differences that change how long backtests take and which optimizations kick in.

In a professional quant research setting, these are not minor annoyances; they undermine the notion that backtests are controlled experiments. If each researcher's environment is effectively unique and constantly drifting, then:

- You cannot reliably compare results across people or machines.

- Experiment tracking loses meaning, because "code version X + data snapshot Y" does not specify behavior fully.
- Debugging becomes slower and less reliable.

The solution is to design and enforce a small number of *standard environments*, and to make the process of recreating them as automatic as possible.

Pinning dependencies

The core idea in environment management is *pinning*: specifying exactly which versions of each dependency are used, and ensuring those versions are installed when the environment is created. Instead of:

> "Install the latest version of library L."

you say:

> "Install library L, version 1.2.3."

and record that choice in a machine-readable specification.

There are several layers of pinning:

Application-level packages.

At the level of language-specific packages (e.g., Python packages), you should maintain explicit version lists. These can take the form of:

- A simple "requirements" file listing each package and version.
- A lockfile generated by a dependency manager. The lockfile records the exact versions of direct and transitive dependencies, and sometimes even their download sources.

Using a lockfile, you can recreate the same dependency tree repeatedly, avoiding surprises when upstream packages publish new releases.

System libraries.

Some dependencies are installed at the operating system level: BLAS libraries, database drivers, compression libraries, etc. For these, pinning may mean:

- Specifying the base OS image (for example, a particular Linux distribution and version).
- Using infrastructure tools to manage and version system packages.

Language runtimes and compilers.

You should also pin versions of language runtimes (for example, Python 3.11 vs 3.9) and compilers (for example, GCC version N). Even minor compiler changes can alter how floating-point code is optimized.

Pinning is not about never upgrading. It is about upgrading *deliberately*, in well-defined transitions, rather than letting the environment drift silently.

Reproducible builds and containers

Pinning versions in text files is a start, but you also need a way to turn those specifications into concrete, reproducible environments on real machines. Two complementary patterns are especially helpful: reproducible builds and containerization.

Reproducible builds.

A reproducible build process is one where, given the same build description (for example, a set of package and system version specifications), you can produce the same environment again. This typically involves:

- Scripting the environment creation (rather than doing it manually).
- Avoiding "latest" or otherwise floating versions in your scripts.
- Using consistent, versioned sources for packages (specific repositories or artifact stores).

The build process can be as simple as a scripted sequence of system and language-specific package installations, as long as it is under version control and produces the same results reliably.

Containerization.

Containers (for example, built using technologies like Docker) provide a way to package an entire environment—operating system image, libraries, and application code—into a unit that can be run on many machines consistently. For our purposes, the key benefits are:

- **Isolation:** containers shield your research environment from differences in the host system.
- **Portability:** the same container image can be run on a developer's workstation, a research cluster, or a continuous integration machine.
- **Versioning:** container images can be versioned and tagged, just like code.

In a container-based workflow, you might define a small number of base images (for example, "research-env-v1," "research-env-v2") that include all the pinned dependencies needed for backtesting. Each experiment then runs inside one of these images, and the experiment record notes which one.

Containers are not magic; you must still manage versions and update paths. But they provide a practical mechanism for making environment definitions concrete and portable.

Deterministic numerics

Even with the same code and dependencies, numerical computations can differ if operations are executed in different orders or with different low-level implementations. This is especially true for floating-point arithmetic, where addition and multiplication are not perfectly associative.

You cannot make floating-point math perfectly exact, but you can often make it *deterministic* by controlling several aspects of the environment:

Threading and parallelism.

Many math libraries and high-level frameworks use multi-threading under the hood. The number of threads and the scheduling policy can affect the order in which partial results are combined. To increase determinism:

- Fix the number of threads used by key libraries.
- Prefer deterministic parallel algorithms where available.
- Be cautious with automatic "use all cores" settings if they change behavior across machines.

BLAS and linear algebra settings.

Different BLAS implementations, and sometimes different versions of the same implementation, can choose different algorithms for matrix operations. Some libraries offer flags or environment variables to favor reproducibility over maximal speed. Where your use case demands strict reproducibility, consider enabling those options, at least for critical parts of the pipeline.

GPU determinism.

On GPUs, non-determinism can arise from thread race conditions, differences in kernel launch ordering, and certain atomic operations. Many deep-learning and numerical libraries provide configuration options to prefer deterministic algorithms. Using them may reduce throughput, but in a research backtesting environment, this is often a reasonable trade-off.

Random number generation.

This was treated in detail in the previous section, but it is worth repeating that your PRNGs should be controlled and independent of hidden library-level defaults. Some libraries silently seed their own generators or use hardware randomness; you should override these behaviors where feasible.

The general principle is: when you rely on a library for numerical work, you should understand the main environment and configuration variables that influence determinism and set them explicitly.

Hardware assumptions

Even with containers and pinned dependencies, hardware differences can matter. A container running on a different CPU architecture or with different vector instructions can still behave differently. Similarly, GPU-accelerated code may behave differently on different card generations.

To manage this, you should:

Document hardware baselines.

Define and document a small number of reference hardware profiles for your research environments, for example:

- "CPU-only, x86_64, AVX2"
- "CPU with AVX-512"
- "GPU-enabled, specific family and driver version"

When you run experiments, record which hardware profile was used.

Avoid silent fallback behavior.

Some frameworks will silently fall back to different implementation paths if certain hardware features are not available. For instance, they might use a slow, different-precision path when a vector instruction set is missing. You should try to detect such fallbacks (through logs or configuration flags) and treat them as environment differences.

Stabilize performance-dependent behavior.

Occasionally, code paths may depend on timing or measured performance (for example, choosing an algorithm at runtime based on benchmark results). These can introduce non-determinism across hardware. Where possible, disable such auto-tuning features in favor of fixed, declared choices in research environments.

The goal is not to eliminate all hardware variation—that may be impractical—but to be aware of it, constrain it as needed, and record it as part of the environment fingerprint of each experiment.

Environment fingerprints

To tie everything together, you should assign each concrete environment a *fingerprint*: a structured summary of its key components and versions. An environment fingerprint might include:

- OS name and version.
- Language runtimes and versions.
- Key library names and versions (numerical, ML, backtesting frameworks).
- BLAS implementation and version.
- GPU driver versions, if applicable.
- Compiler versions.
- Settings for important environment variables (thread counts, determinism flags, etc.).
- Container image identifier, if using containers.
- Hardware profile identifier.

This fingerprint should be:

- **Automatically captured** at experiment runtime, so researchers do not have to record it manually.
- **Stored with the experiment record**, alongside code version, data snapshot IDs, and random seeds.
- **Queryable**, so you can find all experiments that used a particular environment or specific component version.

When a future researcher wants to reproduce or extend an experiment, they can look up its environment fingerprint and provision a matching environment—for example, by pulling the corresponding container image or by invoking an environment-build script tied to that fingerprint.

Continuous integration for environment consistency

Just as you test your code for correctness, you should test your environment for consistency over time. Continuous integration (CI) systems are a natural place to do this. A CI pipeline can:

- Build or pull the standard research environments.
- Run a set of deterministic test backtests or numerical checks.
- Compare results to stored baselines, ideally bit-wise.

If differences appear, they may indicate:

- A change in dependency versions (for example, a package source was updated unexpectedly).
- A change in the base OS image used by container builds.
- A change in compiler behavior or system libraries.

By detecting these deviations early, before researchers rely on the affected environments for serious experiments, you can either:

- Fix the environment to restore exact compatibility, or
- Deliberately accept the change, create a new environment version, and update your baselines and documentation accordingly.

In both cases, environment changes become controlled and visible, rather than silent and accidental.

Evolving environments deliberately

No research organization can use the same environment forever. Libraries improve, security patches are needed, new hardware becomes available, and new research directions require new tools. The key is to treat environment changes as versioned, reviewable events, not as continuous background noise.

A disciplined evolution strategy might look like this:

- **Define environment versions.** For example, "research-env-v1" through "research-env-v5," each with a documented set of components and fingerprint.
- **Deprecate, do not delete.** When you retire an environment, you may prevent new experiments from using it, but you keep enough information (and preferably images) to reproduce old experiments.
- **Test migrations.** When planning a new environment version, choose a representative suite of backtests and run them under both the old and new environments. Compare results carefully, and document any expected differences due to, say, improved numerical stability or bug fixes.
- **Communicate changes.** Make clear to researchers when a new environment is available, what has changed, and how to switch. Encourage them to treat environment version as a key part of their experimental design.

By managing environments this way, you separate the need to move forward technologically from the need to maintain reproducibility for past work.

Bringing it all together

Environment and dependency management may feel distant from the excitement of new strategies and signals, but it is a core part of rigorous quant research. Without it, your carefully designed workflow, deterministic randomness, and versioned data sit on shifting sand.

When every experiment records:

- A precise code version.
- Fixed random seeds and PRNG stream structure.

- Explicit dataset snapshots and their hashes.
- An environment fingerprint tied to a versioned, reproducible environment.

then a backtest is no longer "something that once ran on someone's laptop." It is a well-specified, re-runnable object. Anyone with access to the same ingredients can replay it and obtain the same results, or intentionally vary one ingredient at a time to study its impact.

In the final section of this chapter, we will see how to tie all of these pieces—workflow, randomness, data, environment—into a coherent experiment configuration and tracking system. That system will be the user-facing layer that makes reproducible research not only possible in theory, but practical in daily work.

1.5 Experiment Configuration & Tracking

The preceding sections of this chapter established the building blocks of reproducible research: a disciplined workflow, deterministic randomness, versioned data with clear lineage, and controlled environments. We now add the top layer: a structured way to *define*, *log*, and *query* experiments so that any result can be reproduced, audited, and systematically extended.

Conceptually, this section answers three questions:

- What exactly is an "experiment" in the context of a backtest engine?
- How do we describe experiments in a way that is explicit, machine-readable, and human-understandable?
- How do we record and organize experiments so that an organization can build on past work rather than repeatedly rediscovering it?

What is an experiment? A complete tuple

In everyday research conversation, "experiment" is often used loosely. One person might mean "a notebook I ran once," another "a 500-parameter sweep." For our purposes, an experiment should have a precise and consistent meaning.

We will define an experiment as a *fully specified run of the backtest engine*, characterized by a tuple of components:

- **Code version:** the exact revision of the backtest engine and strategy logic.
- **Configuration:** all run-time parameters and toggles that control the engine and the strategy.
- **Data snapshot(s):** the immutable versioned datasets the run reads.
- **Environment:** the software and hardware stack in which the code executes.
- **Random structure:** master seed and PRNG stream definitions.

To this we add the **outputs**:

- Raw and summarized metrics.
- Time series of portfolio states, trades, and cash flows.
- Derived artifacts such as plots, reports, and model weights.

When these pieces are all captured and tied together, "experiment" becomes a concrete object. You can point to a particular experiment and say: "This is the evidence that supported launching strategy S," or "This is the run that showed our risk model failed in the 2015-2016 period."

Visual overview: the experiment at the center

Before we dive into details, it is useful to visualize how these components relate to each other. At the center is the experiment run itself; around it are the artifacts it depends on and produces. All of them are recorded into an experiment registry.

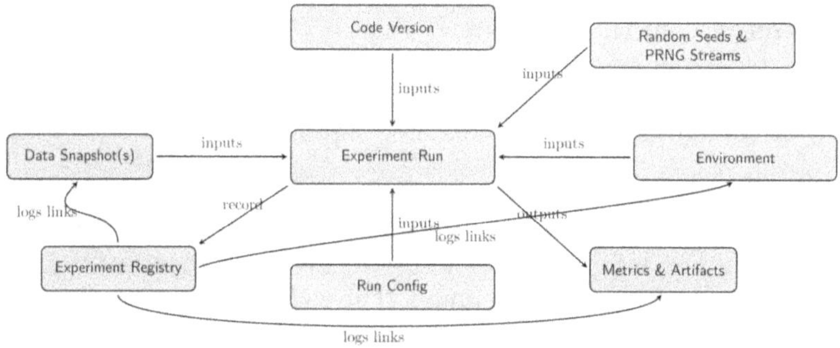

This hub-and-spoke structure captures the central idea of this section: an experiment is not just a number or a plot; it is a structured collection of linked artifacts that live in a registry and can be revisited, compared, and recomposed.

Designing experiment configurations

The first practical step toward structured experiments is to design a configuration schema for your backtests. The configuration is the runtime description of what the engine should do. It should capture, in a machine-readable and human-readable way:

- **Strategy parameters:** lookback windows, thresholds, weights, risk limits, leverage caps.
- **Universe and filters:** included instruments, liquidity cutoffs, listing exchanges, regions.

- **Execution and cost model settings:** slippage assumptions, fee schedules, routing models.
- **Simulation horizon and granularity:** start and end dates, bar frequency, trading calendar.
- **Scenario definitions:** Monte Carlo paths, stress events, bootstrapping options.
- **Feature sets and toggles:** which signals are active, which features go into model training, which optional risk controls are enabled.

A good configuration schema has several properties:

Explicit.

All degrees of freedom that can materially affect results should be expressed in the configuration, not buried in code as "magic constants." If a parameter is important enough that you might tune it or vary it across experiments, it belongs in the config.

Structured.

The configuration should have a clear, nested structure rather than being a flat list of key-value pairs. For example, you might group strategy, data, execution, and risk settings into separate sections. This is easier to understand, validate, and evolve.

Versioned.

The schema itself will change over time. You should assign it a version and record that version with each experiment. When you add or remove fields, you bump the schema version, and any compatibility logic lives in well-defined places, not in ad-hoc patches.

Serializable.

Configurations should live in plain text formats that are easy to diff, review, and store in version control. This also makes it easy to generate them programmatically for parameter sweeps.

By lifting these decisions out of the code and into configuration, you gain two benefits: experiments become more transparent (you can read and understand what was run), and it becomes much easier to vary parameters systematically without editing code.

From configurations to campaigns

Individual experiments are rarely run in isolation. More often, you run many related experiments in a *campaign* — for example, sweeping a parameter grid, testing robustness across universes, or re-running a baseline under updated data.

A campaign can be seen as:

> A set of related experiments generated by systematically varying a subset of configuration fields while holding others fixed.

Structuring campaigns explicitly has several advantages:

- You can tag experiments with a campaign identifier, making it easier to later retrieve all runs related to a given research question.
- You can define shared context (hypothesis, success criteria, notes) at the campaign level rather than repeating it for each run.
- You can perform meta-analysis across the campaign, such as examining how performance varies with a particular parameter.

In practice, a campaign might be represented by a base configuration plus a set of overrides or a parameter grid. The experiment tracking system can create and log a separate experiment record for each combination, each linked to the common campaign.

What an experiment registry does

If configurations define *what* to run, the experiment registry records *what actually happened.* It is the system, whether home-grown or off-the-shelf, that stores experiment records in a structured database.

At a minimum, an experiment registry should:

Assign unique experiment identifiers.

Every run gets an ID that can be referenced in logs, commits, presentations, and tickets. This ID should be stable and globally unique within your organization.

Store core metadata.

For each experiment, the registry stores the tuple we defined earlier:

- Code version (for example, a commit hash and repository name).
- Configuration (as a full serialized object, not just a pointer).
- Data snapshot identifiers and hashes.
- Environment fingerprint (including container image or environment version).
- Random seeds and PRNG structure.
- Timestamps (start, end, duration).
- Author or owner of the run.

Store key results and links.

Alongside metadata, the registry should record:

- Summary metrics (returns, Sharpe, drawdowns, capacity estimates).
- Links to time series outputs (such as location of saved P&L and trade histories).
- Links to derived artifacts such as plots, PDF reports, and trained model files.

Support querying and comparison.

Researchers should be able to query the registry along dimensions like:

- "All experiments where strategy = value_v3, run on dataset snapshot X, with lookback between 6 and 12 months."

- "All confirmatory experiments in campaign Y, sorted by out-of-sample Sharpe."
- "All experiments that used environment version research-env-v2 and data snapshot us_equities_daily_bars_v2 / snapshot_-2024_06_30."

In other words, the registry is both a catalog and a search engine for your research.

Automating experiment logging

Manually recording all this information is impossible in a busy research environment. Logging must be automated and, as much as possible, invisible in day-to-day use.

A practical pattern is:

- **Experiment object in code.** When a run is launched, the backtest engine constructs an "experiment object" in memory that gathers configuration, code version, data snapshots, environment fingerprint, and planned outputs.
- **Pre-run registration.** Before simulation begins, the engine registers this object with the experiment registry, which assigns an experiment ID and records initial metadata.
- **Streaming logs.** As the run progresses, it streams progress logs and partial metrics to the registry, so that researchers can monitor long-running experiments.
- **Post-run finalization.** At the end, the engine writes final metrics and attaches links to output artifacts, then marks the experiment record as complete (or failed, if an error occurred).

From the researcher's point of view, running an experiment may be as simple as launching a job with a configuration. The system takes care of recording the full context.

Tying in pre-registration and workflow

Earlier in the chapter, we introduced the idea of pre-registration: documenting a hypothesis, data boundaries, and success criteria before running extensive experiments. The experiment configuration and registry are natural places to connect pre-registration with execution.

A light-weight integration might work as follows:

- Each pre-registered idea has an identifier and a short document stored in a separate system (for example, your research wiki or ticket system).
- When launching an experiment, the configuration includes a reference to this pre-registration ID, indicating that this run is part of that planned test.
- The experiment registry records this link, so that when you view the pre-registration, you can see all associated experiments and their outcomes.

This helps uphold the separation between exploratory and confirmatory work. Exploratory runs may be unlinked or tagged as such, while confirmatory runs are tied to specific pre-registered plans.

Auditability and governance

In many organizations, especially those managing external capital, research outputs feed into processes with governance and oversight requirements. Experiment tracking directly supports these needs:

Traceability of production strategies.

For each live strategy or model, you can point to the specific experiments that justified its deployment. Each of those experiments is fully specified: code, data, environment, seeds, and configuration.

Reconstruction of decisions.

If a risk event occurs, or if regulators ask how a given model was validated, you can reconstruct the state of knowledge at decision time by re-running or reviewing the relevant experiments, not by relying on memory or partial notes.

Change management.

When a strategy or risk model changes, you can compare the old and new supporting experiments side by side. Differences in performance, risk, and behavior can be examined systematically rather than anecdotally.

Access control and privacy.

The registry can also record which experiments used which datasets, which may be important if some data sources have usage restrictions or privacy constraints. Proper tracking makes it easier to ensure compliance.

Namespaces, tags, and organization

As the number of experiments grows into the thousands or more, a flat list becomes unmanageable. You need ways to organize and navigate the space. Three common tools are:

Namespaces.

You can group experiments into hierarchical namespaces, such as:

- equities/momentum/long_only
- equities/value/multifactor
- macro/trend_following

The namespace may reflect the research area, asset class, or strategy family. It provides a natural way to scope searches and reports.

Tags.

Tags are flexible labels attached to experiments, such as:

- exploratory, confirmatory
- candidate_for_prod, abandoned

- uses_alt_data, stress_test

Because tags are cheap and composable, they are especially useful for quickly marking cross-cutting attributes that might not fit neatly into a hierarchy.

Campaign and project IDs.

As discussed earlier, campaigns correspond to coherent research questions or projects. Explicit campaign IDs tie scattered runs back to the question they were meant to answer.

By using namespaces, tags, and campaigns together, you can keep a complex body of research navigable.

Meta-analysis across experiments

Once experiments are systematically logged, new types of analysis become possible. Instead of treating each run as an isolated event, you can perform *meta-analysis* across many runs. For example:

- Studying how performance metrics depend on particular parameters across a campaign.
- Comparing the same strategy across different data snapshots or environments.
- Measuring how often exploratory signals fail to survive confirmatory tests.
- Quantifying the historical distribution of out-of-sample performance for strategies that made it to production versus those that did not.

This higher-level view can improve your research process itself. You might discover, for instance, that certain classes of ideas rarely clear your confirmatory thresholds, or that some data sources are particularly fragile to updates.

Meta-analysis also supports continuous improvement of infrastructure: tracking how environment changes, data corrections, and engine upgrades affect results across a broad test suite.

Failure modes and common pitfalls

Even with an experiment registry in place, there are several failure modes to watch for:

Incomplete configurations.

If important knobs remain hard-coded in the engine rather than exposed in configuration, experiments may appear identical in the registry while actually behaving differently due to hidden state.

Manual runs outside the system.

Researchers might run "quick tests" in ad-hoc ways without registering them. Over time, these invisible runs can distort intuition and decision-making, because they are not subject to the same review and tracking as official experiments.

Inconsistent naming and tagging.

If namespaces, tags, and project IDs are used inconsistently, querying becomes painful. Establishing a small set of conventions and examples can avoid this.

Registry drift.

The registry itself is a system with its own schema and evolutions. If its schema changes without clear versioning or migration paths, historical experiment records can become difficult to interpret. Treat the registry as a critical component, subject to the same discipline as your data and environments.

Recognizing these pitfalls early allows you to design processes and tools that keep the experiment tracking layer robust.

Closing the reproducibility loop

With experiment configuration and tracking in place, the reproducible research foundations in this chapter come together:

- The **workflow** section taught us to frame research as hypothesis-driven experiments.
- The **determinism** section showed how to tame randomness.

- The **data versioning** section bound experiments to specific, immutable views of the world.
- The **environment management** section stabilized the software and hardware context.
- This section binds these components into a **single object** — the experiment — that can be defined, logged, searched, and revisited.

In such a system, asking "Can we reproduce this result?" is not a philosophical challenge; it is a practical question: "Do we still have access to the code version, data snapshots, environment, and configuration referenced in the experiment record?" If the answer is yes, reproducing the run is as simple as invoking the backtest engine with the recorded experiment definition.

Beyond satisfying curiosity or regulatory demands, this reproducibility is a powerful accelerant for research. New hires can quickly explore and extend prior work. Senior researchers can examine and compare past strategies without digging through old notebooks. Infrastructure teams can make controlled improvements and assess their impact across a rich archive of experiments.

In the rest of the book we will descend from this conceptual layer into more concrete engine design topics — event models, execution simulation, accounting, and bias control. Throughout, the principles established in this chapter will remain in force: every part of the backtest engine should be designed with experiments in mind, so that strategy research is not a sequence of forgettable runs, but a coherent, accumulating body of evidence.

Chapter 2

Market Data & Temporal Foundations

Every backtest stands on a fragile stack of timestamps and ticks. This chapter shows how exchanges actually encode time, prices, and corporate events-and how subtle choices in calendars, storage, and alignment can silently leak information into your simulations or erase edge altogether.

2.1 Market Calendars & Sessions

Backtests do not run on wall-clock time; they run on *market* time. The engine should not simply advance from one raw timestamp to the next. Instead, it should move through a structured notion of trading days and sessions that reflects how exchanges actually operate. This structure is provided by *trading calendars*. A trading calendar tells you, for each date and venue: is this a trading day, when does trading start and stop, are there intraday breaks, and are there special conditions such as half days or auctions. In a well-designed simulation, these calendars drive the backtest clock and all session-aware logic: overnight risk, daily resets, end-of-day batch calculations, and cross-venue coordination.

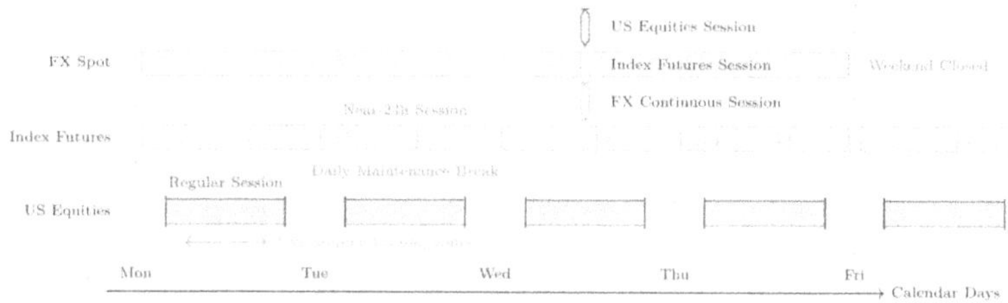

Why Calendars Are the Temporal Backbone

At first glance, you might think that the only temporal information a backtest needs is a timestamp on each tick or bar. In practice, this is not enough. Real markets have:

- Non-trading days such as weekends and holidays.
- Special days such as half days before certain holidays.
- Multiple trading segments within a day: pre-market, regular session, post-market, and auctions.
- Intraday breaks, such as lunch breaks or maintenance pauses.

If your engine simply marches through raw timestamps, it will not "understand" where one trading day ends and another begins, when overnight risk starts, or when daily risk limits and reports should be evaluated. Any realistic portfolio accounting, risk control, or rebalancing logic needs to know: *What is the current session? Where is the engine on the trading calendar?*

For this reason, a robust backtest engine treats the trading calendar as a first-class object. The engine advances from session to session and from day to day according to the calendar. Market data, orders, and fills are then attached to this scaffold, rather than defining the notion of time themselves.

Trading Days and Sessions

The most basic element of a trading calendar is the *trading day*. For a given venue, a trading day is a date on which the exchange is open for trading at least once. This sounds simple, but even here there are subtleties.

Regular vs. non-trading days. Most equity exchanges are closed on weekends and on a set of holidays. Bonds may have their own holiday schedule, which differs from equities. Futures and FX may trade when cash markets are closed. A calendar must encode for each venue and date whether it is:

- A *full trading day*.
- A *partial trading day* (for example, closing early).
- A *non-trading day*.

Sessions within a day. Within each trading day, trading is divided into *sessions*. A session is a contiguous block of time during which the market is in a well-defined trading state. Typical examples include:

- Pre-open or pre-market: order collection, indicative prices, but possibly no continuous matching.
- Regular session: the main continuous trading period.
- Post-market: after-hours trading with reduced liquidity.
- Opening and closing auctions: short windows with specific auction mechanics.

Many backtests only trade during the regular session, but even then, knowing that you are, say, five minutes before the close is critical. For example, you might impose a rule: "No new positions opened after 15:55 local time." The engine must map that rule onto calendar-aware session boundaries, not onto arbitrary timestamps.

Intraday Breaks and Special Segments

Not all markets trade from open to close without interruption. Some futures markets pause for a short maintenance break each day. Several Asian and Middle Eastern equity exchanges have a lunch break. Some venues interleave auction phases with continuous trading.

From a simulation perspective, intraday breaks matter for several reasons:

- **Price gaps.** When trading restarts after a break, the price may jump. That jump should be treated like an overnight move even though it occurs within the same date.
- **Order handling.** Should resting orders survive the break or be cancelled? Are new orders allowed during the break? Your execution model may need to emulate these rules.
- **State transitions.** Risk metrics, such as high-water marks or intraday drawdown limits, may need to consider whether a break is part of the same session or a separate one.

A good calendar representation therefore does more than label days as open or closed. It enumerates each session and intraday break with explicit start and end times. The backtest engine can then reason about transitions, such as:

- End of pre-market → start of regular session.
- Start of lunch break → end of lunch break.
- End of regular session → start of post-market.

At each transition, session-specific logic may fire: cancelling good-for-day orders at the end of the regular session, rolling positions, or triggering routine calculations such as end-of-day portfolio valuations.

Driving the Backtest Clock from Calendars

Once you have a structured calendar, you can use it to drive the internal clock of the backtest. Instead of asking "What is the timestamp of the next bar?" the engine asks questions like:

- What is the current trading date and venue?
- Which session (pre-market, regular, post-market) am I in?
- What is the next boundary: next bar close, session close, or day close?

This leads to a more robust event loop. Conceptually, the engine cycles through:

1. **Determine the current session** from the calendar and the current time index.
2. **Process all market data events** (ticks, bars) that fall within that session.
3. **Allow strategy decisions and order submissions** within permitted windows, for example, until a cut-off time before the close.
4. **Apply session-end logic** at the close: finalize positions, update risk metrics, trigger daily reports.
5. **Advance to the next session** as defined by the calendar.

By centering everything around calendar sessions, you ensure that daily accounting and risk monitoring align with the actual structure of the market being simulated. It also becomes easier to insert new logic at well-defined points: for example, to model a closing auction, you can define a short "auction" session at the end of the day and attach specialized execution behavior to it.

Cross-Venue Calendars and Strategy-Level Trading Days

Most realistic strategies touch more than one market. You might trade a basket of US equities, hedge with futures, and overlay FX hedges for non-USD exposures. Each of these venues has its own calendar and sessions, often in different time zones. The engine must reconcile these into a *strategy-level* notion of time.

Independent venue calendars. The starting point is to maintain a separate calendar for each venue (or, at least, for each distinct schedule of trading hours). For example:

- US equities calendar: Monday–Friday, with US equity holidays and a regular session from morning to afternoon local time.
- US index futures calendar: near-24-hour trading from Sunday evening to Friday afternoon, with short daily maintenance breaks.
- FX spot calendar: continuous from Monday morning in Asia through Friday evening in New York, with minor liquidity changes but no formal daily close.

Each calendar should know, for any given timestamp, whether the venue is trading and what session it is in.

Defining a strategy trading day. When you combine venues, you must decide what constitutes a "day" for the strategy as a whole. There is no single correct answer; it depends on your accounting and risk conventions. Common choices include:

- **Home-market day.** Use the calendar of your primary venue or reporting currency. For example, treat each US equity day as the strategy day, even if some FX or futures trades occur slightly outside that window.
- **24-hour rolling day.** Define a day as a 24-hour window in a chosen time zone (often UTC) and accept that some venue sessions will straddle these boundaries.
- **Composite day.** Define custom boundaries, such as from the opening of the Asian session to the close of the US session, if that better matches how you view risk and P&L.

Whichever convention you choose, you must apply it consistently and encode it in the engine. This affects how you compute daily returns, overnight gaps, and end-of-day risk metrics.

Overlapping and disjoint sessions. In cross-venue strategies, sessions may overlap or be disjoint. For example:

- US index futures begin trading for the next day while US equities are still trading for the current day.
- FX markets remain open when most equity markets are closed.

Your calendar framework should be able to answer questions such as:

- During a given US equity session, which other venues are open?
- At a given FX timestamp, what is the most recent equity close?

This is crucial when you, for instance, hedge an equity position using futures that trade ahead of the next equity open, or when you mark FX hedges relative to a specific equity close time.

Handling Holidays, Half Days, and Ad-Hoc Closures

Exchange schedules are not static. They include:

- Recurring holidays that may follow complex rules, such as "the third Monday in February."
- Half days before or after certain holidays, where trading closes earlier than usual.
- Ad-hoc closures due to technical issues, natural disasters, or regulatory decisions.
- Historical changes in session hours over the years.

A naive approach is to hard-code a list of holidays and treat everything else as a full trading day. This may work for a short, recent period, but it quickly breaks down as your backtest horizon widens.

A more robust design is to treat calendars as data-driven objects that can respond to queries such as:

- Is this date a trading day for this venue?
- What sessions exist on this date, and what are their start and end times?
- Did any special rules apply on this date (for example, early close)?

To achieve reproducibility:

- **Explicitly version calendars.** A calendar used today may differ from the one that was correct 20 years ago. You should be able to reproduce a backtest by referring to the specific version of the calendar used.
- **Record calendar sources.** For example, if you derived the schedule from exchange bulletins, store those references or snapshots so that future users can verify the logic.
- **Include ad-hoc events.** When an exchange closes unexpectedly, update the calendar and treat that change as a data update with its own version.

This may seem like bookkeeping, but it is essential for reproducibility. A seemingly small change—such as adding an early close that you previously missed—can alter end-of-day prices, overnight gaps, and therefore strategy performance.

Calendars in the Code: Design Patterns

From an implementation perspective, calendars should be represented as immutable, queryable objects that can be shared across the engine. Several patterns help here.

Immutable calendar objects. Once constructed, a calendar instance for a given version should never change. If you discover an error or need to incorporate new information (such as a previously missing holiday), you create a new calendar version. This ensures that rerunning a backtest with the same calendar version produces the same session structure.

Cached session queries. Many parts of the engine will ask calendar-like questions repeatedly:

- "What is the next trading day for venue X after this timestamp?"
- "What is the session that contains this timestamp?"
- "What are the boundaries of today's regular session?"

To avoid recomputing these answers, calendars often cache results internally or rely on compact data structures (such as precomputed arrays of session boundaries). This improves both performance and determinism; the same query, given the same inputs, always yields the same result quickly.

Separation of concerns. The calendar should focus on structural information: days, sessions, and their times. It should not be burdened with pricing logic, order book structure, or execution rules. Those higher-level components can *query* the calendar to make decisions. For example:

- The execution model might ask, "Is this time inside the closing auction session?" and adjust its behavior.
- The risk module might ask, "Has the regular session for the primary venue closed?" before computing daily VaR.

This separation keeps the calendar simple, testable, and reusable across strategies and products.

Session-Aware Logic in Backtests

Once calendars are in place, you can express strategy and engine logic in terms of trading sessions rather than raw timestamps. This is more natural and less error-prone. Some common examples:

Overnight position handling. The engine can define "overnight" as the time between the close of today's last relevant session and the open of tomorrow's first relevant session. Risk limits, margin requirements, or position caps can be applied specifically to overnight holdings.

End-of-day batch calculations. Many analytics, such as daily returns, risk metrics, and accounting summaries, are computed at the end of each trading day. Rather than guessing that "end of day" is the last bar before midnight, the engine uses calendar boundaries. This is especially important when markets close early or when venues operate in different time zones.

Session-specific strategies. Some strategies only trade during certain parts of the day, such as the opening or closing auctions, or avoid low-liquidity periods. With session-aware calendars, you can say "only trade during the first hour of the regular session" and have that rule applied correctly even on special days with shifted hours.

Cross-venue coordination. When trading multiple venues, you may need to coordinate actions at the close of one market and the open of another. For instance, you might close equity positions at the US close and immediately adjust futures hedges on an index future that trades later. Calendar-driven logic allows the engine to sequence these events correctly and consistently.

Reproducibility and Historical Changes

Finally, trading calendars change over time. Exchanges adjust their hours, add or remove holidays, or introduce new sessions and auctions. A backtest that spans decades will traverse several distinct eras of trading structure.

To maintain reproducibility:

- **Tie calendars to historical periods.** The calendar for a venue should know when certain rules applied. For example, before a given year there may have been a different close time or no after-hours session.
- **Version calendar definitions.** When you update a calendar to correct or extend its rules, assign a new version identifier and

record which backtests used which version.

- **Test edge dates.** Write tests that focus on dates where rules changed: the first day with a new close time, the first occurrence of a new holiday, or the first day after a schedule adjustment. Ensure that your engine handles these transitions without gaps or overlaps in sessions.

By treating calendars as carefully managed, versioned datasets rather than as loose collections of rules, you align your temporal model with the broader goal of reproducible research. Anyone rerunning your backtest in the future—with the same data and the same calendar version—should see exactly the same sequence of sessions, transitions, and end-of-day boundaries.

Trading calendars and sessions provide the temporal skeleton upon which your entire backtest is built. They define which days are tradable, how each day is structured, when sessions and breaks begin and end, and how multiple venues relate in time. Driving the backtest clock from these calendars—rather than from raw timestamps—makes your simulation more realistic, your accounting and risk logic more coherent, and your results more reproducible. In the following sections, we will build on this scaffold to discuss the precise handling of time zones, timestamp normalization, and event ordering on top of these calendar-defined sessions.

2.2 Time & Timezone Handling

In the previous section, we treated exchange calendars and sessions as the backbone of market time: they tell us on which days and during which local clock intervals trading can happen. We now turn to the more technical question that underlies every data record in a backtest: *what is the exact time of this event, and how do we compare it to others?*

Modern markets operate across the globe. A trade on a Tokyo equity, a quote on a London-listed ETF, and a futures fill on a Chicago exchange may all occur "at the same time" in some physical sense, yet show very different local clock readings. On top of this, governments periodically adjust clocks due to daylight saving time (DST) rules, sometimes changing those rules over history. If your backtest engine does not handle these details correctly, you will end up with:

- Events appearing out of order.
- Bars with missing or duplicated intervals.
- Overnight returns calculated over the wrong horizon.
- Trading cut-offs triggered at the wrong moment.

This section explains how to normalize timestamps across time zones and daylight saving rules so that your engine maintains a monotonic, high-precision event timeline. We focus on intuitive understanding first, then on practical design choices.

Local Exchange Time vs. Canonical Time

Every exchange calendar is defined in a *local* time zone. For example:

- New York equity markets use US Eastern time.
- London markets use UK time.
- Tokyo markets use Japan Standard Time.

Traders on those venues think and speak in local clock time: "The auction is at 9:00," "No orders after 15:55," and so on. Your session boundaries from the previous section are also defined in local time. This is natural and necessary.

However, when you want to compare or merge events from multiple venues, local time quickly becomes confusing. Consider this situation:

- A trade occurs in London at 14:30 London time.
- A trade occurs in New York at 09:45 New York time.

Which happened first in real time? The answer depends on the time difference between London and New York *on that specific date*, which may be five hours, or four hours, or something else entirely if one of them just switched DST. You do not want to re-evaluate that logic ad hoc every time you align two feeds.

The standard solution is to convert all timestamps into a single *canonical* time scale, independent of local time zones. The usual choice in finance is Coordinated Universal Time (UTC). Conceptually:

- Local time is what humans use and what exchange calendars are written in.
- Canonical time is what the engine uses internally to order events and align data.

Every event thus has two different but related time notions:

- A *local timestamp* tied to a specific time zone.
- A *canonical timestamp* (for example, UTC) derived from the local one.

Your engine should be able to move back and forth between these two representations without ambiguity.

The Goal: A Monotonic Event Timeline

The key property you want from canonical timestamps is *monotonicity*. This means that if event B happened after event A in real life, then the canonical timestamp of B is strictly later than that of A. There should be no backwards jumps, no repeated moments, and no gaps that break the logical ordering of events.

Monotonicity is critical when:

- Building bars from ticks by accumulating trades until the bar close time.

- Applying an execution model that depends on the sequence of quotes and trades.
- Running a strategy whose logic is "if X has happened up to time t, then do Y."

If two events seem to share the same instant because of rounding or ambiguous local time, your engine cannot unambiguously say which information was available first. That is a recipe for subtle look-ahead bias.

By choosing a canonical scale such as UTC and converting *all* events into that scale with sufficient precision, you create a single, global, monotonic event timeline. The rest of the engine can then reason in terms of the order of events on this timeline, while mapping back to local calendar time only when needed (for example, to check if a cut-off time has passed in the venue's local clock).

Time Zones: Offsets and Rules

Time zones are usually described by two things:

- A *base offset* from UTC, such as "UTC+1" or "UTC-5".
- A set of *daylight saving rules* that change this offset during parts of the year.

For example, New York time is often described as "UTC-5," but this is only true in winter. In summer it is "UTC-4" due to daylight saving time. London is similar: it can be "UTC+0" or "UTC+1" depending on the season. Many countries have changed their DST rules over the years, sometimes more than once.

In practice, this means that a proper time-zone system is not just a number of hours. It is a database of rules:

- On this date range, use offset A.
- On that date range, use offset B.

- On this specific date at this time, switch from offset A to offset B.

Your engine should rely on a mature time-zone library that encodes these rules, rather than reimplementing them. Reimplementation is error-prone and very easy to get wrong at the edges, exactly where trading schedules may be sensitive.

Daylight Saving Transitions: Gaps and Overlaps

Daylight saving transitions create two distinct awkward situations from the perspective of local time:

- **Spring forward (gap).** At some point, the clock jumps ahead. For instance, it may go directly from 01:59 to 03:00. The local times between 02:00 and 02:59 do not exist at all on that date.
- **Fall back (overlap).** At another point, the clock is set back. Time goes from 01:59 back to 01:00. The local times between 01:00 and 01:59 occur *twice* on that date. Without extra information, "01:30" is ambiguous: do you mean the first or second occurrence?

From an engine's point of view, these behaviors cause trouble if you only look at local timestamps:

- During a gap, you may think that no events can occur in a span of local clock time, even though in UTC everything is fine and continuous.
- During an overlap, two different events may both claim to have happened at the same local time, yet one actually occurred an hour earlier in real time.

This is one of the strongest arguments for always working in canonical time internally. In UTC, there is no gap and no overlap: time moves smoothly forward. The strange behavior exists only in the local view.

However, you cannot ignore local time altogether because:

- Exchange calendars and session schedules are defined in local time.
- Trading rules often refer to local times: "no new orders after 15:55."

The challenge, then, is to correctly convert between local and canonical time around DST transitions and to treat ambiguous local times with care.

Best Practices for Storing Timestamps

To support a reliable event timeline and clean conversions, you should adopt consistent conventions for how timestamps are stored and passed through the engine.

Store canonical time as UTC. The simplest and most robust approach is:

- Store the *primary* timestamp of each event in UTC.
- Use a fixed unit with enough precision, such as microseconds or nanoseconds.

Having a single reference scale simplifies alignment and comparisons. All causal logic and event ordering can be carried out on this UTC time.

Attach explicit time-zone metadata. For every piece of data, it should be clear what local time zone it is associated with. This does not necessarily mean you store a local timestamp in each record, but you must be able to answer:

> "To which venue and time zone does this event belong?"

This allows you to convert the UTC timestamp back to local exchange time whenever you need to consult the calendar for that venue.

Maintain high precision. Modern feeds can contain events spaced microseconds or even nanoseconds apart. Even if your strategy only trades on minute bars, higher precision in the raw event time helps avoid ties and ordering ambiguities. If you round too aggressively, you risk:

- Misordering trades and quotes.
- Placing multiple distinct events at the same apparent instant.
- Blurring the boundaries of bars or cut-off times.

Choose a precision level that is higher than the finest time resolution you expect in your data, and keep it consistent across the system.

Round-Tripping Between Local and Canonical Time

Once you have UTC timestamps and time-zone metadata, you will often need to move back to local time. Typical operations include:

- Labeling bars by local open and close times.
- Checking whether an event occurred during a given local session.
- Applying local rules such as "no new orders after 15:55 local."

The conversion should be a *round-trip*: if you convert an event from local time to UTC and back, you should end up with the same local time, unless the original moment was ambiguous or invalid.

To achieve reliable round-trips:

- Always convert using a time-zone library that knows about historical DST rules for that zone.
- When converting from local to UTC, handle ambiguous or invalid local times explicitly.

Handling DST Gaps (Invalid Local Times)

During the spring-forward transition, some local times do not exist. For example, between 02:00 and 02:59 on a particular date, the clock may have jumped. If your data claims that an event happened at "02:30 local time" on that date, then one of the following must be true:

- The data provider has already converted from another scale and chosen a representation that does not match civil time.
- There is an error in the time stamp.

Your engine should not silently accept such times. Options include:

- Reject them and flag a data-quality issue.
- Adjust them according to a clearly documented rule (for example, snapping them to the nearest valid instant) and record that transformation.

In many cases, exchanges avoid scheduling regular trading in these non-existent time slots, but you may still encounter them in off-market data or poorly processed feeds.

Handling DST Overlaps (Ambiguous Local Times)

During the fall-back transition, some local times occur twice. If you simply see "01:15 local time," you do not know whether this is the first or second occurrence. A robust time library will require you to provide an additional hint, often called a "fold" or similar flag, to indicate which occurrence is intended.

In backtesting, there are two main scenarios:

- If your data provider already supplies UTC timestamps, use them and treat the apparent local duplication as just a visualization issue; in UTC, the two events differ and ordering remains clear.

- If your data is only in local time and falls into the overlapping interval, you must either infer the correct ordering from context (for example, knowing that continuous trading was suspended during part of the interval) or accept that the data is ambiguous and may not support clean event ordering.

In all cases, avoid making silent guesses in your engine code. Ambiguous local times should trigger explicit decisions and documentation.

Impact on Bars, Overnight Returns, and Cut-Off Rules

Timezone handling is not a purely technical detail; it has concrete effects on how you construct market features and apply trading rules.

Bar labeling. When you construct bars (for example, 1-minute or 5-minute bars), you face the question: should a bar be labeled by its start time, its end time, or some other convention? Whatever convention you choose in local time must translate consistently into canonical time.

Around DST transitions, the length of a "minute" or "hour" bar in local time may not align with a fixed span in UTC. A minute that crosses the spring-forward gap may correspond to less than 60 seconds in real time, while a minute in an overlapping hour may correspond to more. Your engine should use canonical time to define exact bar boundaries, then map those boundaries into local labels.

Overnight returns. When you compute "overnight" returns, you are effectively measuring from the last tradable price of one day to the first tradable price of the next. As discussed in the previous section, those boundaries are defined by the local exchange calendar. However, from a risk and accounting perspective, the period may span different durations in UTC due to DST or time-zone crossing. If you ignore these details, you may mis-measure volatility or misalign index levels with your internal P&L records.

Trading cut-offs. Strategy rules such as "no new orders after 15:55 local time" must be applied using the correct local clock, including DST adjustments. Internally, you can:

1. Convert the local cut-off time for a given session into UTC using the calendar and time-zone rules.

2. Compare each event's UTC timestamp to this UTC cut-off.

This avoids errors where you accidentally apply a fixed offset that does not match the actual offset on that date.

Time Libraries and Abstraction Layers

Given the complexity of time zones and DST rules, it is crucial not to embed ad hoc time calculations throughout your code base. Instead:

Choose a robust time library. Use a library that:

- Encodes the historical rules for major time zones.
- Can represent both local and UTC time.
- Supports explicit handling of ambiguous and invalid times.

Define a time abstraction layer. Within your backtest engine, concentrate all time manipulation in a small number of well-tested components. These components should:

- Convert between local and UTC time using the chosen library.
- Interface with exchange calendars to answer questions such as "What session is this UTC timestamp in for venue X?"
- Enforce invariants such as monotonicity of canonical time and correct use of time zones.

By abstracting away low-level details, you reduce the risk that strategy or data-processing code will mishandle time.

Assertions and Temporal Invariants

Because time-handling bugs can be subtle and hard to detect by eye, your engine should proactively check for inconsistencies. Some useful invariants and assertions include:

- **Monotonic canonical time within a feed.** For any single venue and instrument, the sequence of events should have non-decreasing UTC timestamps. If you observe a decrease, either the data is out of order or the time conversion is wrong.
- **Local time falls within calendar sessions.** When you map an event's UTC timestamp back to local time for its venue, it should either fall inside a known trading session or be clearly outside any session (for example, an off-market event). Strange cases such as an event during a declared closure should raise flags.
- **Stable conversions over time.** Converting an event's UTC timestamp to local time and back should yield the original UTC time, barring rounding within your chosen precision. Large discrepancies indicate a misuse of time-zone rules or an inconsistent library configuration.

You can also include dedicated test cases for dates known to involve DST transitions or rule changes. By intentionally stressing those edge conditions, you catch problems early rather than discovering them after a live strategy behaves strangely around a clock change.

Time and time zones are not an optional refinement; they are central to building a trustworthy backtest engine. Exchange calendars and sessions live in local time, but your engine needs a single, monotonic canonical timeline to order events, build bars, and apply causal logic without ambiguity.

By consistently:

- Storing timestamps in a canonical scale such as UTC with high precision.
- Attaching explicit time-zone metadata for each venue and data source.

- Using robust time libraries to handle DST and historical rule changes.
- Carefully round-tripping between local and canonical time, especially around DST gaps and overlaps.
- Embedding invariants and assertions that detect temporal inconsistencies.

you create a solid temporal foundation. The next sections—on market data models, storage, and alignment—will build directly on this foundation, relying on your engine's ability to tell exactly when each event occurred and how it fits into the broader, calendar-aware structure of market time.

2.3 Market Data Models (Bars, Trades, Quotes)

So far, we have focused on *when* trading can occur: calendars, sessions, and time normalization. We now turn to *what* happens at those times. A backtest engine sees the market through a stream of records: trades, quotes, order book updates, and bars. These records are its only window on reality. If they are ambiguous, inconsistent, or poorly structured, every downstream calculation inherits that weakness.

This section defines canonical schemas for the main record types used in simulation:

- Instruments and their stable identifiers.
- OHLCV bars (open, high, low, close, volume).
- Trades (executed transactions).
- Quotes (best bid and ask).
- Order book depth (snapshots or updates).

Our aim is not to describe every possible field from every vendor. Instead, we identify a *minimal, consistent core* that works across asset classes and venues, and that supports reproducible backtests. Once this core is clear, extending it for special cases is straightforward.

From Ticks to Bars: A Unified View

At the lowest level, markets generate *events*:

- A trade is printed: a certain quantity changes hands at a given price.
- A quote changes: the best bid or ask moves, or its size changes.
- A deeper level of the order book changes: an order is added, modified, or cancelled.

These are often called "ticks." Backtests may work directly on ticks, or they may operate on aggregated data such as 1-minute or daily bars. Even if you only use bars, those bars are summaries of some underlying sequence of trades and quotes.

To keep things clear, we will distinguish between:

- Raw records that come from the exchange feed or a close derivative of it (trades, quotes, depth).
- Derived records that you construct from raw data (bars, mid-prices, spreads, classification flags).

The rest of this section defines schemas for these records. Throughout, we focus on three themes:

- **Stable identifiers:** every record must refer to instruments in a way that does not change over time.
- **Consistent units:** prices, sizes, and notionals must be comparable across instruments.
- **Clear semantics:** fields must have unambiguous meanings, with derived quantities kept separate from raw data.

Instruments and Stable Identifiers

Before you can define trades or bars, you must define what they refer to: the instrument. In practice, this is not as simple as using the symbol string.

Symbols change. A company may change its ticker. A future may roll from one contract month to the next. An ETF may switch its listing exchange. Relying on symbol alone creates two serious problems:

- Different instruments may share the same symbol at different times.
- The same economic instrument may have multiple symbols over its life.

To avoid this, every instrument in your research universe should have a *stable, non-recycled identifier* that is internal to your system. You can think of this as a numeric or opaque key that:

- Is created once when the instrument first appears.
- Never changes, even if the public symbol, exchange, or contract code changes.
- Is never reused for a different instrument, even after delisting.

Around this key, you maintain instrument metadata such as:

- Current and historical symbols.
- Asset class (equity, future, option, FX pair, bond, etc.).
- Listing exchange or primary venue.
- Currency of quotation.
- Contract size or lot size (for futures, options, and FX).
- Trading calendar reference (which calendar object applies).

Every bar, trade, quote, or depth record will then include:

Instrument identifier, timestamp, venue (if needed), price, size, and other details.

Because the instrument identifier is stable, you can join, filter, and aggregate records over long historical horizons without being broken by symbol changes or corporate events.

OHLCV Bars: Semantics and Variants

Bars are compact summaries of trading activity over a time interval. A standard price bar has the fields often abbreviated as OHLCV:

- **Open:** the first traded price in the bar interval.
- **High:** the highest traded price in the bar interval.
- **Low:** the lowest traded price in the bar interval.
- **Close:** the last traded price in the bar interval.
- **Volume:** the total traded quantity in the bar interval.

On top of this, you may record:

- Bar start time and end time (normally in canonical time, with a local-time label).
- Number of trades in the bar.
- Open interest (for futures and options, usually at end of day).

Built from trades vs. quotes. It is important to be explicit about what bars represent:

- *Trade bars* summarize executed trades: OHLCV is based on actual transaction prices and sizes.
- *Quote or mid-price bars* summarize indicative prices: OHLC may be based on midpoints or quotes, and "volume" may represent something else (for example, quoted depth or an average).

You should not mix these types silently. A backtest that interprets quote-based bars as if they reflected actual transactions will mis-estimate liquidity and slippage. For reproducibility, include a field in your bar schema that clearly states the bar type and source (trades vs. quotes, and which feed).

Timestamp conventions. Bars need a time label. Common conventions are:

- Label by bar *end* time: the close time of the interval.
- Label by bar *start* time.

Choose one convention and document it. Store both start and end internally if needed, but pick a single *canonical* bar timestamp for indexing and joins. This is essential when you later align bars with other data sources.

Units and currencies. Every bar must specify:

- The unit of price (for example, dollars per share, euros per contract point).
- The currency of quotation (USD, EUR, JPY, etc.).
- The unit of size or volume (shares, contracts, notional).

For futures and FX, price alone is not enough to know economic exposure; you may need the contract multiplier or point value to compute notional. Keep that metadata with the instrument, and keep bar quantities clearly in "shares/contracts" rather than mixing notional and quantity in the same field.

Trades: Executed Transactions

A *trade record* represents a transaction that actually occurred in the market: a certain quantity of an instrument exchanged between a buyer and a seller at a given price and time.

A canonical trade schema includes:

- Instrument identifier.
- Timestamp (canonical, with implicit or explicit venue time zone).
- Price.
- Size (quantity traded).
- Venue or market center (if multiple exist).
- Trade condition or flags (regular trade, opening auction, late print, etc.).
- Trade identifier (if provided by the feed).

Semantics of price and size. The trade price is the agreed transaction price. The size is the quantity that changed hands. This seems obvious, but there are special cases:

- Block trades or off-exchange prints that are reported with some delay.
- Corrections or cancellations of earlier trades.
- "Out of sequence" trades that are recorded with an earlier trade time but reported later.

Your canonical schema should reserve fields for condition codes or flags that indicate such situations. In research, you may later filter or treat them differently. What matters is that your schema can represent them without overloading meaning into the basic price and size fields.

Direction and aggressor side. Sometimes you want to know whether a trade was buyer-initiated or seller-initiated. This is *not* inherent in the raw trade record; it is inferred by matching trades to the prevailing quotes. If you classify trades in this way, you should store the classification as a derived field *separate* from the raw trade. This keeps your core schema simple and lets you recompute or update the classification with newer methods without changing the underlying data.

Quotes: Best Bid and Ask

Quotes describe the current willingness to buy or sell. A simple quote record represents the *top of book*: the best bid and best ask.

A canonical quote schema includes:

- Instrument identifier.
- Timestamp.
- Best bid price and size.
- Best ask price and size.
- Quote condition or flags (for example, indicative, firm, crossed/locked).
- Venue or book identifier (if there are multiple order books).

Derived mid-price and spread. Two very common derived fields are:

- Mid-price: the average of best bid and best ask.
- Spread: the difference between best ask and best bid.

Although these are simple, they should *not* be stored as primary fields in your canonical schema. Instead, compute them as needed and, if you wish, store them in a derived dataset alongside the raw quotes. This helps avoid inconsistencies when quotes are updated or when you change your definition (for example, to volume-weighted mid).

Handling stale or crossed quotes. Real-world quote feeds include messy cases:

- Stale quotes that persist beyond a reasonable time.
- Locked markets where bid equals ask.
- Crossed markets where bid exceeds ask (due to latency or feed issues).

Your schema should be able to represent these situations—for example, by allowing bid to be greater than ask and by including a condition flag. Decisions about whether to filter or adjust them belong in your data cleaning layer, not in the core schema.

Order Book Depth: Snapshots and Updates

For more detailed execution modeling, you may need a view of the *order book*: multiple levels of bid and ask prices with their available sizes. There are two common ways to represent depth:

- Snapshots that capture the entire book (or the top N levels) at a particular time.
- Incremental updates that apply changes to a previously known state.

A canonical depth snapshot schema includes:

- Instrument identifier.
- Timestamp.
- For each level on each side:

- Price.
- Aggregate size at that price.
- Level index (for example, 1 for best, 2 for next best).

- Book type (full depth, top N, aggregated by price, etc.).
- Venue or book identifier.

For incremental updates, each record typically includes:

- Instrument identifier.
- Timestamp.

- Side (bid or ask).
- Price.
- Size change or new total size at that price.
- Action type (add, modify, remove).

From a schema design perspective, the key is to keep depth records *separate* from quotes and trades, while clearly relating them via common keys (instrument, timestamp, venue). This allows your engine to reconstruct the state of the book at any moment, simulate order placement, and compute slippage or market impact.

Canonical Relationships Between Records

Once you have defined instruments, bars, trades, quotes, and depth, you can think of them as related entities in a conceptual schema. Every record type shares some core fields:

- Instrument identifier.
- Timestamp (canonical).
- Venue or book identifier (where applicable).

Other fields are specific:

- Bars: OHLCV, bar type, interval boundaries.
- Trades: price, size, condition.
- Quotes: bid/ask prices and sizes, quote condition.
- Depth: multiple price/size levels, side, level index.

This conceptual picture emphasizes that bars, trades, quotes, and depth are all different "views" on trading activity for the same instruments, anchored by shared identifiers and timestamps. It also hints at how you might join them: on instrument and time, possibly with a tolerance window for as-of joins.

Normalizing Units and Currencies Across Asset Classes

A multi-asset backtest must deal with instruments that behave very differently:

- Equities trade in shares, priced in a currency per share.
- Futures trade in contracts, with a tick value or point value that defines monetary impact.
- Options trade in contracts whose notional depends on the underlying and contract size.
- FX trades in currency pairs, often quoted as units of one currency per unit of another.

To build consistent inputs, your schemas should separate:

- Price fields which always store the quoted price in the instrument's native quotation convention.
- Quantity fields which always store the number of units traded or available (shares, contracts, lots).
- Instrument metadata that tells you how to translate price and quantity into notional exposure.

For example:

- A futures trade has a price (index points) and a size (contracts). The notional is price times contract size, not just price times size.
- An FX spot trade in EUR/USD has a price (USD per EUR) and a size (EUR amount if you treat the base currency as the quantity). The notional in USD is price times EUR size.

Your core trade and bar schemas should *not* try to precompute notional exposure per record. Instead, they should:

- Keep price and size fields simple and consistent.
- Rely on instrument metadata to translate into notional in a chosen reference currency when needed.

This discipline prevents you from hard-coding a particular accounting viewpoint into the raw data and gives you flexibility to change notional conventions or base currencies later.

Raw vs. Derived Fields

Across all record types, there is a recurring tension between convenience and purity. It is tempting to add many derived fields directly into the core schema for convenience. Examples:

- Including mid-price and spread in quote records.
- Including notional trade value in trade records.
- Including log returns in bar records.
- Including trade classification flags (buy/sell initiated) in trades.

From a reproducibility standpoint, this is risky. Derived fields encode assumptions and algorithms: how mid-price is computed, how returns are defined, how aggressor side is classified, and so on. These assumptions change over time. If you embed them into your "raw" schema, you make it harder to revise methods without breaking historical backtests.

A robust design follows a simple rule:

> Keep core schemas as close as possible to exchange reality.
> Put all analytics and features into separate, derived layers
> that cite the raw data and the methods used.

Concretely, this means:

- Raw records store what the exchange or feed directly reports, translated only as needed into canonical units and timestamps.

- Feature datasets or research tables store derived fields, along with metadata that identifies the source code and raw data version from which they were generated.

This separation also simplifies testing: you can check that raw data is structurally sound and that derived features obey their own invariants, without mixing concerns.

A Minimal but Extensible Schema for Backtests

To close, it is useful to summarize a minimal yet practical schema for multi-asset backtests. The following ingredients are usually sufficient to support a wide range of strategies:

- Instrument table with stable identifier, asset class, currency, contract size, calendar, and symbol history.
- Trade table with instrument identifier, canonical timestamp, price, size, venue, and condition codes.
- Quote table with instrument identifier, canonical timestamp, best bid/ask prices and sizes, venue, and quote condition.
- Order book table (optional, for more detailed execution modeling) with instrument identifier, timestamp, venue/book id, side, level index, price, and size.
- Bar table with instrument identifier, bar timestamp (plus start/end), OHLCV, bar type (trade/quote-based), and source.

On top of this, you can build:

- Feature tables (for example, moving averages, volatility estimates, spreads).
- Classification tables (for example, trade direction, regime labels).
- Aggregation tables (for example, index-level or sector-level summaries).

What makes this schema powerful is not its complexity but its consistency:

- All records are anchored by stable instrument identifiers and canonical timestamps.
- Units and currencies are clearly defined and separated from notional calculations.
- Raw and derived information are kept distinct, preserving the ability to regenerate features if methods change.

With such a foundation in place, the later parts of the chapter—on storage formats, alignment, corporate actions, and data quality—can focus on making access to these records fast, compressed, accurately adjusted, and trustworthy, without having to revisit the core question of what a "trade," "quote," or "bar" actually means.

2.4 Data Storage Formats & Compression

The previous sections defined *what* your market data looks like: instruments, trades, quotes, depth, and bars, all timestamped on a clean, calendar-aware timeline. We now turn to a more mundane but equally critical question: *where and how do you store all those records so that backtests remain fast, compact, and reproducible as your research scales?*

Historical market data is large. Even a modest intraday equities universe can produce billions of ticks per year. Naive choices—scattered CSV files, ad hoc directory structures, undocumented reprocessing—may work for a single analyst over a short window, but they quickly collapse under team-scale or decade-scale research. The goal in this section is to design storage patterns that:

- Make common research queries fast and predictable.
- Keep storage and I/O costs under control via appropriate compression.

- Support reproducible backtests by clearly versioning and validating data.

We proceed from simple formats to more sophisticated layouts, always with the backtest workload in mind.

What Backtests Need from Storage

Before choosing formats or tools, it is helpful to articulate the typical access patterns of a backtest engine and a research workflow:

- **Scan by time.** "Give me all trades for instrument X on this day," or "all 1-minute bars for my universe over this month."
- **Scan by instrument.** "Give me the full history of quotes for instrument X over five years."
- **Join across datasets.** "Join these bar records with corporate actions, fundamentals, or signals by instrument and time."
- **Batch backtests.** Run the same strategy logic over many instruments or many parameter settings, often scanning similar slices repeatedly.

Unlike many transactional systems, backtest workloads are mostly *read-heavy*, sequential or semi-sequential, and often column-oriented (you might read many rows but only a few fields). This suggests that:

- Write performance is important but secondary to read throughput.
- Columnar layouts and compression are usually beneficial.
- Partitioning data by time and/or instrument can drastically reduce I/O.

With this in mind, we can assess practical storage options.

Baseline: Text Files (CSV and Friends)

The simplest and most familiar format is plain text, often comma-separated values (CSV). Many data vendors provide data in this form, and most tools can read it. CSV has some advantages:

- Human-readable and easy to inspect.
- Simple to generate from almost any system.
- Tool-agnostic: every language and platform can parse it.

However, CSV has serious drawbacks for large-scale backtesting:

- **Space-inefficient.** Repeating field names or redundant textual representations (for example, timestamps written as long strings) consumes space and hurts I/O.
- **Slow to parse.** Text parsing is CPU-intensive. Re-reading large CSVs repeatedly can dominate runtime.
- **Weak typing and schema enforcement.** Everything is text; you must interpret types and formats on each read, with room for inconsistency.

Plain text formats can be acceptable for small prototyping tasks, but for a serious research archive they should usually be treated as *ingest formats*: you convert them into more efficient internal representations as early as possible.

If you do use CSV as an intermediate format, enforce:

- A fixed, documented field order and delimiter.
- Explicit representations for missing values.
- Consistent timestamp, price, and size formats.

These practices at least improve reliability and reproducibility, even if they do not solve performance issues.

Row-Oriented Databases

Relational databases and row-oriented storage engines (such as many traditional SQL systems) store data record-by-record: all fields for a given row are stored together. This works well for transactional workloads where you frequently read or write entire records by primary key.

For market data workloads, row stores offer:

- Strong schema enforcement and typing.
- Mature indexing and query languages.
- Built-in transactional guarantees (useful if you are continuously ingesting new data).

However, they can be a poor fit for large, analytical scans:

- Scanning billions of rows with only a handful of columns often reads more bytes than necessary.
- Heavy indexing to speed up range queries can bloat storage and complicate maintenance.
- Scaling out to cluster-wide analytics requires more infrastructure and expertise.

Row-oriented databases can be useful for metadata, reference tables (such as instruments and calendars), and smaller or more transactional datasets. But for bulk historical tick or bar data, columnar formats are typically more efficient.

Columnar Storage: Parquet, Feather, and Similar Formats

Columnar formats store data by column rather than by row: all values of a given field are grouped together on disk. Apache Parquet and Feather are common examples used in research environments.

Columnar layouts have several advantages for backtesting:

- **Efficient column selection.** If a query only needs timestamps, prices, and sizes, it avoids reading other fields like condition codes or auxiliary flags.
- **Better compression.** Values in the same column tend to be similar or repeated, which compression algorithms exploit well.
- **Vectorized processing.** Many analytical libraries can process columns as contiguous arrays, improving CPU efficiency.

Parquet, in particular, supports:

- Nested schemas, which can represent more complex structures (for example, depth levels).
- Column-level compression and encoding options, so you can tune each field.
- Embedded schema definitions, which helps with consistency and validation.

For most research-scale archives of trades, quotes, and bars, a columnar format like Parquet offers an excellent balance between flexibility, performance, and tooling support. Feather and similar formats can be useful as lighter-weight, high-speed interchange formats, especially for intermediate results or in-memory caching.

Custom Binary Layouts

Some institutions design custom binary formats tailored to their exact data and engine. These formats can be extremely efficient:

- Minimal overhead per record.
- Fixed-width fields for fast indexing and random access.
- Application-specific encodings that compress very well.

However, custom formats come with costs:

- Engineering time to design, implement, and maintain the format and its readers/writers.
- Tool lock-in: fewer off-the-shelf tools can read the data, making debugging and ad hoc analysis harder.
- Higher barrier to entry for new team members or collaborators.

For most teams, the right balance is to start with well-supported columnar formats and only consider custom layouts if:

- You have clearly identified performance bottlenecks that standard formats cannot address.
- The benefits outweigh the long-term maintenance and interoperability costs.

Even then, it is often wise to keep a documented pathway back to an open, standard format for portability and longevity.

Compression and Encoding Techniques

Regardless of the base format, compression is central to making historical data manageable. For columnar formats, compression typically operates at the column level and can exploit patterns specific to each field.

Important encoding strategies include:

Dictionary encoding. Repeated values (for example, venue codes, condition flags, or symbols within a partition) are stored as small integer indices into a dictionary of unique values. This is highly effective for low-cardinality columns.

Run-length encoding (RLE). Sequences of repeated values are stored as a value plus a run length. For example, if many consecutive rows have the same venue or flag, RLE can compress them efficiently.

Delta encoding. Rather than storing full values, store the difference between consecutive values. This is especially useful for monotonically increasing fields such as timestamps or sequence numbers, and for prices that move in small increments.

Bit-packing. When values fall within a small range, they can be represented with fewer bits than the machine word size. Combined with delta encoding or dictionary encoding, this can compact fields like tick counts or small enumerations.

On top of these encodings, a general-purpose compression algorithm (such as LZ4, Zstandard, or Snappy) often achieves additional gains by exploiting remaining redundancy.

When choosing compression settings, consider:

- **Read pattern.** If you frequently read entire columns, heavier compression may pay off despite extra CPU cost. If you favor low-latency random access, faster but less aggressive compression may be better.
- **Hardware.** On modern CPUs, algorithms like LZ4 and Zstandard can decompress very quickly, so I/O bandwidth, not CPU, is often the bottleneck.
- **Simplicity.** Use a small number of well-understood codecs. Exotic choices can complicate debugging and long-term access.

As a rule of thumb, design for *fast decompression*, since backtesting is read-heavy and often CPU-bound by strategy logic rather than by decompression itself.

Partitioning Strategies: Time, Instrument, Venue

Format and compression are only half the story. How you break your data into files or partitions has a huge impact on performance and manageability. Good partitioning keeps related records together and isolates unrelated records, so that common queries touch as little data as possible.

Common partitioning dimensions include:

By time. For example, one file per day per table, or per month, or per year. Time partitioning aligns well with:

- Backtests that run over specific date ranges.

- Operational tasks like daily ingest and validation.
- Archival strategies (older partitions can be moved to cold storage).

By instrument. For example, one file per instrument per month. This suits workflows where you:

- Frequently scan a single instrument's full history.
- Perform instrument-level analytics or feature construction.

By venue or asset class. Grouping by venue or asset class can simplify handling of different schemas or trading calendars, and can improve locality for strategies that focus on particular markets.

In practice, partitioning often uses a combination, such as:

```
/asset_class=equity/date=YYYY-MM-DD/part-*.parquet
```

or

```
/asset_class=future/instrument=ES/date=YYYY-MM/part-*.parquet
```

The right scheme depends on your dominant query patterns.

Balancing File Granularity

Partitioning too finely—for example, one file per instrument per day with small numbers of rows—leads to a "small files problem." The overhead of opening and closing many tiny files can dominate I/O, and metadata management becomes unwieldy.

Partitioning too coarsely—for example, a single file for an entire decade of global trades—makes every query read far more data than necessary and slows down incremental updates.

As a rough guideline:

- Aim for individual files that are at least tens of megabytes but not many gigabytes.
- Choose time slices (day, week, month) so that common query windows hit a small number of contiguous files.
- Adjust grain differently for high-frequency vs. low-frequency datasets. Tick-level trades may warrant daily partitions; daily bars may fit comfortably into yearly files.

You can refine this over time as you observe real workloads.

Directory Structures and Dataset Layout

Beyond individual files, your directory layout communicates structure and supports automated processing. A clear, predictable layout enables tools and humans to answer questions such as:

- "What data do we have for this asset class over this period?"
- "Which files should today's ingest process write or validate?"

A simple pattern is to reflect partitioning keys in directory names:

- Top-level separation by logical dataset: trades/, quotes/, bars/, orderbook/.
- Within each dataset, directories for asset class or venue.
- Within those, directories for time partitions (year, month, day).

For example:

```
/data_archive/
  trades/
    equity/
      venue=NYSE/
        date=2023-01-02/
          part-0001.parquet
          part-0002.parquet
        date=2023-01-03/
          ...
```

or similar. The exact naming convention is less important than consistency and documentation. Your backtest engine should be able to derive file paths from logical queries (instrument, date range, dataset) using a small, well-tested mapping function.

Versioning, Manifests, and Checksums

Reproducible backtests depend not only on the logical schema and calendar definitions, but also on the exact *bytes* of data used. Over time, your datasets will evolve:

- New days are appended.
- Historical errors are corrected.
- Corporate actions or metadata are revised.

To keep track of these changes and be able to reproduce a past run, you should introduce explicit versioning and validation via:

Dataset versions. Assign a version or snapshot identifier to a particular state of a dataset (for example, trades up to a given date with a particular cleaning pipeline). Strategies can then record which dataset version they depend on.

Manifests. For each version, maintain a manifest file that lists:

- All files included in the dataset.
- Their sizes and checksums (for example, cryptographic hashes).
- Optional metadata such as generation date, data source, and processing software version.

This manifest acts as an index and an integrity check. A backtest can store a reference to the manifest it used; later, you can verify that the same set of files, unchanged, is still present.

Checksums. Computing checksums for each file (and possibly for the manifest itself) helps detect silent corruption or accidental modification. This is especially important when datasets are replicated, backed up, or moved between storage systems.

Together, these mechanisms strengthen the link between code, data, and results. When someone asks, "What data did you use to produce this backtest?" you can point to a specific dataset version and manifest, not just a directory path.

Append-Only vs. Rewrite Workflows

How you update datasets influences both reproducibility and operational simplicity.

Append-only. In an append-only workflow, new data (for new dates or instruments) is added in new partitions or files, and existing files are treated as immutable. Corrections are either:

- Applied in new versions of the dataset, leaving older versions intact.
- Logged as deltas that the engine applies at read time.

Append-only designs naturally support snapshotting and versioning. They also align well with distributed filesystems and object stores, which favor immutable objects.

Rewrite. In a rewrite workflow, you may periodically regenerate entire partitions or datasets to apply improved cleaning or compression. This can simplify data logic but complicates reproducibility, because the same path may point to different bytes over time.

If you adopt a rewrite approach, it is even more important to:

- Use explicit dataset versions and manifests.
- Keep older versions accessible for as long as needed to reproduce past results.

In practice, many teams use a hybrid: append-only within a given version, with occasional wholesale recomputation to produce a new version, referenced by a new manifest and identifier.

Cold Archives and Research Caches

Not all data needs to be equally fast to access. You can save cost and simplify scaling by separating:

- **Cold archive.** A comprehensive, perhaps slower, long-term store of all raw and normalized data. It optimizes for durability and completeness rather than query speed.
- **Research cache.** A curated, smaller subset of data optimized for frequent analysis and backtesting. It may include:

- A focused universe of instruments.
- Precomputed bars and features.
- Higher-compression or lower-latency formats tailored to common workloads.

The key is to define deterministic derivation rules: the research cache is always produced from the archive using documented code and parameters. If you change the derivation process, you create a new cache version, again with a manifest and identifier.

This separation allows you to:

- Keep the full historical record without worrying about its immediate performance.
- Iterate rapidly in research using the cache, which is smaller and more focused.
- Rebuild or extend the cache as universes or strategies evolve.

Storage Choices, I/O, and Engineer Time

Finally, all of these design choices exist within a broader trade-off between storage cost, I/O bandwidth, and engineer time. Over-optimizing the storage format can consume months of engineering effort for marginal gains; under-optimizing can lead to slow, fragile backtests that discourage proper experimentation.

A pragmatic approach is:

- Start with well-supported columnar formats (such as Parquet) and reasonable partitioning by time and asset class.
- Use moderate, fast-to-decompress compression (for example, LZ4 or Zstandard) with simple encodings.
- Implement manifests, checksums, and clear directory structures early, since they are hard to retrofit.
- Profile real backtest workloads to identify bottlenecks before attempting exotic optimizations.

Remember that *clarity and reproducibility* are design goals alongside raw speed. A slightly slower but well-documented, verifiable storage system is often preferable to an opaque, over-tuned one that only one engineer fully understands.

With robust storage and compression foundations in place, the next section on time alignment and resampling can assume that your engine can quickly and reliably read consistent slices of market data—the raw material for building causal, bias-resistant signals.

2.5 Time Alignment & Resampling

Up to this point we have built three pillars: a precise notion of market time (calendars and sessions), a reliable handling of time zones and daylight saving, and well-structured schemas for trades, quotes, and bars stored in efficient formats. We now come to one of the most error-prone steps in quantitative research: *putting different data sources onto the same timeline without accidentally looking into the future.*

In realistic workflows you rarely use a single homogeneous feed. Instead, you combine:

- Intraday prices at 1-minute or tick resolution.

- Daily fundamentals updated once per day or less.
- Event data, such as earnings announcements or index rebalances, at irregular times.
- Alternative data sources with their own reporting lags and timestamps.

To feed these into a backtest or a machine learning model, you need a common time axis: a sequence of "decision points" (for example, bar closes) at which your strategy observes inputs and decides what to do. The challenge is to align everything to this axis while ensuring that, at time t, you only use information that was actually available at or before t.

This section introduces three core techniques for this alignment problem:

- **As-of joins** to align slower-moving series (for example, daily fundamentals) to faster ones (for example, minute bars).
- **Resampling** to aggregate high-frequency data into coarser bars, or to regularize irregular observations.
- **Lagging** to enforce realistic delays and avoid subtle forms of look-ahead bias.

We will explain each technique in turn, then discuss how to combine them into a reusable "time alignment engine" for your backtests.

The Alignment Problem: Different Clocks, Different Grids

Consider three simple series for a single equity:

- 1-minute trade bars during the regular session.
- Daily balance-sheet and income-statement fundamentals, recorded once per day after the close.

- Corporate events such as earnings announcements, each tagged with a timestamp (for example, "today after close").

Your strategy might rebalance once per minute, using the latest intraday price, the most recent fundamentals, and a flag indicating whether an earnings announcement has already occurred. These series live on different "clocks":

- Minute bars define a dense grid of times within the day.
- Fundamentals are piecewise-constant across days, but only become known at specific release times.
- Events are at irregular timestamps, not necessarily aligned to bar boundaries.

If you simply join everything by date or by nearest timestamp, you will likely introduce look-ahead bias. For example:

- Using a fundamental that was released after the close when trading before the close.
- Using an event that happens at 15:45 when making a decision at 15:44 because its date is the same.

The correct approach is always causal: at each decision time t, you may only use information from records whose true availability time is $\leq t$. This causal principle is what guides our alignment techniques.

Choosing a Reference Time Axis

The first design choice is: *What is the reference time axis for alignment?* In most backtests this is:

- A regular bar grid (for example, 1-minute or 5-minute bars) defined using the exchange calendar, or
- A daily grid of session closes or opens, also defined by the calendar.

From the earlier sections, your calendar and timezone logic already provide a clean, canonical bar schedule: a sequence of bar start and end timestamps (in UTC, with local labels) for each instrument or venue. This schedule is your "spine" or "grid."

Every other dataset will be aligned to this grid. For each bar end time t, you will:

- Take the bar's own OHLCV values (by construction).
- Find the most recent valid observation from slower or irregular series whose availability time is $\leq t$.
- Apply lags where appropriate to simulate reporting delays.

This is where as-of joins and resampling step in.

As-Of Joins: Last Observation Carried Forward, Done Right

An *as-of join* answers the question:

> "At time t, what was the most recent known value of variable X for this instrument?"

Formally, given:

- A reference timeline: for example, bar end times $t_1, t_2, \ldots$.
- A slower series: for example, fundamentals recorded at times $s_1, s_2, \ldots$.

We want, for each t_i, the latest s_j such that $s_j \leq t_i$, and the corresponding value of X at s_j. If no such s_j exists (for example, before the first observation), the result is typically missing.

This is sometimes called "last observation carried forward," but that phrase can be misleading if you apply it indiscriminately. A robust as-of join has a few important properties:

Causality. You only look backwards in time. You *never* peek at $s_j > t_i$, even if the nearest point in absolute time would be a forward-looking one.

Maximum staleness. You may want to limit how far back you are willing to reach. For example, you may say:

> "Use the last fundamental observation if it is at most 90 days old; otherwise treat it as missing."

This prevents extremely old values from being carried forward into long gaps.

Session awareness. Alignment should respect market sessions. You generally do not want to carry a value across non-trading days or across large market breaks without being explicit about it.

Instrument and key matching. As-of joins are typically done per instrument, and sometimes per additional keys (such as accounting standard or vendor id). The join logic must be clear about which keys define a unique time series.

Visualizing As-Of Joins and Resampling

To make these ideas concrete, it helps to see a timeline where multiple input series are aligned onto a shared bar grid.

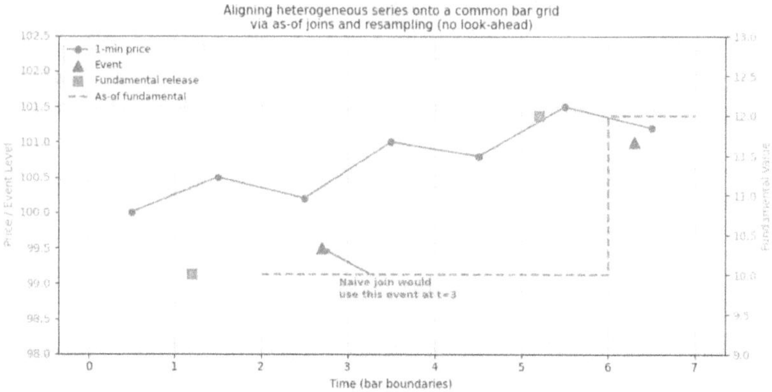

This chart illustrates three layers:

- A regular bar grid (vertical lines).
- A high-frequency price series (blue).
- Slower fundamentals (green) and events (red), with an as-of-aligned fundamental series (green dashed) that respects causality.

The annotation highlights how a naive "nearest timestamp" join might incorrectly use an event at time 2.7 when making a decision at bar boundary 3.0; a causal as-of join would only use that event from bar boundaries at or after 2.7.

Resampling: Building Bars and Regularizing Time

Resampling is the process of aggregating or transforming observations from one time resolution or grid to another. There are two common directions:

Downsampling: from high frequency to lower frequency. For example:

- Building 1-minute bars from tick-level trades or quotes.
- Building daily bars from 1-minute bars.

For price bars, downsampling typically uses OHLCV aggregation consistent with the semantics defined earlier:

- Open: first trade in the interval.
- High: maximum price in the interval.
- Low: minimum price in the interval.
- Close: last trade in the interval.
- Volume: sum of traded size.

Crucially, bar boundaries must be defined using the exchange calendar and timezone rules, not by naive wall-clock arithmetic. For example, you should not assume that there are always exactly 390 one-minute bars in a US equity session; half days and schedule changes can break this.

Upsampling or regularizing: from irregular to regular. For example:

- Mapping irregularly timestamped events onto the bar grid, using as-of joins or explicit lags.
- Filling gaps in series (carefully) to create a regular time index for modeling.

The key point: *Resampling is not just about resizing buckets; it is about respecting time semantics.* That means:

- Always use canonical timestamps tied to the calendar to define intervals.
- Treat non-trading periods and gaps explicitly rather than blurring them.
- Be cautious with forward-filling across session boundaries; often you should reinitialize indicators at the start of each session.

Avoiding Look-Ahead in Resampling

Resampling itself can introduce look-ahead bias if you are not explicit about information availability. For example:

- If you create a daily bar using all trades from 09:30 to 16:00 and then use the daily close to make *intraday* decisions, you are using future information.
- If you compute a rolling 20-day average and use a window that includes today's close when making a trade at today's open, you are again looking ahead.

To avoid this:

- Align features to the *end* of the interval used to compute them, and only use them from that point onward.
- For intraday strategies, either:
  - Use previous-day aggregates (for example, yesterday's close) when trading during today's session, or
  - Recompute intraday features only based on data up to the current time.

A good mental model is: "Every derived feature has a timestamp that marks the first instant at which it is fully known." Your engine must enforce that this timestamp is always $\leq$ any decision time that uses the feature.

Lagging: Modeling Delays and Publication Lags

Not all information becomes usable in the market at the moment it is recorded. Common examples include:

- Fundamentals released after the close but timestamped by their effective date.
- Index reconstitutions announced days or weeks in advance but effective on a later date.
- Vendor feeds that deliver end-of-day data the next morning.

If you align these series purely by their "effective date," you will often assign information too early. For instance, using a new earnings number for the entire day on which it is announced, even though it was only released after the close.

Lagging solves this by explicitly shifting the availability of information:

- A *calendar lag* applies a delay measured in trading days or calendar days. For example, "fundamentals become usable one trading day after their report date."

- A *time lag* applies a delay in clock time. For example, "earnings are usable from their actual announcement timestamp onward."

In practice, you often combine both:

1. Determine the true publication or effective timestamp in local exchange time; convert to canonical time.
2. Apply an additional conservative lag if the data vendor's delivery is known to be delayed.
3. Use this lagged availability time in your as-of joins and resampling.

By encoding lags directly in your alignment rules, you make your modeling of information flow explicit and testable, rather than relying on fuzzy date conventions.

Causality and Multi-Source Alignment

Real strategies may draw on dozens of data sources. To maintain causality when aligning them:

- Define, for each dataset, a function that maps a record to an *availability timestamp*, which may be later than the raw timestamp if lags apply.
- Use these availability timestamps in your as-of joins, not just the raw event times.
- When combining multiple aligned sources into a feature matrix at time t, ensure that every contributing value has availability time $\leq t$.

This approach treats the alignment engine as a kind of "information filter": at each time point it asks, "What did the strategy reasonably know by now?" Different strategies may even adopt different lag assumptions depending on how conservative they wish to be.

Edge Cases: Corporate Actions, Index Rebalances, and More

Some data types have particularly tricky timing:

Corporate actions. Splits, dividends, and similar events often have:

- An announcement date.
- An ex-date (when prices adjust).
- A payment date.

For price adjustments used in backtesting, you typically care about the ex-date, but for information flow you care about the announcement date and time. Your alignment engine should:

- Use the *announcement* timestamp plus any assumed lag when deciding if the action is "known."
- Use the ex-date to adjust prices and shares, as discussed in the corporate actions section.

Index rebalances. Many indices announce constituent changes ahead of their effective dates. A strategy that tries to anticipate or react to rebalances must be clear about whether it:

- Trades on the announcement (using data available at the announcement time).
- Trades at or around the effective date (using information that might have been known in advance).

Again, availability timestamps and lags should capture these choices.

Designing a Time Alignment Engine

Given the complexity of alignment and the risk of subtle bugs, you should encapsulate the logic in a dedicated "time alignment engine" rather than scattering ad hoc join code throughout your research stack. Such an engine typically supports:

Configuration of reference grids. Ability to define:

- Bar grids (for example, 1-minute, 5-minute, daily) using the calendar and timezone layer.
- Strategy-specific decision times (for example, just after the close, or at both open and close).

Registration of data sources. For each dataset:

- Its native time resolution and timestamp semantics.
- A function mapping records to availability timestamps.
- Default lags and maximum staleness rules.

As-of-join and resampling operations. Core methods to:

- Align a dataset to a reference grid using as-of joins with staleness control.
- Resample high-frequency data to the grid with appropriate aggregations.
- Create feature matrices that combine multiple aligned series without violating causality.

Testing and invariants. Built-in checks that:

- No aligned value has availability time later than the decision timestamp.
- Staleness limits are respected; overly old values are flagged or set to missing.
- Session boundaries are honored; no forward-filling across non-trading periods unless explicitly configured.

By treating alignment as a central, testable component, you dramatically reduce the probability that each new strategy inadvertently reintroduces old mistakes.

Test Scenarios for Alignment Bugs

Because alignment errors often produce plausible-looking time series, you need targeted tests to catch them. Useful scenarios include:

- **Synthetic data with known lags.** Create a toy dataset where a signal changes at known times and verify that aligned features only change after the appropriate lag.
- **DST transition days.** Use days with daylight saving transitions and ensure that event ordering and as-of joins behave correctly across local time gaps or overlaps.
- **Corporate event windows.** Surround splits, dividends, and earnings with tests that check when adjusted prices and event indicators become available.
- **Index reconstitution dates.** Validate that index membership indicators used by strategies respect the announced timing.

These tests should be part of your core validation suite, run whenever you change the alignment engine or underlying time libraries.

Time alignment and resampling sit at the boundary between raw market data and strategy logic. Done well, they provide a clean, causal view of a complex, multi-source information flow; done poorly, they quietly inject look-ahead bias and mis-timed features into your research.

The key principles are:

- Define a clear reference time axis using your calendar and time-zone machinery.
- Use as-of joins that only look backwards in time and respect maximum staleness.
- Resample data using bar boundaries defined by the exchange calendar, not naive wall-clock assumptions.
- Model delays explicitly by lagging features to reflect realistic information availability.

- Encapsulate alignment logic in a reusable engine with strong tests and invariants.

With these tools, you can turn heterogeneous, messy feeds into consistent, causal inputs for backtests and models, preserving the temporal discipline that is essential for trustworthy quantitative research.

2.6 Corporate Actions & Adjustments

Up to this point, we have treated price and volume records as if one share of an instrument today is directly comparable to one share yesterday. In reality, issuers routinely change the number of shares outstanding, the capital structure, and the way cash flows to investors. Stock splits, reverse splits, cash and stock dividends, rights issues, spin-offs, and other restructurings all change the mechanical relationship between prices, quantities, and economic value.

If you ignore these events in a backtest, your results will be distorted. If you handle them incorrectly, you can achieve something worse: a beautifully smooth price series that bears no resemblance to the returns an investor could actually earn. This section explains how to represent corporate actions using *adjustment factors* that preserve the continuity of your price series without corrupting the underlying economics.

What Corporate Actions Do, Economically

Let us begin with intuition rather than formulas. Consider a simple stock:

- A **stock split** (for example, 2-for-1) doubles the number of shares outstanding while halving the price per share. If you owned one share at 100 before the split, you own two shares at 50 after. Your total economic value, ignoring small frictions, is the same.
- A **reverse split** (for example, 1-for-10) reduces the number of shares and increases the price per share, again leaving total economic value roughly unchanged.

- A **cash dividend** pays you cash per share. If the stock pays a 2-unit dividend, its price usually drops by about 2 units when it goes ex-dividend. Your economic value is now partly in stock, partly in cash.
- A **stock dividend** or **bonus issue** gives you extra shares, often with a mechanical price adjustment.
- A **spin-off** distributes shares of a new or existing subsidiary to current shareholders. The parent's price drops, but you now own two securities instead of one.

In all these cases, a naive chart of the raw price alone will show jumps that are not genuine gains or losses. A 2-for-1 split will show the price suddenly halving; a large dividend will show a sharp drop on the ex-dividend date. If you compute returns directly from such raw prices, you will misinterpret mechanical adjustments as losses and payouts as negative performance.

The goal of corporate action adjustments is to:

- Remove these mechanical jumps from the *price path*, so that price-based returns reflect true economic gains and losses.
- Preserve the correct relationship between prices, share counts, and cash flows, so that simulated portfolios behave economically like real ones.

Raw vs. Adjusted Data

A fundamental design decision is to distinguish between:

- **Raw data:** as close as possible to what the exchange reported on each day, in original price and share-count units.
- **Adjusted data:** transformed versions of prices and volumes using corporate action information, designed to be convenient for backtesting and performance analysis.

You should *never overwrite* raw data with adjusted values. Instead, you should:

- Keep raw and adjusted series side by side.
- Store explicit metadata describing how adjustments were computed and what corporate action records were used.
- Make it easy to regenerate adjusted series if you change your methodology or receive corrected corporate action data.

This approach supports reproducibility: backtests can record which adjusted dataset (and adjustment rules) they used, while researchers retain the option of revisiting assumptions without corrupting the original record.

Adjustment Factors: The Core Concept

The central tool for corporate action handling is the *adjustment factor*. Conceptually, it is a time-indexed multiplier that maps raw prices and volumes into adjusted ones.

For each instrument and date, you define an adjustment factor $A(t)$ such that:

- Adjusted price at time t = raw price at time t multiplied by $A(t)$.
- Adjusted volume or share quantity at time t = raw quantity at time t divided by $A(t)$ (or multiplied by the inverse, depending on convention).

The factor changes stepwise at corporate action dates. For example, consider a 2-for-1 split effective at some ex-date. For dates on or after the split, $A(t)$ might be 1. For dates before the split, $A(t)$ might be 0.5, so that old prices are scaled down to be comparable to post-split prices.

There are two broad families of adjustment:

- **Backward adjustments:** You keep recent raw prices unchanged and adjust *history* so that older prices are made consistent with the latest share count.
- **Forward adjustments:** You keep early prices unchanged and adjust *future* prices so that they evolve as if no action occurred.

Both can be expressed with appropriate choices of $A(t)$. The choice between them depends on your use case, as we will see.

Splits and Reverse Splits

Splits and reverse splits are the cleanest case. A k-for-1 split (with $k > 1$) means:

- After the split, each pre-split share is replaced by k shares.
- The price per share is divided by k.

Economically, nothing changes except the "unit" of one share. Adjustment is straightforward:

- For backward-adjusted prices, you multiply pre-split prices by $1/k$ so that the adjusted history shows a smooth series across the split.
- For volumes, you multiply pre-split volumes by k so that total traded *value* is preserved when you compute turnover in adjusted units.

Reverse splits are the same idea with $k < 1$ (for example, 1-for-10 means $k = 0.1$). You then adjust historical prices and volumes with the inverse factor.

Splits can be chained. If a stock undergoes multiple splits over its lifetime, the cumulative adjustment factor at each date reflects the product of all individual split factors that affect that date. This cumulative factor is exactly what you store in $A(t)$.

Dividends: Cash Leaving the Asset

Dividends are more subtle because value leaves the asset. A cash dividend of D per share reduces the stock's price by roughly D on the ex-dividend date, but your total wealth remains the same if you hold both stock and dividend cash.

There are two main philosophies for incorporating dividends into adjusted prices:

- **Price-only adjustment:** Treat dividends as separate cash flows and leave prices unadjusted. You compute total return by combining price change with reinvested or non-reinvested dividends.
- **Total-return adjustment:** Adjust historical prices so that the adjusted price series behaves as if all dividends were reinvested back into the stock. In this view, the adjusted price alone captures both price appreciation and dividends.

In backtesting, total-return adjustments are often convenient, especially when you want to compare returns across many instruments or focus on long-term performance. However, execution models and P&L accounting still need to be aware of actual cash flows and raw prices, so the choice depends on context.

When you build a total-return adjusted series:

- You treat the ex-dividend date as a point where the raw price drop is mostly due to the dividend.
- You define adjustment factors so that the adjusted price does *not* jump down on that date; instead, it follows a smoother path that internalizes the dividend.

Mechanically, this is similar to a split, but with a factor based on the dividend relative to price rather than on share count alone.

Backward- vs. Forward-Adjusted Series

Let us contrast the two adjustment directions in more detail.

Backward-adjusted series. Here you fix the most recent segment of the price series in raw terms and adjust the past. This is the most common form for research datasets. Its properties:

- The last date's adjusted price equals its raw price.

- Past prices are scaled down (for splits and dividends) so that the adjusted series looks like a smooth evolution leading to the present.
- Historical returns computed from adjusted prices correspond to total returns including splits and (often) dividends.

This is useful for:

- Estimating volatility, beta, and other risk measures using recent data.
- Training models on long histories where the latest regime is most relevant.
- Comparing instruments with different split histories on a common basis.

Forward-adjusted series. Here you fix the earliest segment of the series and adjust the future:

- The first date's adjusted price equals its raw price.
- Future prices are scaled up when splits or dividends occur.
- The series shows how a position held from the start would grow with all corporate actions reinvested.

This is conceptually closer to an investor's cumulative wealth, but it is less commonly used for cross-sectional research because current prices are no longer in "real" units.

In practice, many research platforms provide backward-adjusted series for day-to-day analysis and a separate set of forward-adjusted indices or returns for long-horizon performance metrics.

Volumes, Shares Outstanding, and Liquidity

Adjustments do not stop at prices. Splits and stock dividends change share counts and therefore the interpretation of volumes and liquidity.

Key quantities include:

- **Shares outstanding:** total number of shares in existence.
- **Free float:** shares available for trading, excluding locked-up or strategic holdings.
- **Traded volume:** number of shares traded in a period.

When you adjust prices for splits, you should also adjust historical volumes and share counts so that:

- Turnover in adjusted units corresponds to actual trading activity.
- Liquidity measures (such as average daily volume) remain meaningful.

For example, in a 2-for-1 split, pre-split volumes and shares outstanding should be multiplied by 2 to express them in post-split units. This way, if you estimate "average daily volume in current share units" over a long history, you are not artificially deflating liquidity in earlier periods.

Dividend adjustments, when represented as total-return factors, can also affect adjusted volumes if you choose to maintain a notion of "dividend-reinvested shares." However, for many applications it is sufficient to:

- Adjust prices and leave traded volumes in raw units.
- Use separate fundamental data (shares outstanding, free float) to interpret liquidity and market capitalization.

The critical point is consistency: whatever convention you choose, document it and apply it consistently across the dataset.

Special Cases: Rights Issues, Spin-Offs, and Others

Not all corporate events fit neatly into "split" or "dividend." A few important special cases:

Rights issues. A rights issue gives existing shareholders the right to buy additional shares, usually at a discount, often with a trading period for the rights themselves. Economically, this is similar to a combination of:

- A stock dividend (you obtain rights as an entitlement).
- A capital raising (if you exercise and pay additional cash).

For price adjustments, you often treat the rights issue as generating an implicit "value" that must be accounted for in the total-return adjustment factor. Handling rights formally can be complex; many research datasets approximate them as adjustments to price and shares outstanding that maintain continuity across the ex-rights date.

Spin-offs. In a spin-off, the parent company distributes shares of a subsidiary to existing shareholders. The parent's price drops, but shareholders now own both the parent and the spun-off entity.

There are two ways to handle this in adjusted price series:

- **Parent-only adjustment:** Adjust the parent's historical prices so that the drop on the spin-off date is removed, treating the value of the spun-off shares as if it had been reinvested into the parent. This yields a total-return series for "owning the parent and always holding onto spin-offs."
- **Separate-entity modeling:** Track both the parent and the spin-off as separate instruments and model the distribution as a special dividend in the parent, with a matching initial price for the spin-off.

The right choice depends on how your strategy would have treated the spin-off in reality. Again, what matters is that your adjustment factors are consistent with that choice and that you disclose the assumption.

Ticker and identifier changes. Changes in ticker symbol or listing exchange do not directly change economics, but they can break naive time series if you rely on symbols as identifiers. This is why earlier sections emphasized stable internal instrument identifiers. Corporate action feeds often include symbol change events; your adjustment logic should ensure that:

- Historical series are continuous across symbol changes.
- Adjustment factors are associated with the stable identifier, not with any particular symbol string.

Integrating Adjustments into the Data Pipeline

Where in your data pipeline should you apply corporate action adjustments? There are two broad patterns:

Storage-time adjustment. You preprocess raw prices and volumes, apply adjustment factors, and store adjusted series as separate datasets. Backtests then read either raw or adjusted data as needed.

Advantages:

- Faster access at run time; no per-query adjustment needed.
- Simple for users: they select the appropriate dataset and do not worry about applying factors manually.

Disadvantages:

- If corporate action data or adjustment rules change, you must regenerate the adjusted datasets.
- You need to maintain tight version control so that you know exactly which adjustment rules were in effect for any given dataset.

Query-time adjustment. You store raw prices and volumes plus adjustment factors; backtest code applies adjustments on the fly when reading.

Advantages:

- Flexibility to change adjustment methods without rewriting stored data.
- Easier to offer multiple adjustment views (price-only, total-return, forward- or backward-adjusted) over the same raw archive.

Disadvantages:

- Slightly higher complexity and CPU cost at query time.
- Requires careful implementation in your data-access layer to avoid inconsistent or partial application of factors.

In both patterns, the guiding principles are the same:

- Keep raw and adjusted data separate.
- Version corporate action feeds and adjustment algorithms.
- Log which combination of raw data, corporate actions, and adjustment rules was used for each backtest.

Avoiding Look-Ahead Bias in Corporate Actions

Corporate actions create a special kind of look-ahead risk. Because we know their full historical effects today, it is tempting to apply them retrospectively as if investors in the past had known them in advance.

To stay honest:

- Treat *price and share count adjustments* (such as splits) as mechanical: they are applied at the ex-date because they affect raw trading units. Using adjusted prices in backtests is fine as long as your execution model uses raw trade prices and quantities when simulating fills.
- Treat *information events* (such as dividend announcements, spin-off plans, and rights issue terms) using the time alignment and lagging logic from the previous section. You can only use knowledge of a future event from its announcement onward, not from the effective date backward.

For example, when using a total-return adjusted series that internalizes dividends:

- It is acceptable to use the adjusted series to compute long-run volatility or trend, because you are essentially including the effect of past dividends on wealth.
- It is *not* acceptable to use the future knowledge of a special dividend to alter your trading decisions before its announcement. That decision logic must be driven by an event series aligned causally, not by the adjusted price path alone.

In ambiguous situations, err on the side of conservatism: delay the use of information, or test both conservative and aggressive assumptions and examine the sensitivity of results.

Data Quality and Edge Cases

Corporate action data is itself imperfect. You will encounter:

- Missing actions that cause unadjusted price jumps.
- Duplicated or conflicting records from different vendors.
- Incorrect effective dates, announcement dates, or terms.
- Instruments with complex restructuring histories that are hard to model cleanly.

Your cleaning and validation framework (from the final section of this chapter) should include checks such as:

- Detecting large overnight price moves and verifying whether a corporate action is recorded for that date.
- Reconciling corporate actions across multiple sources when available.
- Flagging instruments whose adjustment factors change frequently due to data corrections.

For severe inconsistencies, it may be better to exclude an instrument from certain analyses rather than risk silently corrupted results. At a minimum, backtests should log when they rely on instruments with known adjustment anomalies.

Corporate actions are not an annoyance to be patched over; they are fundamental to how equity and related instruments evolve. Splits, dividends, rights issues, and restructurings constantly change the unit in which price and volume are measured, and they move value between securities and cash.

Adjustment factors provide a disciplined way to handle these changes:

- They transform raw prices and quantities into adjusted series that are continuous and analytically convenient.
- They can represent both backward- and forward-adjusted views, supporting different research needs.
- They allow you to separate mechanical unit changes from genuine economic returns.

By maintaining both raw and adjusted datasets, versioning your corporate action feeds and adjustment rules, and treating information timing carefully, you can build backtests that are both realistic and reproducible. The next and final section on data quality, cleaning, and validation will tie these threads together, showing how to ensure that all these temporal and structural choices rest on trustworthy, auditable data.

2.7 Data Quality, Cleaning & Validation

By now we have built a carefully structured view of market data: calendars and sessions define when trading can occur; time normalization ensures a monotonic event timeline; data models capture trades, quotes, and bars; storage formats and alignment logic make these records usable at scale. All of this rests on a crucial assumption: that the underlying data are *trustworthy*.

In practice, real-world market data are messy. Feeds drop packets, exchanges correct trades after the fact, vendors change symbol mappings, and corporate actions are sometimes misapplied. If you accept all incoming data at face value, your backtests will sit on a foundation of hidden errors. Worse, small data problems can masquerade as profitable strategies: what looks like an alpha signal might really be a stale quote or a survivorship filter.

This section lays out a systematic approach to data quality, cleaning, and validation, with three goals:

- Detect and classify typical data issues before they contaminate research.
- Apply repair strategies that are conservative, documented, and reproducible.
- Maintain auditability, so that every transformation can be traced and justified.

Typical Data Problems in Market Feeds

It helps to name the problems you will encounter. Common issues include:

Missing days or partial sessions. Entire days may be absent, often due to ingest failures rather than true market closures. Within a trading day, some periods may have no data because of outages or vendor glitches.

Duplicate or out-of-order records. Feeds might replay messages, or records may arrive slightly out of sequence. This is particularly common in tick data.

Stale quotes. Best bid or ask quotes may remain unchanged for an implausibly long time, often because the feed has stopped updating while the underlying market continues to trade.

Crossed or locked markets. The best bid may equal (locked) or exceed (crossed) the best ask, typically due to timing differences between venues or data errors.

Wildly off-market prices. Erroneous trades or quotes can show prices far away from the prevailing market, sometimes by orders of magnitude (for example, a trade at 1000 instead of 10).

Corporate action misapplications. Missing splits, incorrect ex-dates, or misapplied dividend adjustments can create artificial jumps or distort volumes.

Survivorship bias and look-ahead in universes. Instrument lists that only include currently active securities, or that use future knowledge about delistings and index membership, lead to biased strategy evaluations.

These issues are not rare exceptions; they are part of the everyday reality of market data. A professional backtest engine treats them as first-class concerns, not as edge cases to be ignored.

A Layered Approach to Data Quality

Cleaning should not be a single monolithic step where all problems are "fixed" in opaque ways. Instead, think in layers, each addressing different aspects of data quality:

- **Structural validation against schemas.**
- **Range and sanity checks on values.**
- **Cross-source reconciliation.**
- **Statistical anomaly detection over time.**

Each layer produces diagnostics and, where appropriate, controlled transformations. Separating these concerns makes it easier to reason about what you are doing and to reproduce the process later.

Structural Validation: Does the Data "Shape" Make Sense?

Structural validation checks whether records conform to expected schemas and basic ordering properties. You are asking: "Is this even a well-formed feed?"

Typical checks include:

Schema consistency. For each dataset (trades, quotes, bars, etc.):

- All required fields are present (instrument id, timestamp, price, size, etc.).
- Field types are correct (timestamps parse, prices are numeric, enumerated fields have allowed values).
- No unexpected extra fields appear without documentation.

Violations here often indicate ingest issues or upstream changes in vendor formats.

Timestamp monotonicity within a feed. For each instrument and venue:

- Timestamps of trades and quotes should be non-decreasing.
- If out-of-order events are allowed, they should be rare and treated explicitly (for example, sorted and flagged).

If you see frequent time reversals or large negative jumps, something is wrong in either the feed or the time normalization logic.

Calendar consistency. Using your exchange calendars:

- Records should not appear outside trading sessions unless explicitly allowed (for example, off-market prints).
- Days labeled as market holidays should not contain regular session activity.

Misalignments here may indicate incorrect calendars, wrong time zones, or vendor mislabeling.

Structural problems are usually *hard errors*: you should either fix them mechanically (for example, parsing types) or reject/flag the offending records for manual review. Silent tolerance is dangerous.

Range and Sanity Checks: Are Values Plausible?

Once the basic structure is sound, you ask: "Do these numbers make sense?" Sanity checks define bounds and relationships that should almost always hold.

Examples:

Price and spread bounds. For each instrument:

- Prices should be positive and within a broadly reasonable range (for example, not 0 or 10^9 unless those are plausible for the instrument).
- For quotes, best bid should be less than or equal to best ask; persistent violations indicate crossed/locked markets or errors.
- Spreads should not exceed implausible fractions of the price for extended periods.

Thresholds should be instrument-specific where possible: a penny stock has different typical spreads than a large-cap index future.

Volume and size checks. For trades and bars:

- Trade sizes should be positive and not exceed known limits (for example, total shares outstanding).
- Bar volumes should not be negative and should be consistent with sums of constituent trades if both are available.

Derived-field consistency. If you compute mid-prices, returns, or volatility estimates:

- Returns larger than some extreme threshold (for example, hundreds of percent in one minute) should be flagged.
- Derived metrics should not produce undefined or infinite values except where clearly justified (for example, missing data).

Range violations do not always mean the data are wrong; extreme market events do happen. The right response is often to *flag* suspicious points, not automatically delete them. Later, you can decide, based on context, whether to keep them, correct them, or exclude them from certain analyses.

Cross-Source Reconciliation: Trust, but Verify

Relying on a single data source is risky. When possible, obtain multiple feeds or references for key datasets (for example, a primary and a consolidated feed, or two vendors for daily bars) and compare them.

Cross-source checks might include:

Price and volume comparison. For each instrument and date:

- Compare end-of-day prices and volumes across vendors.
- Define tolerances (absolute or relative) beyond which differences are flagged.

Corporate action agreement. For splits, dividends, and other actions:

- Confirm that action types, ex-dates, and terms match across providers.
- Flag mismatches for manual resolution or conservative handling.

Calendar agreement. For trading days and holidays:

- Compare actual presence of trading activity against the calendar.
- If two sources disagree on whether a day is a trading day, investigate.

When sources disagree, you should have a clear policy:

- Which source is primary?
- Under what conditions do you override the primary with secondary?

- When do you mark data as "uncertain" and exclude it from critical backtests?

These decisions should be documented in your data-quality playbook, not made ad hoc in individual research scripts.

Statistical Anomaly Detection: Subtle Problems over Time

Some data issues only become apparent when you look at time-series behavior, not at individual records. Statistical anomaly detection complements structural and range checks.

Examples:

Volatility regime shifts. If the estimated volatility for an instrument suddenly jumps by orders of magnitude and stays high, it may indicate:

- A real structural change (for example, a crisis).
- A change in tick size, trading venue, or price scale.
- A feed change or mis-scaling in the data (for example, prices in cents vs. dollars).

Liquidity profile changes. If average daily volume or quote depth changes drastically overnight and permanently, you should ask:

- Did the instrument re-list, merge, or change symbol?
- Has the vendor altered which venues are included?

Cross-sectional anomalies. Within a universe:

- Instruments with consistently extreme spreads, volumes, or returns compared to peers may be suffering from data issues.
- Instruments that never trade or always trade at the same price may be inactive listings or stale feeds.

These methods do not "prove" data are wrong; they surface candidates for further investigation, and in some cases justify conservative exclusion from universes or particular strategies.

Hard Errors vs. Soft Anomalies

Not every problem should be "fixed" automatically. It is useful to distinguish:

Hard errors. These are violations that almost certainly indicate incorrect data, such as:

- Negative prices.
- Timestamps that cannot be parsed or violate basic ordering.
- Prices off by several orders of magnitude with no supporting event.

Hard errors typically warrant one of:

- Dropping or correcting the record with a deterministic rule (for example, clipping an obviously extra digit).
- Excluding the entire day or instrument from analyses if contamination is severe.

Soft anomalies. These are unusual but possibly legitimate observations, such as:

- Very large but plausible price moves during a crisis.
- Temporarily crossed markets around news events.
- Extended periods of illiquidity in microcaps.

Soft anomalies should be:

- Flagged and logged.

- Left in the dataset by default, unless a particular strategy cannot tolerate them.

By separating these categories, you reduce the temptation to "over-clean" the data in ways that remove real, informative extremes and leave only an idealized, low-volatility world.

Cleaning Strategies for Common Issues

With this framework in place, we can outline practical, conservative cleaning recipes.

Duplicate and out-of-order records.

- Sort events by instrument, venue, and timestamp.
- Drop exact duplicates (same instrument, timestamp, and content).
- For out-of-order but otherwise valid events, reorder them; if reordering requires large corrections (for example, tens of seconds in high-frequency data), flag the day or segment as potentially unreliable.

Missing days or partial sessions.

- Use calendars to identify expected trading days with no data.
- Distinguish between true market closures (holidays, ad-hoc closures) and ingest failures.
- For partial sessions (for example, missing morning data), decide whether to:

- Exclude the day from analyses that rely on intraday structure.
- Use the available segment for lower-frequency analyses (for example, daily closes).

Avoid silently "filling" missing days with forward-filled prices; this can distort volatility and autocorrelation.

Stale and crossed quotes.

- Define a maximum quote age relative to recent trades or to wall-clock time; treat quotes older than this threshold as stale and ignore them in mid-price or spread calculations.
- For crossed markets, you can:

- Use trades to infer a more realistic mid-price.
- Temporarily widen the spread to a conservative level.
- In some cases, drop these intervals from slippage modeling.

Wild price outliers.

- Identify candidate outliers via large relative changes, absolute thresholds, or inconsistency with nearby quotes.
- Where the cause is clearly a data glitch (for example, one throw-away print at 1000 in an otherwise tight range), you may:

- Remove the outlier trade from the dataset used for bar construction.
- Replace the outlier with a nearby value (for example, previous or next trade) but *flag* the correction.

- If the outlier corresponds to a known event (for example, a fat-finger trade that triggered a brief halt), consider whether your strategy could realistically have traded at that price. If so, you may choose to keep it in execution modeling.

Corporate action misapplications.

- Compare price jumps around known ex-dates to expected adjustment factors.

- If missing or incorrect actions are detected, correct the corporate action series and regenerate adjusted prices.
- When in doubt, prefer using raw prices plus explicit action records over pre-adjusted prices of unknown provenance.

Survivorship Bias and Universe Construction

Data quality is not only about individual records; it also concerns which instruments appear in your backtests. Survivorship bias occurs when you only include instruments that survived to some later date, thereby overstating performance.

Typical traps:

- Building a universe from a current index membership list and applying it historically, ignoring past constituents that were later removed or delisted.
- Using a symbol list from the data vendor that silently drops delisted names from older periods.

To avoid this:

- Maintain a *time-varying* universe, where each instrument has a history of inclusion/exclusion and, where applicable, index membership. Universe membership at time t should only depend on information available at or before t.
- Treat delistings and bankruptcies explicitly as events; ensure that your accounting and P&L model includes the corresponding terminal cash flows or write-downs.
- When benchmarking against indices, use historical constituent lists and weights, not reconstituted current memberships.

Survivorship-related logic should be part of your data and universe construction layer, not bolted on in each strategy. Documenting these rules is essential for interpreting performance.

Auditability: Logging and Lineage

Cleaning and validation change data. For reproducible research, you must be able to answer:

> "Given this number used in a backtest, where did it come from, and what transformations were applied to it?"

Achieving this requires:

Transformation logs. When you perform cleaning steps (such as dropping outliers, correcting timestamps, or adjusting for corporate actions):

- Log what was changed, when, by which process, and why.
- Aggregate logs into human-readable reports that summarize the number and type of modifications per dataset, per day, or per instrument.

Data versioning. As discussed earlier:

- Assign version identifiers to datasets after cleaning.
- Store manifests that list all underlying files and checksums.
- Reference these versions explicitly in backtest configuration and results.

Code versioning. Cleaning logic evolves:

- Track the code version (for example, commit hash) of the cleaning and validation routines used to generate each dataset version.
- When you change cleaning rules, create new dataset versions; do not silently overwrite old ones.

Together, these practices form data lineage: the chain from raw source to research-ready dataset. Lineage gives you the confidence to revisit past results, explain differences between runs, and defend your methodology to colleagues, risk managers, or regulators.

Reproducible Validation Suites

Finally, validation should not be an ad hoc activity. You should maintain a suite of automated tests that can be run whenever:

- New data are ingested.
- Cleaning logic is updated.
- Core infrastructure (time libraries, storage formats, calendars) changes.

Such a suite might include:

- Structural and range checks on recent data slices.
- Regression tests on known problematic dates (for example, major market events, DST transitions, corporate action clusters).
- Universe consistency tests to ensure that historical membership and delisting events behave as expected.

The goal is to catch data-quality regressions *before* they reach research or production backtests.

Data quality is not a one-off cleaning pass; it is an ongoing discipline woven into the design of your backtest engine and data infrastructure. By:

- Recognizing common data issues in market feeds.
- Applying a layered approach of structural checks, sanity bounds, cross-source reconciliation, and statistical anomaly detection.
- Distinguishing hard errors from soft anomalies and handling each appropriately.
- Implementing conservative, documented cleaning recipes for duplicates, missing periods, stale quotes, outliers, and corporate action issues.

- Constructing time-varying, bias-aware universes that avoid survivorship and look-ahead.
- Maintaining audit trails, data and code versioning, and reproducible validation suites.

you transform messy, fallible raw feeds into auditable, trustworthy simulation inputs. This closes the loop on the chapter's main theme: robust backtests are not just about clever models or fast engines; they are about respecting the true shape of market time and the imperfections of the data that record it.

Chapter 3

Simulation Architecture & Event Engine

A good backtest isn't a fancy spreadsheet-it's a tiny exchange you control. In this chapter we deconstruct that exchange into clocks, feeds, and an event loop, then show how to wire them so every run is causally correct, reproducible to the tick, and ready to scale from a laptop to a cluster without changing a single line of strategy code.

3.1 Event Scheduling & Clocks

In the previous chapter we treated market data, orders, and portfolio state somewhat informally: "prices arrive," "the strategy reacts," "fills happen," and so on. To turn these ideas into a reliable backtest engine, we must now answer a stricter question:

Exactly when does each action happen, and in what order, relative to every other action?

This section defines the discrete-time backbone of the engine. We will build up three core concepts:

1. A **session-aware simulation clock** that is the single source of truth for "what time it is" in the backtest.
2. A **priority-ordered event schedule** that decides which event happens next when multiple things want to occur at the same time.
3. A **latency model** that inserts realistic delays between cause and effect, without sacrificing reproducibility.

Together, these form the scheduler: the component that moves simulated time forward and orchestrates every interaction between data feed, strategy, execution model, and accounting.

Three Notions of Time

Real-world trading involves several overlapping notions of time. Confusing them is a frequent source of subtle bugs.

Wall-clock time. This is the time on your local machine or server, including network delays, OS scheduling, and logging timestamps. It is often in your system's local timezone and drifts slightly with clock corrections.

Exchange time. This is the time used by the trading venue. Market data and order acknowledgements are timestamped according to the exchange's clock, usually in the exchange's local timezone, with well-defined session hours, holidays, and special events (such as auctions).

Simulated time. This is the time maintained by your backtest engine. It advances only when the scheduler processes an event. It is not tied to how long the backtest takes to run in real life. In a discrete-event simulation, simulated time may jump from 09:30:00 to 09:30:05 directly, if nothing relevant happens in between.

For backtesting, **simulated time must be clearly defined and under your control**. You typically express it in a single canonical timezone (for example, UTC) and derive it from exchange timestamps plus the details of the trading calendar. Wall-clock time is mostly useful for profiling and debugging performance, not for determining trading outcomes.

The Scheduler as Canonical Time Source

Every component in the engine must agree on one thing: *the scheduler's clock is the only authoritative time.* No module reads the system clock to decide anything about trading logic. Instead, the scheduler:

- Maintains the current simulated time.
- Decides which event occurs next.
- Advances simulated time to the timestamp of that event.
- Notifies the relevant module (data feed, strategy, execution, accounting).

When your strategy asks "what time is it?" it is really querying the scheduler's notion of time. When the execution model decides whether an order can be filled during the session, it consults the same clock. This is the foundation for deterministic, replayable simulation: given the same configuration and data, the same sequence of events and timestamps will always occur.

Right after we introduce this idea, it is helpful to visualize how the scheduler relates to the rest of the system.

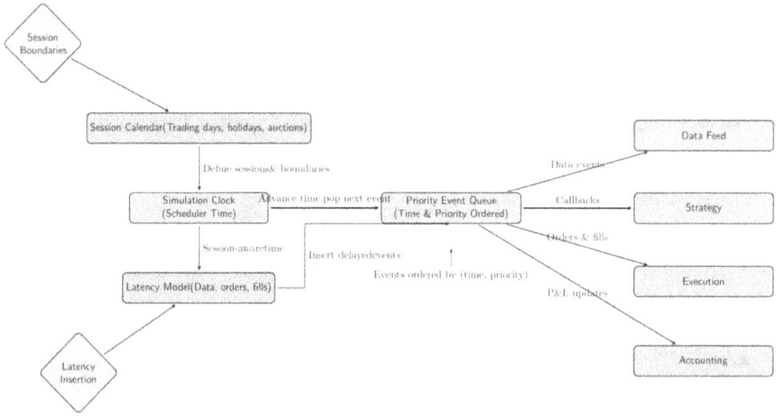

Session-Aware Clocks and Trading Calendars

Financial markets are not open 24/7 in a simple way. They have:

- Regular trading hours (for example, 09:30–16:00).
- Pre-open and closing auctions.
- Lunch breaks in some markets.
- Holidays and ad-hoc closures.
- Early closes on special days.

A robust simulation clock must be **session-aware**: it understands which times are tradable, which belong to auctions, and which are outside the session.

Trading Calendar as a First-Class Input

The trading calendar is a data structure that answers questions like:

- Is this timestamp inside a session?

- What are the open and close times for this date?
- Are there special events (auctions, early close) today?
- What is the next valid trading timestamp after this one?

The scheduler uses the calendar to:

1. Reject events that fall outside any defined session (or map them to appropriate session edges).
2. Insert synthetic events such as:

- *Session open*: initialization logic, opening auctions.
- *Session close*: final accounting, daily roll, performance snapshots.
- *Auction phases*: when special pricing or order rules apply.

3. Advance time correctly when there are long gaps (for example, from Friday close to Monday open, skipping the weekend).

A calendar can be shared across multiple components. The data feed uses it to decide which timestamps are valid for replay. The execution model uses it to check whether orders placed at a given time can be filled. But the scheduler is the component that actually applies the calendar to move simulated time.

Clock Modes: Bars, Intraday, and Ticks

The granularity of the simulation clock determines both the realism and the complexity of the engine.

Bar-close mode. The simplest mode advances time from bar close to bar close: for example, daily or minute bars. The scheduler jumps from one bar timestamp to the next, and the strategy is only called once per bar. This is easy to reason about but cannot model within-bar dynamics, such as intra-minute order placement and fills.

Intrabar or event-driven mode. Here, time advances whenever a new event arrives: a trade, a quote update, a bar boundary, or a timer you scheduled. This allows fine-grained modeling: you can place an order at 09:30:01 and get filled at 09:30:05, even if your performance metrics are ultimately computed on a bar basis.

Hybrid modes. Many engines use a middle ground: the strategy may only receive callbacks at bar boundaries, but the execution model runs at a higher resolution on underlying tick data. In that case, the scheduler still advances through all underlying events, but it decides which ones are visible to which module.

Choosing a mode is not a purely technical decision; it encodes an assumption about what information the strategy can use and when. Once chosen, the clock mode becomes a contract: every module must know how frequently it will be called and what assumptions it can make about time ordering of events.

Events as Timestamped Messages

The scheduler operates on *events*. An event is a message with at least:

- A **timestamp** in simulated time, usually corresponding to exchange time normalized to your canonical timezone.
- A **type**, such as *data*, *order submission*, *fill*, *timer callback*, *session open*, or *session close*.
- A **payload**, which carries the specific information (for example, price and volume for a trade, or order identifier and quantity for a fill).

The scheduler maintains a set of future events and repeatedly:

1. Picks the next event to process.
2. Advances the simulation clock to that event's timestamp.
3. Dispatches the event to the appropriate handler (data feed, strategy, execution, accounting).

4. Allows the handler to create new future events (for example, an order submission may result in a future fill event).

This leads naturally to the need for an ordered data structure.

Priority Queues and Event Ordering

To select the "next" event efficiently, backtest engines commonly use a **priority queue** keyed by timestamp. The concept is simple: at any moment, the next event to process is the one with the smallest (earliest) timestamp.

However, timestamps alone are not enough. Many events can share the same timestamp:

- A data tick at 09:30:00.
- A timer callback at 09:30:00.
- A fill that the execution model schedules at 09:30:00.

Yet the order in which these are processed matters for causality. For example, a strategy *must not* react to a price move that occurs "after" it places an order but has the same timestamp.

To handle this, events need an additional ordering rule—a **priority**.

Defining Event Priorities

Priorities can be encoded as simple integers or as an ordered category. A reasonable, though not universal, ordering at a given timestamp is:

1. **Data events** (prices, trades, quotes, corporate actions).
2. **Timer events and engine callbacks** (for example, end-of-bar computations).
3. **Strategy actions** (order submissions, cancellations).
4. **Execution results** (fills, partial fills).

5. **Accounting updates and bookkeeping** (portfolio value, risk checks).

Within each category, you may still need a deterministic tie-breaker, such as a monotonically increasing sequence number. The key is that the full ordering rule, often written conceptually as "order by (timestamp, priority, sequence number)," is:

- **Global**: it applies to all events, regardless of source.
- **Stable**: given the same inputs, it always yields the same ordering.
- **Documented**: users of the engine know the rules and can design strategies accordingly.

Causal Correctness

A central goal of the event ordering is **causal correctness**. Informally:

> An event should only be able to respond to information that is logically available at its timestamp, and nothing that happens "later" may affect it.

This is why data updates are often processed first at a given timestamp, so that:

1. The data event updates the observable market state (prices, quotes).
2. The strategy is then called and can inspect this state.
3. The strategy submits an order at the same timestamp.
4. The execution model may generate a fill that is also timestamped there or slightly later.

If you were to process fills before strategy callbacks at a given timestamp, you could end up with impossible scenarios where a fill uses prices that the strategy has not yet seen.

Modeling Latency as Scheduled Delays

Real markets have latency:

- Market data takes time to travel from the exchange to you.
- Your orders take time to travel from your system to the exchange.
- The exchange takes time to match orders and send back fills.

A naive backtest typically ignores this and assumes zero latency: orders are filled immediately at the observed price. This can drastically overstate performance for strategies that depend on reacting quickly to short-lived opportunities.

A more realistic model inserts **delays** between cause and effect.

Latency as Event Time Shifts

In an event-driven engine, latency is naturally expressed as a shift in event timestamps:

- A data event may arrive at the exchange at 09:30:00 but only become visible to the strategy at 09:30:00.050 (50 milliseconds later).
- A market order may be submitted by the strategy at 09:30:01.000 but only reach the exchange at 09:30:01.010.
- A fill may be produced by the exchange at 09:30:01.012 and received by your system at 09:30:01.020.

The latency model is responsible for taking a "logical" event (for example, "strategy submits order now") and scheduling one or more "physical" events in the future (for example, "order reaches exchange," "fill received") by adding appropriate delays.

Mechanically, this means:

1. The strategy calls "submit order."

2. The execution module, consulting the latency model, computes the arrival time at the exchange by adding a delay.
3. It then creates one or more new events with later timestamps and pushes them into the priority queue.

Deterministic vs Stochastic Latencies

Latency may be:

- **Deterministic**: for example, a fixed 10-millisecond round-trip.
- **Stochastic**: drawn from a statistical distribution, perhaps depending on time of day or load.

Introducing randomness adds realism but threatens reproducibility. To keep simulations reproducible:

- Latency random draws should come from well-managed pseudo-random number generators, with seeds recorded as part of the configuration.
- The order of random draws must be stable: if event processing order changes, the latencies might change, leading to drift in results.

A practical compromise is to limit where randomness is allowed and strictly define the order in which random draws are consumed. The latency model, integrated with the scheduler, is a natural place to centralize this.

Granularity and Rounding

When modeling latency, you must also choose a time resolution. For low-frequency strategies, milliseconds may be more than enough. For ultra-high-frequency models, nanoseconds might be necessary.

Be explicit about rounding rules. For example:

- If you add a 7.3 millisecond delay, do you round up or down to the nearest microsecond?
- When two events land on exactly the same timestamp after rounding, how are they ordered?

These choices affect both realism and determinism. They should be documented and, ideally, configurable.

Clock Contracts With Downstream Components

The scheduler and its clock form the spine of the engine. Every downstream module interacts with them through a **contract**:

Data feed. The data feed guarantees that all emitted market data events are:

- Timestamped in the canonical simulated time.
- Non-decreasing in time for each symbol stream.
- Inserted into the event queue before their timestamps are reached.

In return, the scheduler guarantees that data events will be delivered in timestamp order and according to the priority rules.

Strategy. The strategy is promised that:

- It will only see time moving forward, never backward.
- Within a single callback, simulated time is fixed.
- Any orders it submits are tagged with the current simulated time and then subject to the latency model.

It must also respect that it cannot "reach back" and influence past events.

Execution model. The execution model relies on:

- Session-aware time to decide when orders are actionable.
- The latency model to schedule when orders are sent, matched, and filled.
- Priority rules to ensure that fills are processed in a well-defined order relative to data and strategy callbacks.

Accounting and risk. Accounting expects:

- To receive all fills and corporate actions in timestamp order.
- To perform margin checks and risk updates at specific times, for example, after each fill or at end-of-bar.

It can then guarantee that portfolio state is always consistent with all prior events at the current simulated time.

Putting It All Together

Event scheduling and clocks are not just implementation details; they are the visible skeleton of your backtest engine. A clear, session-aware clock combined with a well-defined priority event queue and an explicit latency model allows you to:

- Reproduce results exactly, because the sequence of events and their timestamps are fully determined.
- Reason about what information is available to the strategy at each moment, and prevent impossible look-ahead.
- Model realistic delays between observing prices, sending orders, and receiving fills.
- Decompose the system into modules (data, strategy, execution, accounting) that share a common view of time and ordering.

In the next sections we will build on this backbone. First we will look more closely at the data feed and replay subsystem, which is responsible for generating the event stream that drives the scheduler. Then we will assemble the full event-driven backtest engine, showing how the main loop processes events according to the rules laid out here.

3.2 Data Feed & Replay

In the previous section we built the backbone of the simulation: a session-aware clock and a priority-ordered event scheduler. That gave us a clear answer to the question "when does something happen?" We now turn to a complementary question:

What events are we feeding into the engine, and how do we deliver them in a way that is scalable, robust, and reproducible?

This section focuses on the historical data subsystem, which we will call the *data feed*. Its job is to turn raw historical collections-files, databases, object stores-into a clean, ordered stream of events entering the scheduler. Done correctly, this subsystem:

- Aligns many different data types and symbols on a single time axis.
- Streams data incrementally, without loading everything into memory.
- Cooperates with the event engine when downstream consumers are slow (backpressure).
- Supports fault-tolerant replay so that you can interrupt and resume runs without changing results.

We will build up these ideas step by step, using the simulation clock and event queue defined earlier as our anchor.

What Counts as "Data" in a Backtest?

The most obvious form of data is price history, but a realistic engine must handle several categories of events:

Trades. Individual executed trades, each with a timestamp, price, and size. At the tick level this can be very high frequency data.

Quotes. Bid and ask quotes (or full order-book snapshots), representing available liquidity. Quotes evolve rapidly and may contain many updates with no trade occurring.

Bars. Aggregated data such as open-high-low-close-volume over fixed intervals (for example, 1 minute, 5 minutes, daily). Bars are derived from underlying ticks but are often the primary input for lower-frequency strategies.

Corporate actions. Splits, dividends, symbol changes, rights issues. These can abruptly change prices or share counts; they must be represented as explicit events so that the engine can adjust positions and prices consistently.

Reference data. Static or slowly-changing information: ticker to instrument mapping, sector classifications, tick sizes, exchange codes, margin rules, and so on. Some of this may be loaded at initialization; some may appear as infrequent "update" events.

Each of these must be converted into the engine's internal event representation, which includes a timestamp that is compatible with the simulation clock, and a type that the scheduler can use to order and dispatch the event.

Normalization and Timestamp Discipline

Historical data often arrives in heterogeneous formats:

- Different timezones (exchange-local, UTC, local machine time).
- Different timestamp conventions (start-of-interval vs end-of-interval for bars).
- Different resolutions (seconds, milliseconds, nanoseconds).
- Different field names and semantics.

Before such data can safely drive a simulation, it must be **normalized**. At minimum, normalization enforces:

A common time standard. Choose a canonical timezone for your engine, typically UTC, and convert all timestamps to it. Align this with the session-aware clock introduced previously, so that "09:30:00 at the exchange" maps to the same instant everywhere in the engine.

Consistent bar conventions. Decide whether your bar timestamps represent the bar's open, its close, or its center, and keep that consistent. For instance, minute bars might be tagged by their closing time: the bar covering [09:30:00, 09:30:59.999] is labeled 09:30:59.999 (or simply 09:30:00 depending on your convention). This choice directly affects how the strategy interprets "time of last known price."

Monotonic streams per symbol. For each symbol and data type, ensure that timestamps are non-decreasing. If you discover out-of-order records, you must either sort them or explicitly define how to resolve conflicts. The scheduler assumes that for a given symbol and event type, it will never encounter time running backwards.

Uniform field naming & typing. Regardless of original source, an "execution price" means the same thing everywhere, an "ask size" has the same units, and so on. This makes downstream code simpler and less error-prone.

Practically, normalization is often implemented as an offline preprocessing step. However, conceptually, the normalized representation is the only one the data feed should emit into the engine proper.

The Replay Cursor: Walking Through History

Once data is normalized, we need a mechanism to "walk" through it in time order and present events to the scheduler. That mechanism is the *replay cursor*.

Think of a replay cursor as a read head that points to the "next" historical event. For a single data source, such as daily bars for one symbol, the cursor is simply an index into a sorted list. But real backtests usually involve:

- Many symbols.
- Multiple data types (trades, quotes, bars, corporate actions).
- Possibly multiple venues.

In that context, a single cursor per stream is not enough. We need to merge many time-ordered streams into one.

Multi-Stream Merging

Imagine you have:

- One stream of minute bars for AAPL.
- One stream of minute bars for MSFT.
- One stream of corporate actions for all U.S. equities.

Each stream is independently sorted by time, but we must deliver events to the scheduler in *global* time order across all of them. A natural approach is:

1. Maintain one cursor per stream, each exposing its current "next event."
2. At each step, look at all candidate events and choose the one with the earliest timestamp.
3. Advance the corresponding cursor and emit that event into the engine's priority queue.

Conceptually this mirrors how the scheduler itself extracts the next event to process from its queue. Here, instead of processing, we are *generating* events from historical storage.

This merging logic has to respect the session-aware clock: if an event lands outside any trading session, the data feed and scheduler must agree whether it is allowed, adjusted to a session boundary, or discarded.

Preserving Original Exchange Ordering

For some strategies, especially intraday and microstructure models, the relative order of trades and quotes at the same timestamp matters. Historical data sometimes provides sequence numbers, trade IDs, or book update indices that capture this partial ordering.

Your replay cursor must preserve this ordering faithfully. That means:

- Within a single stream (for example, trades for one symbol on one venue), events are emitted in the exact order they appeared in the original data.
- When merging streams with overlapping timestamps, you define a deterministic cross-stream rule, but you never reorder events *within* a stream.

This is conceptually similar to the event priority rules in the scheduler, but at the boundary between raw data and internal events.

Streaming vs Loading: Buffering Strategies

A naive backtester might load all required data into memory before running the simulation. This is often fine for short backtests or small universes but becomes infeasible for:

- Long time spans (many years).
- High-frequency data (ticks, order-book updates).
- Large universes (thousands of symbols).

Instead, the data feed should be **streaming**: it reads and decodes data incrementally, ahead of the current simulation time but not by too much. This is where buffering enters the picture.

Look-Ahead Buffers

The replay cursor can maintain a small buffer of "next" events that have already been read from storage but not yet consumed by the scheduler. The size of this buffer is a trade-off:

- Too small: the simulation may repeatedly stall waiting for I/O.
- Too large: you risk unnecessary memory use, and possibly preloading lots of data that is never reached if the backtest stops early.

A practical approach is to buffer by *time window* rather than by number of events. For example, always keep at least one day of future events in memory for each active symbol, but no more than one week. This aligns well with the idea of a session-aware clock: the buffer can try to stay at least one full session ahead, if resources permit.

Serialization Boundaries

In distributed or multi-process setups, you must decide where to place *serialization boundaries*:

- Do you read raw files in one process and send normalized events over the network?
- Do you have each worker directly read from shared storage and perform its own normalization and buffering?

These choices impact performance and determinism. If multiple workers independently normalize and merge data, you must ensure that they all apply the exact same rules so that two runs with the same configuration produce the same events in the same order.

A clean architecture often centralizes normalization in a preprocessing step that produces "engine-ready" data files. Then, each worker's data feed is relatively simple: just streaming and merging already-normalized event streams.

Flow Control and Backpressure

So far we have assumed that the data feed can push events into the event queue as quickly as it likes. In practice, downstream components (strategy, execution, accounting) may not be able to keep up, especially in complex simulations or when running on constrained hardware.

Backpressure is the mechanism by which slower consumers can signal to the data feed to slow down or pause, avoiding unbounded memory growth and eventual failure.

Push vs Pull Models

There are two broad styles of interaction between the data feed and the scheduler:

Push-based. The data feed reads ahead and pushes new events into the priority queue up to some limit. If the queue reaches a high-water mark (too many future events in memory), the data feed pauses reading until consumers catch up.

Pull-based. The scheduler, when it needs more events at or beyond a certain time, explicitly asks the data feed to advance its replay cursor and produce the next batch of events. The data feed never gets "ahead" of the scheduler by more than one request.

Both approaches can work. A pull-based design often makes backpressure more explicit: the scheduler directly controls how far into the future it wants to see events. A push-based design can better hide I/O latency by prefetching, but must be careful not to overrun memory.

Regardless of style, you should:

- Define clear limits on how many unprocessed events can pile up.
- Decide what happens when limits are reached (block the data feed, drop events, or trigger an error).
- Make these behaviors visible and configurable.

Interaction With Latency and Clock

Backpressure is not only a performance concern; it interacts with your latency model and clock semantics. For instance:

- If the data feed is blocked from loading future events, the scheduler must not advance simulated time beyond the last known data point.
- If latency modeling creates many additional future events (for example, delayed fills), the total number of scheduled events may grow quickly, triggering backpressure even if the raw data rate is modest.

Therefore, queue limits and buffering policies must take into account not only raw historical data but also derived events created during simulation.

Replay Robustness: Checkpoints and Idempotence

For serious research and production systems, you rarely run a backtest in one uninterrupted session. Jobs may be killed by cluster maintenance, configuration changes, or simply by human error. You must be able to:

- Stop a simulation mid-way.
- Restart it from a checkpoint.
- Obtain bitwise-identical results to a straight-through run.

This is not only a convenience; it is a core requirement for reproducible research at scale.

Deterministic Seek Positions

To resume a simulation, the data feed must know "where in history" it left off. This can be represented by a *seek position*, which might include:

- For each underlying stream (for example, each symbol's bar file), the index or byte offset of the next event to read.
- The current simulated time.
- Any pending buffered events that have been read but not yet processed.

These seek positions must be:

- **Deterministic**: given the same seek position, the data feed will replay the exact same subsequent sequence of events.

- **Serializable**: you can write them to disk or to a database as part of a checkpoint.

When the simulation is resumed:

1. The scheduler restores its clock and event queue from checkpoint.
2. The data feed restores its seek positions and internal buffers.
3. The engine proceeds as if it had never stopped.

Idempotent Event Emission

A subtle but important property is *idempotence*: re-emitting the same logical event twice should not corrupt state if you are careful, or, preferably, should not happen at all.

In the context of checkpoints, idempotence means that you must avoid "double-feeding" events that were already processed before the checkpoint. This is why storing precise seek positions and buffer contents is so critical: if upon resume you start reading slightly earlier in the raw data and emit overlapping events, strategy state, positions, and P&L may be incorrectly duplicated.

A robust design guarantees that the prefix of events seen before the checkpoint is exactly the same as the prefix seen in a full, uninterrupted run, and that the suffix after resume is also identical.

Partitioned Backtests

Many large-scale studies partition work by:

- Time slices (for example, Year 1 on worker A, Year 2 on worker B).
- Universes (for example, symbols A-M vs N-Z).
- Scenarios (for example, variations in slippage or latency).

Your replay system must ensure that each partition sees a consistent slice of the event stream and that the union of these slices is exactly the full stream, without gaps or overlaps. This is effectively the same problem as checkpointing, but with the goal of distributing work instead of resuming it.

Data Lineage and Versioning

Although this section is about mechanics, it is worth noting that **data lineage** and **versioning** are closely tied to replay. If you change the underlying data (for example, update corporate actions or re-clean a tick history), the same backtest configuration may produce different outcomes, even with a perfectly deterministic engine.

To remain honest and reproducible:

- Tag each dataset with a version identifier.
- Record which dataset versions are used in each backtest.
- Ensure that a replay or resume run uses the same data versions.

In practice, these metadata can be stored alongside checkpoints and configuration files. Conceptually, the data feed is responsible for enforcing "I am replaying exactly dataset X, version Y," and refusing to mix incompatible sources.

Putting the Data Feed in Its Place

By now, the role of the data feed in the overall architecture should be clear:

- It translates raw historical storage into normalized, timestamped events compatible with the simulation clock.
- It maintains one or more replay cursors that walk many symbol and event streams in global time order.
- It buffers ahead prudently, cooperates with the scheduler to manage backpressure, and avoids unbounded queue growth.

- It supports deterministic checkpoints and seek positions so that runs can be paused, resumed, and partitioned without changing results.

In the next section, we will take the scheduler and data feed together and assemble the complete event-driven backtest engine. There we will focus on the main loop that pops events from the priority queue, calls strategy and execution logic, updates accounting, and enforces the causal ordering rules that give our simulations their interpretability and credibility.

3.3 Event-Driven Backtest Engine

We now have two major building blocks:

- A session-aware scheduler and clock that define *when* things happen and in what order.
- A data feed and replay subsystem that define *what* historical events are supplied to the engine, and how they are streamed and replayed.

In this section we assemble these pieces into the core of the system: the *event-driven backtest engine*. This is the kernel that repeatedly takes the next event, advances simulated time, and invokes the appropriate component (data, strategy, execution, accounting), while maintaining strict determinism and causal ordering.

You can think of this engine as a small operating system for your backtest. Strategies and plugins are applications that run inside it; the scheduler and event queue provide process scheduling; the data feed is akin to a device driver that supplies input.

The Main Event Loop: High-Level View

At the highest level, the engine's main loop does four things, over and over:

- Pop the next scheduled event from the priority queue.

- Advance the simulation clock to that event's timestamp.

- Dispatch the event to the correct handler (data, strategy, execution, accounting, or engine-internal logic).

- Allow handlers to schedule new future events, which are pushed back into the priority queue.

Execution continues until there are no more events (the end of the backtest period), or until some terminating condition is reached (for example, a user-defined stop time or an unrecoverable error).

Because this loop is so central, it is worth visualizing its control flow before we dive into details.

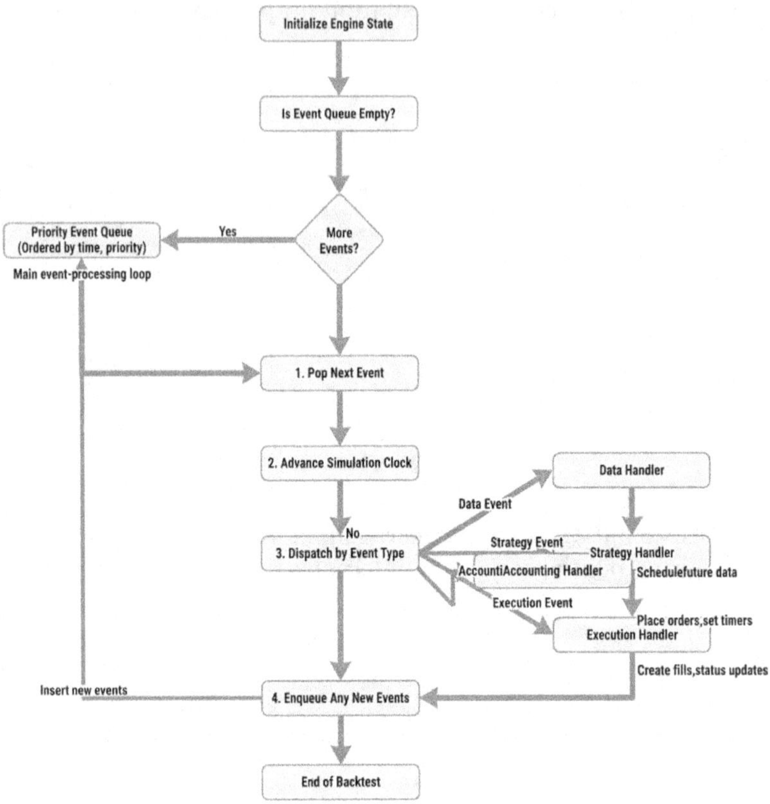

We will now unpack each stage of this loop, paying special attention to determinism (same inputs, same outputs) and causal ordering (no event can react to information that arrives "later" in simulated time).

Initialization: Setting Up the Engine

Before the main loop begins, the engine performs a one-time initialization:

- **Load configuration**: simulation start/end dates, instrument universe, strategy parameters, execution and latency models, risk and accounting settings.

- **Initialize the clock**: set the simulation clock to a well-defined initial value, often the start of the first trading session in the requested period. The clock is wired to the trading calendar chosen earlier.
- **Initialize the data feed**: create replay cursors for each underlying data stream (for example, one per symbol and data type), validate that requested data is available, and prime internal buffers with the earliest events.
- **Seed the event queue**: push any initial events into the priority queue, such as:

- Session-open events.
- The first batch of data events (for example, the first bar or tick for each active symbol).
- Strategy initialization callbacks.

- **Initialize strategy and state stores**: allocate structures for positions, cash, open orders, P&L, metrics, and logs. Run any strategy-level initialization code under a special "engine-init" event so it is logged like everything else.

After this, the event queue must contain at least one event, or the engine will terminate immediately. This condition is checked explicitly at the start of the loop.

Step 1: Pop the Next Event

The first operation in each loop iteration is to pop the next event from the priority queue.

Because the queue is ordered by both time and priority, this guarantees:

- No event with an earlier timestamp exists.

- Among all events at that timestamp, the one with the highest precedence (for example, data before strategy before fills) is chosen.

This simple rule is the heart of determinism. If the queue is implemented properly and all producers (data feed, strategy, execution, accounting) obey the same event insertion rules, two runs with the same configuration will always pop events in the same sequence.

Step 2: Advance the Simulation Clock

Once the next event is known, the engine advances the simulation clock from its current value to the event's timestamp. This has several important implications:

- **Time monotonicity**: the clock never moves backwards. Any attempt to schedule an event in the past relative to the current clock should be rejected or flagged as an error.
- **Session awareness**: if the event's timestamp crosses a session boundary (for example, from pre-open to continuous trading, or from intraday to after-hours), the engine may insert implicit events:

- Session-open or session-close events.
- Auction start/end events.

These are pushed into the queue and will be processed at the appropriate priorities relative to the original event.

- **Visibility guarantees**: at the moment the clock is advanced, all modules agree that simulated time is now at this new timestamp. Any decisions made during this iteration are based on the world as of that instant.

By separating "advance time" from "process event," we gain flexibility. For instance, some engines interleave additional bookkeeping or logging steps right after advancing time but before dispatching the event, ensuring that the time change itself is observable.

Step 3: Dispatch by Event Type

Every event has a type, which determines which handler will process it. Common types include:

- **Data events**: trades, quotes, bars, corporate actions.
- **Strategy callbacks**: data-driven callbacks (for example, "on_-bar"), timers ("on_timer"), end-of-day hooks, and custom user-defined events.
- **Execution events**: order submissions, cancellations, fills, partial fills, rejections.
- **Accounting events**: portfolio revaluations, margin checks, risk limit checks, periodic reporting.
- **Engine-internal events**: session transitions, checkpoint triggers, diagnostics.

The dispatcher is a simple but critical piece of logic: it routes each event to the correct component and ensures that components do not accidentally handle events they do not understand.

Conceptually, you can think of dispatch as a switchboard that says:

> "If this is a data event, hand it to the data handler. If this is a timer event, invoke the strategy's timer callback. If this is a fill event, hand it to the execution and accounting handlers,"

and so on, according to a well-documented table.

Step 4: Handlers and State Transitions

Once dispatched, each handler performs some combination of:

- Reading the current engine state (positions, open orders, latest prices).

- Updating local or global state (for example, adjusting positions after a fill).
- Emitting zero or more new events to be scheduled in the future.

To keep the discussion concrete, let us walk through the typical responsibilities of each major handler.

Data Handler

The data handler's main tasks are:

- **Update observable market state**: for example, set the latest trade price, bid/ask, or bar values for the affected instrument.
- **Trigger downstream callbacks**: depending on your design, a data event may directly cause strategy callbacks (for example, bar-close triggers "on_bar" for all subscribed strategies) or may simply update state that the strategy will read on its next scheduled call.
- **Advance the replay cursor**: after processing a data event, the data feed may read the next event from storage and, if it lies in the future, schedule it into the queue.

Importantly, the data handler must not alter past data. Any corrections to historical data should be applied before the simulation, to preserve reproducibility.

Strategy Handler

The strategy handler is the main "consumer" of simulated market information. When invoked, it:

- Reads current market state (for example, last prices, indicators), its own internal state (for example, recent signals), and portfolio state (positions, cash).
- Computes decisions (for example, new target positions, orders to submit, timers to set).
- Emits events corresponding to those decisions:

- Order submission events with details (instrument, side, quantity, order type).
- Timer events (for example, "wake me up in 5 minutes of simulated time").
- Custom events for other plugins (for example, risk requests, metrics).

The key invariant is that the strategy only sees information up to the current clock time. The engine and scheduler prevent it from seeing future data. The strategy's decisions are therefore *adapted* to the available history, an essential property for avoiding look-ahead bias.

Execution Handler

The execution handler models how orders interact with the market. When it receives an order event, it:

- Records the order in an internal order book (open orders, their sizes, and constraints).
- Consults the latency model to schedule when the order will reach the exchange and when potential fills could occur.
- Creates one or more future execution events:
- Order-acknowledged or order-rejected.
- Full or partial fills with prices and sizes.

When a fill event is dispatched, the execution handler:

- Updates the order's remaining quantity.
- Marks orders as fully filled or cancelled when appropriate.
- Emits downstream events for accounting and for the strategy's "on_fill" callback (if supported).

Execution modeling can be very simple (for example, assume immediate fill at bar close) or sophisticated (for example, order-book simulation). Regardless of complexity, the event-driven skeleton remains the same: orders in, fills and status events out.

Accounting Handler

The accounting handler maintains the portfolio and risk state. When it receives fills or corporate action events, it:

- Updates positions and cash.
- Recomputes portfolio value using the latest prices.
- Applies transaction costs (commissions, fees) and slippage models if they are not already captured in execution prices.

It may also run periodic events, such as:

- Margin checks after each fill or at fixed intervals.
- End-of-day rolls that realize P&L, update funding costs, and store daily snapshots.
- Risk limit checks that may trigger forced liquidations or stop the simulation if limits are breached.

Accounting is where much of the "truth" of the backtest resides. If accounting is incorrect or out of sync with event ordering, even a perfectly ordered event stream will produce misleading results.

Enqueuing New Events: Closing the Loop

Every handler can schedule future events by pushing them into the priority queue with appropriate timestamps and priorities. This is how:

- The data feed extends the event stream by reading the next piece of history.
- The strategy requests future callbacks (for example, timers or end-of-session hooks).

- The execution model inserts delayed fills and acknowledgements.
- The engine schedules internal tasks like checkpoints or periodic logging.

This action closes the loop: events beget more events, and the engine continues processing until no future events remain within the configured simulation horizon.

Because the queue is a global structure, you must take care to:

- Attach correct timestamps that respect the latency and session rules.
- Assign priorities that maintain causal correctness (for example, data before strategy before fills at the same timestamp).
- Preserve reproducibility by ensuring that event insertion does not depend on uncontrolled factors such as wall-clock time or thread scheduling (in single-threaded engines, this is straightforward; in parallel engines, it requires more care and is discussed in a later section).

Causal Ordering and Invariants

The structure we have built so far is flexible: you can add new event types and handlers as needed. But flexibility can also introduce subtle ordering errors. To avoid them, define and enforce explicit *invariants*.

Three particularly important invariants are:

Time monotonicity. The simulation clock never moves backwards, and no event with a timestamp earlier than the current clock may be processed.

Information availability. When a handler runs at time T (conceptually), it may only read state derived from events with timestamps less than or equal to T. Future data must not be visible.

Atomic state updates. Each event is processed atomically: its handler sees a consistent snapshot of state at the start, and when it finishes, its updates are fully applied before the next event starts. There is no interleaving of updates from different events.

While we are avoiding formal mathematics, it can be helpful to think in simple "before/after" pictures: for each event, draw a line between state at time T^- (just before processing) and state at time T^+ (just after), and require that every piece of state updates consistently along that line.

State Management: Central vs Modular

Where should engine state live? There are two broad patterns:

Central state store. A single, well-structured object (or set of objects) holds all mutable state: positions, cash, orders, latest prices, strategy variables, and so on. Handlers receive references to this store and update it in-place.

Modular state stores. Each component maintains its own state (for example, execution keeps the order book, accounting keeps positions and P&L, the strategy keeps its own indicators), and communication happens through well-defined messages (events) or through controlled read-only views.

Both patterns can work, but they have different trade-offs:

- Central stores make global invariants and snapshotting easier, as you can capture the entire state in one place. However, they risk becoming monolithic and tightly coupled.
- Modular stores encourage separation of concerns and cleaner interfaces but require careful design to ensure that all modules agree on the order and visibility of updates.

For reproducible simulation, what matters is not which pattern you choose, but that:

- The mapping from event sequence to state transitions is precisely defined.
- No hidden side effects cross module boundaries without going through well-defined events or interfaces.

- Snapshotting and checkpointing of state can be done consistently (this topic is expanded later when we discuss parallelization and checkpoints).

Determinism and Randomness

Even with a perfectly ordered event loop, randomness can break reproducibility if not managed carefully. Randomness may appear in:

- Execution models (for example, randomization within a slippage model).
- Latency models (stochastic delays).
- Strategy logic (for example, randomized exploration in reinforcement learning-style algorithms).

To preserve determinism:

- Use controlled pseudorandom generators with explicit seeds.
- Document where random draws occur and in what order.
- Ensure that event scheduling does not change the order of random draws between runs with the same configuration.

In practice, this often means that random draws are tied to specific events or stages in the loop. For example, an execution model may say: "for each fill event I generate, I take exactly one random draw from my private generator." As long as the sequence of fill events is deterministic, the randomness remains reproducible.

Handling Edge Cases and Failures

No engine is complete without a plan for edge cases and failures. A few common scenarios:

Simultaneous events across assets. Two events with the same timestamp may affect multiple instruments (for example, an index-level news shock). Your priority rules must handle these consistently.

Often, data events are processed first for all instruments, then strategies are called, then execution and fills, and finally accounting.

Mid-event failures. If an error occurs while processing an event (for example, a strategy raises an exception), you must decide:

- Do you abort the entire backtest?
- Do you mark the strategy as failed and continue with others?
- Do you attempt recovery and retry?

Whichever policy you choose, it should be deterministic and leave the engine in a well-defined state. For reproducible research, "fail fast, record diagnostics, and stop" is often safer than silent recovery.

End-of-data conditions. When the data feed runs out of history for some symbols but not others, the engine must decide whether to:

- Continue simulation for instruments with remaining data.
- Stop the entire run at the earliest "exhaustion" point.
- Treat the missing data as an outage (for example, prices frozen) and model its impact explicitly.

This policy affects how you interpret results near the edges of your backtest window and must be documented.

From Kernel to Full System

The event-driven backtest engine described here is deliberately minimal. It focuses on:

- The core loop that processes events in time and priority order.
- The contracts between clock, data feed, strategy, execution, and accounting.
- The invariants that guarantee deterministic, causally ordered simulations.

On top of this kernel, real systems add many layers:

- Parallelization and checkpointing to run large studies efficiently.
- Logging, metrics, and tracing for observability.
- Plugin architectures and extension points for custom execution models, risk modules, and metrics sinks.
- User interfaces and configuration management.

But all of these build on the same skeleton. If the event loop is well-designed—simple, deterministic, and explicit about ordering—the rest of the system will inherit those desirable properties. In the following sections we will see how to scale this kernel across cores and machines, and how to expose it safely to user strategies through a stable, testable Strategy API.

3.4 Parallelization & Checkpointing

So far we have focused on correctness: a single event-driven engine with a clear notion of time, ordering, and data replay. In practice, you will rarely run only one backtest. You will run hundreds or thousands of simulations:

- Sweeping over parameter grids or model variants.
- Testing robustness across different market regimes and slippage assumptions.
- Running portfolio-level simulations with large universes and long histories.

To make this work at realistic scales, we must exploit modern hardware: multiple cores on a machine and multiple machines in a cluster or cloud environment. At the same time, we cannot sacrifice the core promise of this book: **deterministic, reproducible results**. If a run is distributed today and repeated six months from now, it should produce the same event sequences and outputs, provided the code and data versions are the same.

This section explains how to scale the event-driven engine while preserving determinism. We will:

- Distinguish types of parallel workloads and their natural partitioning schemes.
- Discuss the management of randomness (pseudorandom generators) in parallel, so that results are stable across runs.
- Show how to define checkpoints and restart logic so that long simulations can be paused, resumed, and recovered from failure without altering outcomes.

Two Kinds of Parallelism

It is useful to distinguish two broad categories of work.

Embarrassingly Parallel Workloads

These are jobs that are logically independent:

- Running the same strategy over 100 different parameter combinations.
- Testing 50 different transaction cost models on the same historical period.
- Performing walk-forward or cross-validation runs on disjoint time windows.

Each run is a full backtest with its own event engine, data feed, and strategy configuration. There is no need for communication between runs during simulation time. These workloads are "embarrassingly parallel" because you can simply launch one run per core or per machine, and aggregate results when all are done.

Determinism is straightforward here:

- Each run has its own configuration, random seed, and data slice.

- The event loop we already built guarantees deterministic behavior within a run.
- There is no cross-talk between runs that could introduce nondeterministic scheduling effects.

Most research platforms gain huge speedups simply by exploiting this level of parallelism.

Tightly Coupled Simulations

More challenging are workloads where different parts of the simulation interact:

- A multi-asset portfolio with cross-asset position limits, where decisions for one symbol depend on fills and prices in others.
- A futures curve trading model that needs consistent margin and risk computed over all contracts.
- A market-impact model that aggregates orders from multiple strategies or symbols to simulate shared liquidity.

Here, you cannot trivially split the universe into independent pieces that run without talking to each other. Events in one partition may affect state in another.

Scaling tightly coupled simulations requires careful *partitioning* and sometimes more complex concurrency control. It is still possible to be deterministic, but you must design the partitioning and communication model deliberately.

Partitioning Strategies

Partitioning is how you divide a large problem into smaller chunks that can be processed in parallel. In backtesting, three common schemes are:

- By scenario or configuration.
- By symbol or instrument.

- By time.

Partitioning by Scenario

Partitioning by scenario is the simplest and overlaps with embarrassingly parallel workloads. For example:

- Scenario A: base slippage, latency model 1.
- Scenario B: double slippage, latency model 2.
- Scenario C: stressed volatility scaling, different risk controls.

Each scenario runs its own event engine from start to finish. Determinism is simply handled by the per-engine design. Parallelization is handled by a job scheduler or cluster manager that allocates one scenario per core or machine.

Because this is so straightforward, many systems treat “scenario parallelism” as the first lever to pull.

Partitioning by Symbol

Partitioning by symbol divides the universe into disjoint subsets of instruments, for example:

- Group 1: symbols A–M.
- Group 2: symbols N–Z.

Each group is processed by a separate worker, which maintains its own event queue, data feed, and local strategy or execution logic for those symbols. This can work well when:

- Strategies are largely per-symbol and do not depend heavily on cross-asset constraints.
- Cross-asset information (such as index levels) can be modeled as read-only data shared across workers, rather than as mutable state.

Aggressive global constraints (such as "total portfolio leverage across all symbols must not exceed X") complicate this picture, because each worker only sees a partial portfolio. You can handle this in two main ways:

- Keep global risk and accounting centralized, with workers sending their per-symbol events to a central aggregator that enforces global constraints and feeds back decisions.
- Periodically synchronize summaries (for example, partial positions and risk metrics) to a coordinator, which then broadcasts updated constraints.

The more frequent and fine-grained the interactions, the more your symbol partitioning will feel like a distributed system problem, not an embarrassingly parallel one.

Partitioning by Time

Partitioning by time divides the full historical period into contiguous segments:

- Segment 1: 2010–2012.
- Segment 2: 2013–2015.
- Segment 3: 2016–2018.

Each segment can be processed by an engine that is initialized with the ending state of the previous segment. This is very useful for:

- Processing extremely long histories where a single run would be impractically large or long.
- Running out-of-core simulations where you wish to load and process one time block at a time.

However, partitioning by time introduces a new requirement: **the state at the boundary between segments must be faithfully captured and passed along**. This is essentially the same problem as checkpointing. If you mishandle it, results from the concatenated segments will differ from a single, uninterrupted run.

Determinism in Parallel Execution

Parallelization introduces new sources of nondeterminism:

- Different cores or machines may process tasks at different speeds.
- Operating systems and schedulers may interleave threads in varying orders.
- Network delays may vary.

If you let these factors influence the order in which events are processed or random numbers are drawn, your results will change from run to run, even with identical inputs.

To prevent this, the core rule is:

> All simulation-relevant ordering and randomness must be determined by *logical* rules in your engine, not by how the operating system or cluster happens to schedule tasks.

Concretely, this implies:

- Keep each event engine single-threaded at the simulation level, if possible. Parallelize by running many engines in parallel, not by multithreading within one engine's event loop. This keeps event ordering within an engine under your explicit control.
- When you need multiple threads or processes inside a single logical engine (for example, for I/O or heavy calculations), make sure they feed events into the central event queue in a way that preserves the same total order you would get in a single-threaded implementation.
- Avoid using wall-clock time or "time since start" inside the simulation. The engine's simulation clock should be the only source of temporal information for trading logic.

In short: parallelize around the engine, not through its core loop, unless you are prepared to reason carefully about concurrency.

Managing Pseudorandomness in Parallel

Randomness appears in many quantitative systems: stochastic execution and slippage, Monte Carlo scenario generation, randomized strategies, and more. In a single-engine setting, we can manage this by:

- Using a pseudorandom number generator (PRNG) with a fixed seed.
- Drawing numbers in a fixed, documented order tied to event processing.

In parallel settings, we must additionally prevent different engines or workers from stepping on each other's random streams.

Seed Partitioning

A simple pattern is to assign each engine its own seed, derived from a global root seed and the engine's index:

- Root seed: a number recorded as part of the experiment configuration.
- For engine k: derived seed = some deterministic function of (root seed, k).

Each engine then uses only its own derived seed and does not share a PRNG with any other engine. As long as:

- The number of engines and their indexing are fixed by configuration.
- The mapping from index to derived seed is stable.

you will obtain the same random sequences for each engine across runs.

Stream Partitioning Within an Engine

Within a single engine, you might want distinct random streams for different components:

- One stream for execution randomness.
- One stream for latency randomness.
- One stream for the strategy's own sampling.

This can make reasoning about behavior and debugging much easier. You can again derive per-component seeds from the engine's base seed in a deterministic way.

An important rule is to avoid sharing one PRNG across many independent parts of the engine if their order of use might change between versions or configurations. Otherwise, a small change in execution (for example, adding a new random draw in one place) can shift the entire sequence of downstream random draws, leading to surprising differences between runs.

Checkpointing: Freezing Engine State in Time

Long simulations and large experiments seldom run perfectly from start to finish. Machines fail, jobs are preempted, bugs are discovered. To make progress in this imperfect environment, you need **checkpointing**: the ability to save the engine's state at specific points in simulated time and resume later, reconstructing exactly the same future evolution.

Checkpointing has three main elements:

- Choosing *where* in the event stream to cut and save state.
- Defining *what* to save to be able to resume deterministically.
- Designing checkpoints as *versioned artifacts* that remain interpretable across reasonable code and data changes.

Consistent Cut Points

A "cut point" is a point in simulated time where you decide to take a snapshot. A good cut point has these properties:

- All events with timestamps less than or equal to the cut time have been fully processed.

- No event that should logically belong to the past is still pending in the queue.
- The system is in a clean state, such as end-of-session or end-of-day, where many accounting and risk quantities are naturally defined.

In practice, checkpoints are often taken at:

- End-of-day, after daily accounting rolls are complete.
- End-of-month or end-of-year, for long-term studies.

The engine can schedule special "checkpoint events" at these times. When such an event is processed, it triggers the snapshot logic.

What to Capture in a Checkpoint

To resume a simulation exactly, a checkpoint must include enough information to reconstruct:

- **Simulation clock**: the current simulated time and any session-related flags.
- **Event queue**: all pending events with timestamps greater than the cut time, including their types, payloads, priorities, and any internal identifiers.
- **Data feed positions**: for each underlying data stream, the seek position (file offset, index) of the next event to read, plus any buffered events that have been read but not yet scheduled.
- **Engine state**: positions, cash, open orders, latest prices, strategy internal variables, risk metrics, and any other mutable state that influences future behavior.
- **PRNG state**: the internal state of each pseudorandom number generator in use.
- **Configuration and metadata**: code version identifiers, data version identifiers, engine configuration, and any environment information that affects behavior.

If any of these pieces is missing or inconsistent, a resumed run may diverge from an uninterrupted one.

Checkpoint Artifacts as Versioned Objects

A checkpoint is not just an in-memory structure; it is a serialized object stored in a filesystem, object store, or database. Over time, your code and data may evolve. To avoid confusion and silent incompatibilities:

- Give each checkpoint a **schema version**, indicating the format of its serialized contents.
- Record **code version identifiers** (for example, commit hashes) and **data version identifiers** alongside the checkpoint.
- On resume, verify that the current engine can understand the checkpoint's schema and that it is appropriate to combine the checkpoint with the current code and data.

Sometimes you will deliberately break compatibility (for example, after a major redesign of the accounting model). In such cases, old checkpoints should be marked as obsolete for new code, rather than being misinterpreted.

Resuming From Checkpoints

Resuming a simulation is conceptually simple:

- Load the checkpoint from storage.
- Reconstruct the engine's internal state, clock, event queue, and data feed positions.
- Restore PRNG states.
- Continue running the event loop until completion or the next checkpoint.

The crucial test of a checkpointing system is this:

> If you run the simulation straight through without checkpoints and then run it again with checkpoints and resumes at the same cut points, do you obtain exactly the same outputs?

You should design regression tests to verify this property. If the two runs diverge, it means:

- Some state was not captured correctly.
- The event queue or data feed was not restored at the right position.
- PRNG states did not match, causing random draws to differ.

Fixing these issues is usually a matter of extending what you save in the checkpoint or tightening the definition of cut points.

Fault Tolerance and Cluster Environments

In a cluster or cloud setting, failures are normal: nodes may be preempted, networks hiccup, and disks fail. Checkpointing is your main defense against losing work.

A typical pattern is:

- Run each engine as a job with periodic checkpoints (for example, once per simulated day or week).
- If a job fails or is preempted, restart it from the most recent checkpoint rather than from the beginning.
- Use a job scheduler that is aware of this pattern and can mark partially complete jobs as "retryable from checkpoint."

Here again, determinism means that a retried job produces the same results as if it had never failed, just with extra wall-clock time spent.

One subtle issue is the aggregation of results from many parallel jobs. If you combine outputs in different orders (for example, summing floating-point values across scenarios), you may see slight numerical differences. While these are usually negligible for trading decisions, if you care about bitwise-identical reproducibility, you should:

- Define a canonical order for aggregating results (for example, sort jobs by a stable key and reduce in that order).
- Use numerically stable aggregation methods when large reductions are involved.

Putting It All Together

Parallelization and checkpointing transform the event-driven engine from a correct but limited toy into a practical research tool:

- **Parallelization** lets you explore broad hypothesis spaces—parameter grids, scenario sweeps, multi-universe studies—in a reasonable amount of time, by exploiting all available cores and machines.
- **Deterministic PRNG management** ensures that adding hardware or changing job scheduling does not change scientific conclusions; the same logical experiment remains the same numerical experiment.
- **Checkpointing** provides robustness and flexibility, allowing you to pause and resume long runs, recover from failures, and partition work across time or space while maintaining equivalence to a single uninterrupted run.

All of this rests on the foundations built in earlier sections: a clear simulation clock, an ordered event engine, and a disciplined data feed. If those pieces are deterministic and well-specified, scaling them out and making them restartable is a tractable engineering problem rather than a guessing game.

In the final section of this chapter, we will turn to the user-facing boundary: the Strategy API and plugin architecture. There we will see how to expose the power of this engine to research users while preserving the invariants that make parallel, checkpointed simulations scientifically trustworthy.

3.5 Strategy API & Plugin Architecture

Up to this point, we have treated the backtest engine as a closed system: a scheduler advancing a session-aware clock, a data feed replaying normalized events, an event-driven kernel coordinating execution and accounting, and optional parallelization and checkpoints. In practice, however, a backtester exists to serve *users*—quant researchers and portfolio managers—who will constantly push new ideas into the system.

This final section is about how to open the engine safely. We will define:

- A minimal but expressive **Strategy API** that lets users write trading logic without touching core engine internals.
- A broader **plugin architecture** for execution adapters, risk modules, metrics sinks, and other extensions.
- The **contracts and invariants** that keep the engine deterministic and testable even as user code evolves.

The goal is to allow rapid innovation at the edges while preserving a stable, well-understood core.

Why an API Matters for Reproducibility

It is tempting to let users write arbitrary code anywhere in the engine: query global variables, mutate accounting state directly, spawn threads, and so on. This might work for quick prototypes, but it quickly destroys the properties we care about:

- **Determinism**: uncontrolled side effects can make results depend on execution order, hardware, or timing.
- **Testability**: if strategies touch everything, it becomes impossible to test the engine in isolation.
- **Evolution**: any change to engine internals risks breaking existing strategies.

A good API creates a clean boundary:

> Inside the engine: carefully controlled, deterministic, and well-tested.
>
> Outside the engine: user strategies and plugins that can be versioned, swapped, and iterated on quickly, as long as they respect a small set of stable interfaces.

Designing this boundary is as important as designing the event loop itself.

The Strategy as a First-Class Component

A *strategy* is user code that decides what to trade given a stream of market and portfolio information. Within our architecture, strategies are one type of pluggable module, but they are special because they sit at the center of most research workflows.

We will model a strategy as an object with:

- A small set of **lifecycle callbacks**.
- A well-defined **configuration surface**.
- Clear rules about **what state it owns** vs **what the engine owns**.

Lifecycle Callbacks

The engine runs strategies by invoking a handful of callbacks at specific points in the event stream. A typical set might include:

- `initialize`: Called once before the simulation starts. The strategy can set up internal variables, subscribe to instruments, and register any recurring timers. At this point no market data has been processed yet, but configuration and calendars are available.

- on_data: Called when new data events become visible to the strategy. Depending on clock mode and design, this might correspond to:

- Bar-close events (for bar-based backtests).
- Specific tick or quote events (for higher-frequency simulations).

Inside on_data, the strategy can read the latest prices and indicators and place orders.

- on_timer: Called when a user-defined timer fires. Timers are scheduled in simulated time (for example, "every 5 minutes" or "at 15:59 each day"). This is useful for tasks such as periodic rebalancing or intraday risk checks that are not tied to a particular data tick.
- on_fill: Called when an order submitted by the strategy is filled or partially filled. The strategy can update its internal view of positions, risk, and pending orders, or react to slippage and execution quality.
- on_close: Called near the end of the simulation or at the close of each session, depending on design. The strategy can perform final cleanup, compute summary statistics, and flush any internal logs.

These callbacks are not magical; they are simply event handlers wired into the event engine:

- Data events in the engine lead to on_data calls.
- Timer events lead to on_timer calls.
- Fill events lead to on_fill calls.
- A special engine event leads to on_close.

The crucial point is that the *timing and order* of these callbacks are determined solely by the event loop and scheduler described earlier. Strategies cannot arbitrarily change the clock or inject out-of-band behavior; they act only when the engine calls them.

Configuration Surfaces

Strategies must be configurable without changing their source code. Typical configuration elements include:

- Parameter values (lookback windows, thresholds, position limits).
- Instrument universe and filters (for example, "top 500 by market cap").
- Execution and risk preferences (for example, maximum participation rate).

From the engine's perspective, configuration is a structured object that:

- Is provided at initialization time.
- Is immutable for the duration of a run.
- Is recorded as part of the experiment metadata so that runs can be reproduced.

Strategies read from configuration but do not modify it. This separation allows you to sweep over parameter grids and scenario definitions systematically, and it ensures that "the same configuration" truly means the same behavior.

Engine-Owned vs Strategy-Owned State

A frequent source of bugs is ambiguity about who owns which pieces of state. We recommend drawing a clear line.

Engine-owned state includes:

- Portfolio positions and cash.
- Official record of open orders and their statuses.

- Official P&L, risk metrics, and performance statistics.
- Latest canonical market data (prices, corporate actions) as seen by the engine.

Strategies can read engine-owned state through a stable interface (for example, a "context" or "portfolio view" object passed into callbacks) but must not mutate it directly. They influence engine state only through structured actions such as submitting orders or registering timers.

Strategy-owned state includes:

- Internal indicators and signals (for example, moving averages, scores).
- Local bookkeeping, such as intended target positions or recent decisions.
- Temporary data used for calculations.

This state lives inside the strategy object. It is the strategy's responsibility to keep it consistent with observable engine state (for example, reconciling its view of positions with fills seen in on_fill).

This separation has two benefits:

- It keeps the engine's accounting and risk logic independent of any particular strategy.
- It makes it easier to snapshot and restore engine state without needing to understand every internal detail of user strategies.

If you choose to support strategy state checkpointing, you can do that via an explicit serialization interface, but it should be clearly delineated from engine state.

Safe Actions Strategies May Take

Within callbacks, strategies should be allowed to do a small number of well-defined things:

- **Read**:
- Current simulated time.
- Latest market data for subscribed instruments.
- Portfolio and risk state exposed by the engine (for example, current positions, cash, margin usage).
- **Submit**:
- New orders or cancellations.
- Timer registrations (for future `on_timer` calls).
- Optional custom events to other plugins (for example, sending a risk check request).
- **Log**:
- Structured messages for later inspection and debugging.

Any action that changes engine-owned state must flow through these structured channels and be reflected in the event stream. Strategies should *not*:

- Directly adjust positions or cash.
- Manually edit the event queue or simulated time.
- Access external systems (for example, the internet, local databases) in ways that affect trading logic without being captured as part of the experiment configuration.

Restricting side effects in this way is a key ingredient of reproducibility.

Sandboxing and Safety

Even with a clean API, user code can misbehave: infinite loops, excessive memory usage, or numerical errors. The engine should protect itself and other runs from such failures.

Practical safety measures include:

Execution time limits. Set a maximum allowed wall-clock time per callback (for example, per on_data call). If the strategy exceeds it, the engine can:

- Abort the run and surface a clear error.
- Mark the strategy as failed and skip further callbacks.

While wall-clock time is not used for trading logic, it is appropriate for guarding against runaway computations.

Exception handling. Wrap strategy callbacks in try/catch logic:

- If user code raises an exception, capture the stack trace and inputs.
- Shut down the run cleanly, ensuring that partial state does not leak into other runs.

Silent failures must be avoided; they are a direct threat to trust in the engine.

Resource limits. In shared environments, consider limiting memory or disallowing certain operations (for example, opening files or launching threads) from within strategy code. This can be done via process-level controls or by running strategies in separate sandboxed processes that communicate with the engine via a narrow IPC interface.

Beyond Strategies: General Plugin Architecture

Strategies are just one kind of extension. A mature backtest platform usually supports a broader range of plugins, such as:

- **Execution adapters**: alternative models of how orders are filled, from simple bar-based fills to detailed order-book simulations.
- **Risk modules**: custom margin rules, drawdown constraints, or scenario stress tests.
- **Metrics and reporting sinks**: modules that consume events or summary statistics and produce reports, visualizations, or exports.
- **Data transformers**: on-the-fly feature generators, resamplers, or data quality monitors.

Rather than invent a different integration model for each, you can treat them uniformly as *plugins* that:

- **Register** with the engine at startup, declaring which event types and callbacks they are interested in.
- **Handle** certain events when dispatched by the core loop (for example, a risk plugin may receive fill and P&L events; a metrics plugin may receive end-of-day summaries).
- **Emit** additional events or logs if needed (for instance, a risk plugin might emit "risk limit breached" events that the engine turns into forced liquidations).

Conceptually, plugins are peers of strategies. They differ mainly in purpose and in which APIs they are allowed to use. For example, a metrics plugin may be read-only with respect to engine state, while an execution plugin is allowed to create fills.

Capability Descriptors and Permissions

To keep plugins manageable, it helps to define *capability descriptors*. Each plugin declares what it can do and what it needs:

- Which event types it wants to subscribe to.

- Which actions it is allowed to perform (for example, submit orders, update risk limits, log metrics).
- What configuration fields it expects to receive.

The engine uses these descriptors to:

- Wire up event subscriptions at initialization.
- Enforce permissions at runtime (for example, prevent a metrics plugin from modifying positions).
- Provide meaningful error messages if a plugin requests unsupported capabilities.

This explicitness is important as your plugin ecosystem grows. It prevents accidental privilege creep and keeps the core engine's invariants intact.

Backward and Forward Compatibility

Once strategies and plugins depend on your APIs, you must evolve those APIs carefully. Two complementary goals are:

- **Backward compatibility**: old strategies and plugins should keep working when you upgrade the engine, at least for some period.
- **Forward compatibility**: new strategies should not rely on engine-internal details that might change frequently.

Practical guidelines include:

- **Version your APIs**. Assign version numbers to major interfaces (for example, Strategy API v1, Execution Plugin API v2). When you introduce breaking changes, increment the version and support both old and new versions for a while.

- **Deprecate gradually**. When you plan to remove or change an interface, mark it as deprecated and provide clear migration paths.
- **Favor additive changes**. Whenever possible, add new optional parameters or callbacks instead of changing the meaning of existing ones.

From a reproducibility standpoint, it is also crucial to log which API versions each run used, alongside code and data versions. This way, if results differ across time, you can attribute changes to specific upgrades.

Observability for Strategies and Plugins

Determining why a backtest behaved a certain way often requires detailed insight into both engine and strategy behavior. The architecture should provide observability without granting uncontrolled access.

Common observability tools include:

Structured logging. Instead of free-form text logs, encourage or enforce structured logs: messages with fields such as time, instrument, order ID, event type, and user-defined tags. This makes it much easier to filter and analyze behavior after the fact.

Metrics. Provide simple APIs for strategies and plugins to emit metrics:

- Counters (for example, number of trades, number of signals generated).
- Gauges (for example, current leverage, average spread).
- Histograms (for example, distribution of slippage).

The engine can collect these metrics and export them alongside P&L and risk results.

Traces. For debugging complex interactions, you may want lightweight traces showing how a single order or instrument moved through the system:

- When was the signal generated?
- When was the order submitted, acknowledged, and filled?
- What did risk and accounting do at each stage?

Exposing traces as a read-only stream to plugins (for example, a debugging or visualization plugin) can be powerful, provided that reading them does not affect the simulation.

Design Guidelines for a Pleasant but Safe API

We can now summarize practical guidelines for designing the Strategy API and plugin architecture:

- **Keep the core loop and state model simple.** Do not expose internal details unnecessarily. If users can express what they need with a few callbacks and well-defined actions, that is a feature, not a limitation.
- **Make time and ordering explicit.** For every callback, document:
  - What simulated time the strategy sees.
  - What events must have been processed before this callback.
  - Whether the callback can generate events at the same timestamp or only in the future.
- **Minimize mutable shared state.** Prefer read-only views of engine-owned data and structured actions that trigger state changes, rather than letting strategies poke directly at accounting internals.
- **Embrace composability.** Treat strategies, execution models, risk modules, and metrics sinks as plugins following similar patterns. This reduces the number of mechanisms users must learn.
- **Respect the experiment record.** Make it easy to log configuration, API versions, and dependencies automatically for each run, so that users can reproduce results without manually tracking everything.

From Engine to Research Platform

With a carefully designed Strategy API and plugin architecture, the event-driven engine becomes more than a simulator; it becomes a research platform:

- Researchers can rapidly experiment with new ideas by changing only their strategies and configurations, not core engine code.
- Execution and risk teams can plug in alternative models and policies without rewriting strategies.
- Infrastructure teams can upgrade the engine, data pipelines, and parallelization layer while preserving old results, thanks to stable interfaces and explicit versioning.

Most importantly, this openness does not come at the expense of rigor. By keeping extension points narrow and well-specified, we preserve the deterministic, causally ordered nature of the simulation. That is the foundation on which reliable quantitative research is built.

Chapter 4

Strategy, Orders & Execution Modeling

In a live trading system, nothing magical happens between a model's signal and the broker's fill report-only code and market microstructure. This chapter opens that black box. We'll turn abstract predictions into concrete orders, march them through a simplified yet realistic market, and account for every execution, fee, and constraint. By the end, you'll be able to trace any backtest P&L line back to a fully specified decision and execution path-no hidden heuristics, no hand-waving, just reproducible mechanics.

4.1 Feature Engineering Pipeline

In the previous chapters we treated the strategy mostly as a black box: the engine delivered time–aligned market data, and the strategy responded with signals or target positions. In a real system, there is a substantial layer in between: the *feature engineering pipeline*. This pipeline transforms raw data into cleaned, lagged, and normalized inputs that your signal models can consume.

This section focuses on how to design that layer so that it is:

- **Deterministic**: the same inputs and configuration always produce the same features.
- **Leakage–free**: no feature at time t uses information that would only be observable after t.
- **Structured as a DAG**: a directed acyclic graph of computations, so dependencies are explicit and there are no cycles.
- **Cached and reproducible**: intermediate results are stored and can be recomputed or invalidated in a controlled way.

We will walk from the conceptual level—what a feature DAG is and why it matters—down to practical concerns like partitioning by instrument and calendar, handling point–in–time versus revised data, and exposing metadata such as latency and sampling frequency.

From Raw Data to Features: Why Structure Matters

The raw inputs to a backtest engine are messy: trades, quotes, bars, corporate actions, fundamentals, news, and possibly proprietary data. Downstream models, however, want clean tables of features: for each instrument and each backtest timestamp, a set of numbers that represent "the state of the world as it was known then."

You *could* write ad hoc code inside each strategy that pulls data from various tables and transforms it on the fly. This is tempting for simple experiments, but it quickly breaks three important requirements for a serious backtest engine:

- **Reusability**: every strategy ends up reimplementing similar transformations (e.g., moving averages, volatilities) in subtly different ways.
- **Reproducibility**: it becomes hard to answer, "Which exact inputs produced this signal on this date?" months later.
- **Auditability**: risk and research teams cannot easily see which transformations were applied and whether they introduced look–ahead bias.

A feature engineering pipeline addresses these issues by moving data transformations into a first–class, shared subsystem. That subsystem exposes a clean interface: given a timestamp, instrument, and feature name, it returns a value that is guaranteed to have been computed in a controlled, leakage–free, and versioned way.

The Feature DAG Concept

The natural way to organize feature computations is as a *directed acyclic graph* (DAG):

- **Nodes** represent data objects: raw data tables (e.g., minute bars, corporate actions) or derived features (e.g., a 20–day average return).
- **Edges** represent dependencies: if feature B uses feature A, then there is an edge $A \to B$.
- **Acyclicity** means there are no loops: no feature depends, directly or indirectly, on itself.

The DAG is *time aware*: not only does B depend on A, but at each backtest time t, $B(t)$ depends on some well–defined window of past values of A (for example, $A(t-1)$ to $A(t-20)$). The graph structure lets the engine compute features in topological order: all prerequisites are available before a node is evaluated.

This structure is the backbone of determinism and reproducibility:

- Because dependencies are explicit, you can check for cycles and invalid constructions before a backtest runs.
- Because the DAG is separate from any specific strategy, multiple strategies can share the same feature computations.
- Because each node has a well–defined computation, you can hash its definition and inputs to ensure that recomputing it later yields identical outputs.

Right after introducing the DAG, it is useful to visualize it.

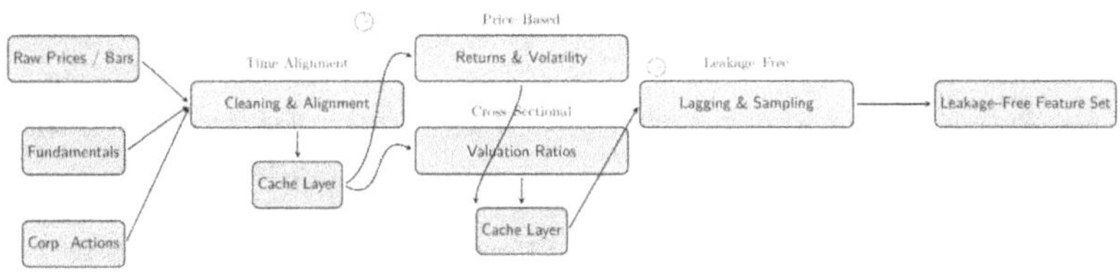

Deterministic, Leakage–Free Computation

A feature pipeline is only as trustworthy as its handling of time. Two rules are non–negotiable:

- **No look–ahead**: a feature at time t must be computable using only data that would have been observable at or before t in the real world.
- **Deterministic evaluation**: given a specified version of the raw data and configuration, the same query always returns the same feature value.

In practice, enforcing these rules has several components.

Explicit observation timestamps. Every raw data item needs a timestamp that answers the question: "When could a trader have first used this information?" For trades and quotes, this is the event time. For daily bars, it is typically the bar close time plus any reporting delay. For fundamentals, it is the announcement time, not the period end.

Feature nodes must be defined in terms of *observation times*, not just calendar times. For example, a trailing 20–day volatility of returns at 16:00 on March 15 must be computed from returns whose prices were observable before 16:00 on March 15, given your market calendar and any reporting lags.

Lagging all inputs. Even when data is timestamped correctly, it is easy to accidentally sneak in future information through alignment choices. A common safeguard is to define a global convention such as:

> "Features computed on bar t can only use prices and other data from bars $t-1$ and earlier."

In that scheme, if your signal is evaluated once per day at the close:

- Prices from today's close contribute to features used for *tomorrow*'s orders.
- Features used for today's orders depend only on data up to yesterday's close.

The pipeline should enforce this convention mechanically. For example, any rolling operation can automatically shift its outcome by one bar when exposed as a feature. This removes manual decision–making from the strategy code and reduces the risk of inconsistency.

Handling infrequent or delayed data. Some data, like fundamentals or analyst estimates, arrives irregularly and may be revised. Here, leakage occurs in more subtle ways. You must distinguish at least three concepts:

- **Economic date**: the period that the data refers to (for example, "Q4 2024 earnings").
- **Initial release time**: when the first version became publicly available.
- **Revision times**: when adjustments or restatements were later released.

A leakage–free pipeline stores all of these, but for backtesting it uses a *point–in–time* view: at any backtest time t, you see only the data versions released on or before t. Later revisions are not retroactively applied to earlier timestamps.

Partitioning by Instrument and Calendar

The feature pipeline operates over a large cross–section of instruments and multiple calendars. This complicates basic questions like "What is the 20–day average volume?" because:

- Not all instruments trade every day.

- Different instruments may follow different trading calendars or time zones.
- There may be missing data or trading halts.

To remain deterministic and interpretable, the pipeline should partition state along two dimensions:

By instrument (or instrument group). Each instrument (for example, each stock, future, or pair) has its own independent time series of raw data. Features such as rolling volatility or average volume are computed *per instrument*, using only that instrument's history.

This avoids accidental cross–talk where the behavior of one asset influences the features of another, unless you have explicitly defined a cross–sectional feature (for example, ranking within a sector).

By calendar. Each instrument's time series lives on a specific trading calendar and time zone. When you define a feature that uses a window of past data (for example, 10 trading days), the pipeline must interpret "past 10 days" in terms of that calendar, skipping non–trading days.

When combining cross–sectional features (say, sector averages) across instruments, the pipeline needs a *canonical backtest time grid* (for example, daily at New York close) and explicit rules about how to align data from different calendars onto that grid.

These partitioning rules become part of the formal definition of each feature node. A properly documented node states not only its formula but also: "This feature is defined per instrument on its native trading calendar, then sampled onto the global daily close grid with one–bar lag."

Point–in–Time vs Revised Data

Data rarely stays fixed after its initial release. Vendors may patch errors, companies restate financials, and historical bars can be adjusted for splits or dividends. For a reproducible backtest, you must make a clear choice about what you mean by "the data."

There are two main perspectives:

- **Point–in–time (as known then)**: what a trader could have seen at each historical time, warts and all.
- **Revised (as corrected later)**: a cleaner, more accurate history, but not strictly what was known in real time.

For strategy testing, especially when exploring predictability, point–in–time is usually the gold standard. However, there are valid reasons to use revised data for certain tasks (for example, risk model calibration) as long as you are explicit.

In a feature DAG, the cleanest solution is to treat *data version* as part of the node identity. For example, you might have:

- raw_prices_pit — point–in–time prices.
- raw_prices_revised — fully adjusted and patched prices.

Downstream features like returns can then choose their parents explicitly. You might define:

> daily_return_pit depends on raw_prices_pit and inherits its point–in–time behavior.

By encoding this into the DAG, you can run backtests with different data–version policies simply by selecting different root nodes, without rewriting strategy code.

Caching and Hash–Based Fingerprinting

Feature computations can be expensive. Some may require scanning long histories, joining multiple datasets, or performing complex transformations. Recomputing everything from scratch for every backtest run is usually impractical.

Caching solves this but introduces its own reproducibility concerns. The challenge is to cache aggressively *without* accidentally mixing results from different configurations or data versions.

A straightforward approach combines two ideas:

Node–level caching. Each feature node can be cached at a suitable granularity, such as:

- By instrument and time slice (for example, chunks of dates).
- By market calendar segment (for example, per day or per bar).

When the engine needs a feature value, it first checks whether the relevant slice for that node, instrument, and time is already cached. If so, it loads it instead of recomputing.

Hash–based fingerprints. To know whether a cached slice is compatible with the current backtest, you compute a fingerprint for each node that includes:

- The node's definition (the transformation logic and parameters).
- The fingerprints of its parent nodes.
- Identifiers for the underlying raw data versions.

This fingerprint can be stored alongside the cached data. When you rerun a backtest, the engine recomputes the node's fingerprint. If it matches the one on disk, you can safely reuse the cached slice. If not, the cache entry is invalid and must be recomputed.

This mechanism guarantees that when you change a parameter (say, the lookback window from 20 days to 30) or switch from point–in–time prices to revised prices, the change propagates through the DAG and forces the appropriate caches to refresh.

Feature Metadata: Making Latency and Validity Explicit

Features are not just numbers; they have properties that affect how they should be used. To keep the rest of the engine clean and auditable, those properties should be captured as metadata attached to each node.

Useful metadata fields include:

- **Units**: for example, price in currency, return in percent, volume in shares, ratio in dimensionless units.
- **Sampling frequency**: tick, minutely, hourly, daily, weekly, or event–driven.
- **Latency**: how long after an underlying event the feature becomes available for trading decisions.
- **Validity window**: how long the feature remains "fresh" before it must be recomputed or can be considered stale.
- **Dependency structure**: references to parent nodes in the DAG, so that tools can trace how the feature was constructed.

Two fields deserve special emphasis in a backtest engine: latency and validity window.

Latency. Even if a raw data point has a timestamp, you may want to encode additional delays. For example:

- Exchange feeds might arrive with a small delay.
- Some fundamentals are only processed overnight in your production system.

By attaching a latency value to each feature—say, "1 bar" for closing price–derived features and "1 day" for certain fundamentals—the backtest can mimic production timing. When the strategy requests features at time t, the pipeline only returns those whose latency has elapsed.

Validity window. Some features are stable over time (for example, a country classification or an industry code). Others become outdated quickly (for example, a short–term volatility metric computed intraday).

A validity window tells the engine how far into the future a feature value can be reused. For instance:

- A daily momentum feature may be considered valid for the entire next trading day.

- An intraday order book imbalance feature might be valid only for one bar.

This matters when sampling features onto a coarser backtest grid. If a feature is requested at a time when its last computed value is outside its validity window, the engine should either recompute it or mark it as missing.

Putting It All Together: A Deterministic, Reusable Layer

Designing the feature engineering pipeline as a deterministic, leakage–free DAG with caching and rich metadata brings several benefits that ripple through the entire backtest architecture:

- **Consistency across strategies**: multiple strategies can share the same features and be confident they are computed identically.
- **Reproducibility**: given a backtest run identifier, you can reconstruct exactly which data, feature definitions, and cache versions were used.
- **Safety**: leakage checks and time alignment conventions live in the pipeline, not scattered across strategy code.
- **Performance**: caching intermediate nodes lets you scale to larger universes and higher frequencies without prohibitive recomputation.
- **Inspectability**: risk, compliance, or audit teams can inspect the feature DAG and understand what went into signal generation.

Once this layer is in place, the strategy logic that sits above it can focus on *what* to predict and *how* to map predictions to positions, instead of wrestling with low–level data handling. In the next section, we will build on this foundation to define how signals themselves are represented, how they age and decay over time, and how their provenance can be traced back through the feature DAG to the underlying raw data.

4.2 Signal Representation & Lifecycle

In the previous section we built a disciplined feature engineering pipeline: a deterministic, leakage-free graph that turns raw data into model-ready features. The natural next question is: what do we do with those features?

Most quantitative strategies take features as inputs and emit *signals*. These signals are the strategy's opinion about what to hold or how to trade. In a small research script, you might think of a signal simply as "a number per asset per day." In a production-grade backtest engine, that is not enough.

This section standardizes what we mean by a signal and how it evolves over time. The goal is that every downstream module—sizing, portfolio construction, execution, risk, and reporting—can interpret signals in a consistent and unambiguous way. We will focus on four main questions:

- What does a signal *numerically represent*?
- How is its *size* interpreted and normalized across assets?
- What is its *horizon* and how does it *decay* as time passes?
- How do we track its *provenance* and reconstruct its state at any backtest time?

Throughout, we treat signals as explicit, versioned data objects, not as ephemeral byproducts of some model code. This is central to building a reproducible and auditable backtest engine.

What a Signal Represents

Before we talk about sizes, horizons, or decay, we must settle the most basic question: when your strategy outputs a signal value, what is that number?

There are several common interpretations:

- **Expected return**: the number is a forecast of the asset's return over a given future horizon.
- **Risk-adjusted score**: the number is a forecast scaled by risk, such as a Sharpe-like score.
- **Probability**: the number is the probability of a particular event, such as the probability that the price will increase.
- **Direct target**: the number is already a desired exposure, such as a target weight or target dollar position.

All of these can be valid, but mixing them within one engine without clear labelling leads to confusion. For example, a portfolio construction module that assumes every signal is an expected return may behave very differently if it is fed probability scores instead.

A robust backtest engine therefore standardizes a *signal type* for each stream of signals. Each signal record should carry a field that encodes what the numeric value means, such as:

- "expected return over one day, in percent",
- or "target weight in the portfolio",
- or "z-score of valuation factor".

In practice this is a structured label rather than free text, but the key idea is that downstream code can read it and interpret the number correctly.

Once you commit to a small number of signal types, you gain two advantages:

- **Simpler sizing logic**: if all signals presented to a given sizing policy mean "expected excess return over one day", you can write generic rules that map them to positions without instrument-specific hacks.
- **Clear interfaces**: strategies that directly output target weights can plug in at a different layer than strategies that output forecasts.

Signal Size and Normalization

Signals are typically computed per asset and can vary widely in scale. For example, expected one-day returns on a volatile small-cap stock might be much larger in magnitude than those on a stable large-cap stock. If we feed raw numbers into downstream modules, the interpretation of "0.5" or "2.0" in one asset may differ greatly from another.

To design a reusable signal layer, we need two related concepts:

- **Signal size**: how strong is the strategy's opinion in some absolute sense?
- **Normalization**: how do we make that strength comparable across different assets?

There are several common normalization schemes:

Volatility scaling. One intuitive approach is to measure signals in units of the asset's own volatility. For instance, a signal of +1 could mean "buy enough that the position contributes one unit of target risk," while -1 means "short one unit of target risk." The underlying forecast may be an expected return, but by dividing by recent volatility, you create a risk-normalized score.

This aligns naturally with position sizing: a given signal value leads to roughly similar risk across assets, regardless of their price level or raw volatility.

Cross-sectional ranking. Another widely used approach is to convert raw signals into ranks or percentiles across the traded universe at a given time. For example, you might rank all stocks from worst (0) to best (1) based on their raw alpha score.

This makes signals directly comparable across assets, and downstream modules can treat them as preferences: buy the top decile, sell the bottom decile, and ignore the middle.

Direct target scale. Some strategies prefer to skip further transformation and define signals directly on the output scale. For example, a signal might be a target weight between -1 and +1, where -1 represents a full short allocation and +1 a full long allocation, relative to some risk budget.

In this case, "signal size" already has an operational meaning: it tells the engine exactly how much of the asset to hold, once risk and leverage constraints are applied.

Regardless of which scheme you choose, the important part for the engine is that the *meaning of the scale* is standardized and recorded. Every signal should carry metadata such as:

- its numerical range (for example, unbounded, between -3 and +3, between 0 and 1),
- whether higher values always mean "more long" or "higher probability of the event",
- whether the scale is absolute (like expected return) or relative (like rank).

This makes it possible to combine or compare signals, and to plug them into generic policy modules without worrying about hidden conventions.

Signal Horizon: How Far Ahead It Looks

A feature at time t is a description of the world as observed up to t. A signal at time t is a statement about some future behavior. To use signals sensibly, we must know *which part of the future* they are about.

We call this the signal's *horizon*. At a high level, the horizon answers the question, "Over what future period is this signal trying to be right?" Here are some typical examples:

- One bar ahead: the signal is about the next bar's return (for example, the next day or the next minute).
- Fixed window: the signal forecasts the average return over the next week or month.
- Open-ended: the signal suggests a longer-term tilt that does not have a fixed expiry.

In a backtest engine, horizon is not just a research detail; it affects how you:

- evaluate forecast accuracy,
- align signals with realized returns,
- decide when a signal is stale and should be dropped or replaced.

Therefore, each signal record should explicitly encode its intended horizon. At minimum, this includes:

- a measurement unit (for example, number of bars, calendar days, or volume-based bars),
- a value (for example, one bar, five bars, or twenty trading days).

A one-bar-ahead signal and a twenty-day-ahead signal are not directly comparable, even if they are on the same numeric scale. If you later choose to evaluate performance or optimize a portfolio based on a mix of horizons, that should be a deliberate design decision rather than an accident.

Signal Decay: Aging and Expiry

Signals do not stay fresh forever. As time passes and new information arrives, the original forecast becomes less relevant. A robust engine must model this *decay* explicitly, rather than leaving it as an implicit assumption.

There are three common patterns:

Hard expiry. A signal is assumed to be valid up to a specific future time or bar, and then instantly becomes obsolete. For example, a one-day reversal signal generated at today's close might be considered valid only for trades executed tomorrow; beyond that, it is discarded.

In this case, each signal record includes an *expiry time*. The engine ensures that, at any given backtest timestamp, it only considers signals whose expiry is in the future.

Gradual decay. Some signals are thought of as "fading" over time rather than suddenly switching off. For instance, a medium-term momentum signal might be strongest right after it is generated, but still somewhat informative for several weeks.

This can be modeled by associating a decay profile with the signal, such as:

- a schedule of multipliers over future bars,
- or a half-life, defining how quickly the effective size shrinks.

Each time the engine advances, it updates the *effective* signal value by applying the appropriate decay, even if no new signal is generated.

Superseded by updates. Many strategies produce updated signals frequently. In these cases, the natural rule is that a new signal for an asset replaces the previous one. The decay of the older signal is effectively cut short by the arrival of new information.

The engine should have a clear policy for this: when a new signal arrives, the previous one is either marked as expired or flagged as superseded, and the active signal state for that asset is updated accordingly.

Signal Events and State: A Lifecycle View

To tie the preceding ideas together, it helps to think in terms of a signal's *lifecycle*. From the engine's perspective, each signal passes through identifiable stages:

- **Creation**: the signal is generated based on the current feature snapshot and model parameters. At this point, we record its value, type, horizon, and metadata, as well as a timestamp for when it became available.
- **Active life**: while the signal is not expired or superseded, it influences downstream decisions. During this period, its effective contribution may shrink due to decay.
- **Expiry or replacement**: either the signal reaches its natural expiry time, or a newer signal takes precedence. At that point it stops contributing to new trading decisions.

- **Archival**: the signal remains in storage for later analysis, attribution, or debugging, but is no longer part of the live decision state.

The backtest engine itself operates in terms of *signal events* and *signal state*:

- A **signal event** is an atomic record that something changed: a new signal was created, an existing one was updated, or one expired.
- The **signal state** at time t is what you get when you start from an initial empty state and apply all events up to time t in order.

This distinction is important for reproducibility. Events are what you store and version; state is what you reconstruct on demand. If you want to know, "what signals were active on March 15 at 10:00 for asset X?", you replay events up to that time. This ensures consistency with other parts of the engine, such as order generation and P&L attribution, which also depend on event histories.

Identifiers, Versioning, and Provenance

Signals are the output of models, which in turn depend on features, which depend on raw data. To make backtests truly auditable, we must be able to trace a signal back through this chain. That means capturing *provenance*.

At a minimum, each signal should carry:

- a unique identifier for the signal itself (for example, a combination of asset, strategy, and creation time),
- a reference to the strategy or model that created it,
- a reference to the specific *model snapshot* in use (for example, parameter set, training data version),
- a reference to the feature set version or feature DAG fingerprint used at that time.

The model and feature references tie the signal back to the rest of the deterministic architecture:

- If you change model parameters or retrain on new data, you create a new model version. Signals created under the old and new versions can be distinguished.
- If you change feature definitions or raw data versions, you change the feature DAG fingerprint. Signals generated under different fingerprints are not silently mixed.

This versioning makes it possible to answer questions like:

> "Did the performance change because we changed the model, or because the underlying data vendor backfilled historical prices?"

You can run backtests under different model and feature versions, and compare signals and outcomes while holding other pieces constant.

Storage and Retrieval: Events vs Time-Series Grids

Signals exist over time, across assets, and potentially across multiple strategies. The way you store them affects how easy it is to reconstruct signal state and to run large backtests efficiently.

There are two main perspectives:

Event stream. In this representation, you store each signal creation, update, and expiry as an event with a timestamp. This is similar to how you might store trades or orders. To know the signal state at time t, you apply all events up to t.

This is very natural for systems where signals are sparse or asynchronous, for example:

- A strategy that only updates signals when certain thresholds are crossed.

- A multi-asset system where different assets are updated on different schedules.

Event streams map well to databases and messaging systems used in live trading, which makes it easier to keep research and production in sync.

Time-series grid. In this representation, you store, for each asset and each timestamp on a regular grid (for example, every bar), the current effective signal value. This is convenient for backtesting because you can look up the signal state at a given bar with a single read.

The grid can be constructed on the fly by replaying events and filling forward within validity windows, or it can be precomputed and cached as an intermediate product.

In practice, a robust engine often supports both representations: events as the source of truth, and derived grids or snapshots for fast evaluation. What matters for this chapter is that the mapping between them is deterministic and documented, so that no ambiguity arises about which signals were considered active at any point.

Why Standardization Matters

To close this section, it is worth stepping back from the details. Why invest so much effort into defining signals precisely?

There are several reasons:

- **Interoperability**: Once signals have a standard representation, you can reuse sizing and portfolio construction modules across many strategies.
- **Reproducibility**: Given a backtest run, you can reconstruct not only trades and P&L, but also the exact signals that drove each decision, and how they evolved over time.
- **Risk and compliance**: Risk teams can inspect signals and their horizons, check that they align with approved use cases, and verify that no hidden look-ahead or misuse of data is taking place.

- **Research speed**: Researchers can focus on improving forecasts rather than reinventing the plumbing needed to interpret signals, handle decay, or manage versions.

Signals form the bridge between your feature engineering layer and your position sizing and execution layers. If that bridge is vague or ad hoc, the entire architecture becomes fragile. If it is clear and standardized, you can add new models, change data sources, or adjust constraints without losing track of what your strategies are actually trying to do.

In the next section, we will extend this structure one step further and discuss how standardized signals are turned into target positions, under explicit constraints on leverage, turnover, and concentration.

4.3 Position Sizing & Constraints

So far, we have treated signals as well-defined objects: they have a clear numerical meaning, a horizon, decay rules, and provenance. Signals, however, are still abstract opinions. The portfolio cannot hold "a signal"; it holds shares, contracts, or notionals.

This section describes the layer that turns signals into *target positions*. It is the main bridge between the forecasting side of the engine and the trading side. To be useful in a robust backtest, this layer must satisfy two requirements:

- It must be a *deterministic policy*: given current state and signals, it always produces the same targets.
- It must *enforce constraints*: volatility budgets, leverage limits, turnover and trading frequency controls, and concentration limits.

We will move gradually from simple, intuitive sizing rules to richer constraint handling, and then discuss how to package everything so that it remains reproducible and auditable.

From Signal to Target: Clarifying the Mapping

Recall that a signal is a standardized number attached to an asset at a point in time, with a known interpretation. For concreteness, suppose that for each asset we have a scalar signal at time t that is either:

- an expected excess return over a fixed horizon, or
- a normalized score, such as a cross-sectional rank or risk-adjusted z-score.

The first task of the sizing layer is to define a mapping from this number to a *desired exposure*. That exposure can be expressed in various ways:

- a **weight**: the fraction of portfolio capital to allocate to the asset (for example, +5% long, -2% short),
- a **dollar exposure**: the notional amount to hold long or short (for example, $2 million long),
- a **contract count**: the number of futures or options contracts.

In principle, any of these representations can be the internal language of your engine. In practice, it is convenient to adopt a canonical internal representation, often *target weights*, and convert to dollars or contracts later using instrument metadata and current prices.

Whatever representation you choose, the signal-to-target mapping should be *explicit and documented*. For example, you might decide that:

> "A signal of +1 corresponds to a target weight of +2%, and a signal of -1 to -2%. Signals outside the range -3 to +3 are clipped at the boundaries."

That is a simple linear rule with clipping. Others are possible, but the key is that the relation is fixed and the same for all assets that share a given signal type.

Basic Sizing Rules

Let us start with simple sizing policies, ignoring constraints for the moment. These capture most of the intuition and are building blocks for more complex behaviour.

Linear sizing. The most straightforward rule is proportional:

- Zero signal implies zero target position.
- A positive signal implies a long target, increasing in proportion to the signal size.
- A negative signal implies a short target, again proportional in magnitude.

This aligns naturally with the idea that stronger convictions should lead to larger positions. The proportionality constant encodes your overall risk appetite: a more aggressive strategy chooses a larger constant, leading to larger positions for the same signals.

Nonlinear sizing. In some strategies you may want to de-emphasize weak signals and amplify strong ones. A typical shape is:

- Signals near zero lead to very small or zero target positions.
- Beyond a threshold, position size grows faster than linearly with signal strength.
- At very large signals, the target size saturates to a maximum.

Conceptually, this is a smooth “S-shaped” curve. It reflects a belief that very small signals are not worth trading (once costs and noise are considered), but very strong signals are particularly attractive and should be overweighted, up to a risk limit.

Discrete buckets. For very simple or low-liquidity strategies, you may assign positions in coarse steps:

- Strong negative signal: full short,
- Moderate negative: half short,

- Near zero: flat,
- Moderate positive: half long,
- Strong positive: full long.

This is easy to reason about and can simplify implementation when dealing with instruments that must be traded in large lots.

In all of these cases, the mapping from signal to unconstrained target is a pure function that does not depend on the rest of the portfolio. It transforms each asset's signal into a first guess of its desired exposure.

Risk and Volatility Scaling

Signals are not directly comparable if different assets have very different risk profiles. A naive proportional sizing rule might give the same weight to a low-volatility bond and a high-volatility small-cap stock when they have the same signal. The portfolio would then be dominated by the risk of the more volatile asset.

To address this, the sizing layer typically incorporates a *volatility or risk scaling* component. The intuition is that for a given signal strength, you want each asset to contribute a similar amount of risk, not just a similar weight.

Conceptually, you can think of each asset as having a current estimate of its risk level (for example, a recent volatility measure). The sizing rule then adjusts the target size inversely with that level:

- Higher volatility assets receive smaller position sizes for the same signal.
- Lower volatility assets can receive larger positions without exceeding risk budgets.

This leads to more balanced risk contributions and makes the interpretation of signal size more stable across assets. In practice, this component draws on features computed by the feature engineering pipeline, such as rolling volatility or factor exposures, but the sizing logic itself remains a deterministic transformation.

From Unconstrained to Constrained Targets

The unconstrained target from signal and volatility scaling still ignores the realities of running a portfolio. You cannot allocate unlimited leverage, nor can you concentrate arbitrarily in a single stock or sector. You also may want to limit how much you trade from one period to the next.

We therefore distinguish two conceptual stages:

1. **Unconstrained target**: what the strategy would like to hold if there were no limits other than signal interpretation and risk scaling.
2. **Constrained target**: the actual target positions after applying all portfolio-level policies.

The transition from unconstrained to constrained target is the heart of the "constraints" in this section. It must be modeled as a *deterministic policy layer*: a fixed, versioned set of rules that map any unconstrained target and current state to a valid constrained target.

We will now walk through the main types of constraints and discuss how they fit together.

Leverage and Exposure Limits

The most familiar portfolio-level constraints are leverage and gross exposure limits. Two quantities are especially important:

- **Gross exposure**: the sum of absolute long and short positions.
- **Net exposure**: the difference between total long and total short positions.

A backtest engine should allow you to configure hard limits on both. For example:

- Gross exposure must not exceed 200% of capital.
- Net exposure must remain between -20% and +20% of capital.

There are many ways to enforce such limits. A simple and deterministic approach is to:

1. Compute the gross and net exposures implied by the unconstrained target.
2. If they fall within allowable ranges, accept the unconstrained target as is.
3. If they violate limits, scale the entire set of positions back proportionally until constraints are just met.

More refined rules are possible (for instance, scaling only longs or only shorts), but the crucial point is that the policy is *explicit and deterministic.* Given a particular unconstrained target and limit set, the constrained target is uniquely determined.

By making leverage constraints part of this sizing layer, rather than an afterthought in execution, you ensure that all downstream modules are working with exposures that are actually feasible.

Concentration and Sector Limits

Leverage constraints operate at the portfolio level. You also need controls that prevent excessive bets on individual assets or groups of related assets.

Common examples include:

- **Per-asset limits**: maximum absolute weight or dollar exposure per instrument.
- **Sector or industry caps**: maximum exposure to a sector, industry group, or country.
- **Name count limits**: caps on the number of long or short positions, for manageability or liquidity reasons.

These constraints are often phrased as simple limits on aggregated exposures. For example:

- No single stock may exceed 5% of portfolio capital.
- Total long exposure to any one sector may not exceed 30%.
- Short exposure to any one stock may not exceed 1% of average daily volume.

Implementing these constraints deterministically requires two steps:

1. **Compute implied exposures**: from the unconstrained target, compute per-asset weights, sector aggregates, and any other relevant groupings.
2. **Apply adjustment rules**: if any limit is violated, adjust positions according to pre-specified rules until all limits are satisfied.

Adjustment rules can be as simple as:

- Clipping any position that exceeds its per-asset limit.
- Proportionally scaling all assets within an overexposed sector until the sector total meets its cap.

More complex schemes can prioritize assets with stronger signals when trimming, but the engine should encode these priorities deterministically, not as ad hoc manual tweaks.

Again, the goal is not to find an "optimal" adjustment in a mathematical sense, but to have a clear, reproducible mapping from unconstrained desires to feasible, constrained targets.

Minimum Lot Sizes and Rounding

Real-world trading is not continuous. You can only trade in discrete units: whole shares, whole contracts, or minimum lot sizes. Even in a backtest that uses weights as an internal representation, you must eventually convert those weights into integer trade quantities.

This conversion introduces rounding errors. If done carelessly, rounding can introduce unintended biases or cause apparent violations of constraints (for example, exceeding a cap by a tiny amount after rounding).

To avoid this, the engine should treat rounding as part of the deterministic policy layer. For each instrument, you can define:

- the minimum tradable unit (for example, one share, one contract, one block of 1,000),
- the rounding rule (for example, round to nearest, round down, or round towards zero),
- any special rules for illiquid or restricted instruments (for example, only trade in multiples of a larger block size).

The sizing layer then:

1. Computes target positions in the continuous space (weights or dollars) after all exposure and concentration constraints.
2. Converts those targets into integer quantities according to instrument metadata and rounding rules.
3. Optionally recomputes implied weights to ensure that post-rounding exposures are still within acceptable tolerances.

Treating rounding as a deterministic part of the sizing policy, rather than a separate heuristic in the execution layer, helps keep the backtest's notion of target positions aligned with what is actually tradable.

Turnover and Trade Frequency Controls

So far, we have focused on static constraints: limits that apply to the portfolio at a given time. Another important set of constraints concerns *changes* in the portfolio over time.

Two related concepts are central here:

- **Turnover**: how much of the portfolio is traded over a period, typically measured as traded volume relative to capital.

- **Trade frequency**: how often you trade individual assets, or how frequently you rebalance.

Excessive turnover increases transaction costs and may be operationally infeasible. To control it, the sizing layer can impose explicit policies such as:

No-trade zones. Define a region around the current position within which small changes in the unconstrained target do not trigger trades. For example, if the current weight of a stock is 1% and the unconstrained target moves to 1.1%, the engine might decide to do nothing. Only when the difference exceeds a threshold (say, 0.5%) would a trade be generated.

This introduces intentional *stickiness*: the portfolio does not constantly chase tiny fluctuations in signals.

Minimum signal change thresholds. Similarly, you can require that signals change by more than a minimum amount before their implied target positions are allowed to move. This is particularly useful when signals are noisy estimates.

Turnover caps. At the portfolio level, you can caps on total daily or weekly turnover. If the unconstrained target would require too much trading, the engine can scale back the desired position changes proportionally.

All of these rules must be formulated in terms of current state and unconstrained target, so that the resulting constrained target is a pure function of observable inputs. In particular, they should avoid hidden state or randomness. For instance, if you adopt the rule "never trade before 10:15," that rule should be part of the policy configuration, not an undocumented practice.

Determinism and Policy Versioning

The repeated emphasis on determinism is not an academic preference; it is what makes backtests comparable over time and across environments. In the context of position sizing and constraints, determinism means:

> Given the same sequence of signals, prices, and configuration, the sizing layer always produces the same sequence of target positions.

To achieve this, you should:

- Avoid hidden randomization in sizing policies. If you need to break ties or select among equals (for example, which stock to drop when reducing a sector exposure), use deterministic tie-breaking rules, such as sorting by a stable key and dropping the last.
- Version all policy parameters: leverage limits, concentration caps, rounding rules, turnover thresholds, and so on. A change to any of these creates a new policy version.
- Record, for each backtest run, which policy version was in effect. This allows you to rerun or compare simulations under different constraint sets.

This approach mirrors what we did for features and signals: treat the sizing layer as a first-class component with its own configuration and versioning, rather than as scattered logic across strategy code.

Engine Interfaces and State Dependencies

The output of the sizing layer is typically a set of *target positions* per asset at each backtest time step. To produce these, the layer needs to know:

- the current portfolio state (current positions, cash, exposures),
- the current set of active signals (and their effective values after decay),
- relevant market data (prices, volatility estimates, volume, classification data),
- the policy configuration (limits, rounding rules, turnover controls).

Given these inputs, the sizing layer produces a new target portfolio. It is useful to distinguish conceptually between:

- the **desired change** in positions (how much you would like to trade), and
- the **resulting target** after applying trade frequency and turnover controls.

The execution layer, which we will discuss in later sections, then takes these target positions and decides how and when to place orders to move from the current portfolio towards the target, subject to microstructure and slippage models.

By keeping the interface between sizing and execution clean—in terms of target positions rather than low-level orders—you can modify execution policies without disturbing the logic of position sizing, and vice versa.

Why a Policy Layer, Not Ad Hoc Filters

It is tempting to think of many of these constraints as "filters" applied directly to signals. For example, you might be inclined to:

- zero out signals for illiquid stocks,
- scale signals down when leverage is high,
- clip signal values when turnover is large.

While this can work in simple settings, it entangles forecasting with implementation constraints. It becomes hard to reason about what the signals *mean*, because their values now depend on portfolio-level conditions.

By contrast, treating position sizing and constraints as a separate policy layer has several advantages:

- **Separation of concerns**: signals express beliefs about the future; sizing expresses how aggressively to act on those beliefs, given risk and constraints.

- **Reusability**: the same sizing policies can be applied to many different signal models.
- **Auditability**: risk and compliance can inspect constraint rules without needing to untangle model code.

In a well-designed backtest engine, this policy layer is as central as the feature pipeline and the signal schema. It is the place where abstract forecasts are translated into concrete, feasible portfolios.

In this section we have taken a step further along the strategy pipeline. Starting from standardized signals, we have defined how to map them into target positions while respecting a web of constraints:

- Basic sizing rules transform signal values into unconstrained desired exposures.
- Volatility and risk scaling make position sizes comparable across assets.
- Leverage, concentration, and sector limits ensure exposures remain within acceptable bounds.
- Minimum lot sizes and rounding enforce tradability at the instrument level.
- Turnover and trade frequency controls limit how aggressively the portfolio changes over time.
- Deterministic, versioned policies make the whole process reproducible and auditable.

These targets are not yet trades; they are desired end states. In the next sections, we will see how the engine moves from these target positions to actual orders, how it models order types and market microstructure, and how it accounts for slippage and transaction costs when simulating execution.

4.4 Portfolio Construction Basics

In the previous sections we have walked from raw data, through a disciplined feature pipeline, to standardized signals, and then to asset-level target positions that respect risk and implementation constraints. It may seem as though we already have a portfolio: for each asset we have a target exposure.

In practice, however, there is often an additional layer that we will call *portfolio construction*. This layer decides how to combine multiple inputs—possibly multiple signals, multiple strategies, or multiple risk objectives—into a coherent, diversified portfolio that trades sensibly and respects transaction costs.

This section introduces the basic ideas of portfolio construction in the context of a backtest engine. We will focus on simple, robust methods rather than advanced optimization theory, with an emphasis on:

- how to represent current and desired portfolio state;
- how to turn per-asset targets into coherent portfolios using weighting schemes;
- when and how to use small-scale optimizers;
- how to keep all of this deterministic and reproducible.

What Portfolio Construction Adds Beyond Position Sizing

It is useful to clarify where portfolio construction sits relative to the sizing layer you just saw.

The sizing layer takes, for each asset, a signal and a risk estimate, applies limits and constraints, and outputs a *target position* for that asset. If you run only one strategy and one signal, and if your constraints are already portfolio-aware (for example, you cap gross exposure and sector exposures), you might think there is nothing left to do.

Portfolio construction becomes important as soon as you:

- combine multiple signals or sub-strategies,
- wish to apply higher-level diversification or neutrality goals (for example, factor or sector neutrality),
- wish to explicitly trade off forecast strength versus transaction costs.

In these settings, the per-asset targets from individual components are more like *inputs* to a final decision, not the final portfolio. Portfolio construction is the layer that blends these inputs into a single, actionable set of positions.

To keep the architecture clean, we will think of this layer as operating on *proposed exposures*. The inputs are:

- a representation of the current portfolio (what we currently hold),
- one or more sets of proposed target exposures (from different signals or strategies),
- risk estimates (for example, volatility or factor loadings),
- cost and liquidity estimates (for example, spreads, volumes, fee schedules),
- configuration for constraints and diversification goals.

The output is a *final target portfolio*: the positions we intend to hold after rebalancing.

Representing Current and Desired Portfolio State

Before we can construct portfolios, we must agree on how to *represent* them. In the engine, a portfolio state typically includes:

- Positions per asset: in shares, contracts, or weights.
- Cash and cash-equivalents.

- Derived metrics: gross and net exposures, sector exposures, factor exposures, risk estimates.

The current state is whatever the accounting layer reports at the start of a decision step. The desired state is what portfolio construction will produce.

There are two common internal representations for portfolio construction:

Weights-based representation. Here you express each asset's position as a fraction of total capital. This is natural for long-short equity or other strategies where capital is the basic resource. Many constraints, such as leverage caps or sector weights, are naturally expressed in terms of weights.

Dollar or notional representation. Here you work directly with dollar exposure or contract notionals. This can be convenient when dealing with derivatives, where the notion of "weight" needs to consider underlying exposure and margin requirements.

In most engines, you choose one as the canonical internal representation and convert as needed. What is important for our purposes is that the representation be:

- consistent across current and target states,
- accompanied by the necessary metadata (such as sector labels, factor loadings, and cost parameters),
- unambiguous and deterministic given the underlying positions.

With this in place, portfolio construction reduces to the following question:

> Given the current portfolio and a set of proposed per-asset targets, what new target portfolio should we adopt?

Heuristic Allocation Rules

The simplest approach is to avoid heavy optimization and rely on deterministic heuristic rules. These are easy to understand and debug, and often good enough for many strategies. We will look at several common patterns.

Proportional to Signal Strength

The most direct rule is to set target weights proportional to the signal values, subject to simple scaling and constraints. For example:

- Normalize the signal vector across assets, for example by dividing by the sum of absolute values.
- Multiply by a target risk or leverage budget to get initial weights.
- Apply per-asset caps and sector caps as in the sizing layer.

This leads to a portfolio where:

- Assets with stronger positive signals receive larger long weights.
- Assets with strong negative signals receive larger short weights.
- Assets with zero or small signals receive small or zero weights.

If you have multiple signal sources, you can combine them linearly before this step (for example, an average of two models), or allocate separate "sleeves" of capital to each signal and then sum their resulting portfolios.

Risk-Parity Overlays

Pure signal-proportional portfolios may be dominated by a few high-volatility or highly correlated assets. To encourage diversification, you can overlay risk-parity ideas.

A simple heuristic is:

- Start from signal-proportional weights.
- Estimate each asset's contribution to portfolio risk (for example, using volatilities and correlations).

- Scale down weights of assets whose risk contribution is too high, and scale up those whose contribution is too low, within constraints.

This steers the portfolio toward a state where risk contributions are more balanced, while still respecting the information in the signals. It is not a full optimization; rather, it is an adjustment rule applied iteratively or in closed form using approximate measures.

Sector- and Factor-Neutralization

For strategies that aim to exploit security selection skill rather than broad directional bets, it is often desirable to be neutral with respect to certain groups or risk factors. For example, an equity long-short strategy may want:

- zero net exposure to each sector,
- zero net exposure to the overall market factor.

A heuristic way to achieve this is:

- Construct initial weights from signals.
- Compute sector exposures (sum of weights within each sector).
- Adjust weights in a way that cancels sector exposures while preserving as much as possible of the ranking implied by the signals.

For example, suppose technology is overweight long in your initial portfolio. You could reduce all long tech positions slightly and reduce all short tech positions slightly in absolute value, until net tech exposure is zero. This preserves the relative differences within the sector while removing the net sector bet.

This procedure can be extended to factor exposures using a factor model: compute the factor exposures implied by your weights and then project them onto a neutral subspace by subtracting components along undesired factors. Even when done approximately rather than optimally, such neutralization can significantly change portfolio behaviour and must therefore be modeled explicitly and deterministically in the backtest.

Transaction Costs and Simple Turnover Penalties

Any change from the current portfolio to a new target implies trades. Trades incur costs: spreads, impact, fees, and taxes. A sensible portfolio construction layer takes at least a basic view of these costs, rather than naively jumping to the unconstrained or heuristic target every period.

One way to introduce cost awareness without solving a full optimization is to employ *turnover-aware heuristics*. For example:

- Only move partway from the current portfolio toward the new signal-implied target, with a fixed or state-dependent step size.
- Apply no-trade zones at the portfolio level: ignore target changes that imply trades below a certain notional threshold.
- Allow full rebalancing only when the benefit, as measured by signal changes, exceeds a simple estimate of transaction costs.

These heuristics make the portfolio more conservative in its trading, thereby reducing turnover and costs. They also introduce path dependence: the next portfolio depends not only on the new signals but also on where you currently are. To remain reproducible, all such rules must be encoded in the configuration and applied deterministically.

When to Use Optimizers

Heuristics, while simple, have limits. They may have difficulty enforcing multiple interacting constraints or producing stable portfolios when signals are noisy. In many real strategies, some form of small-scale optimization is used for portfolio construction.

From the perspective of a backtest engine, an *optimizer* is just another deterministic mapping:

Inputs: current portfolio, forecasts (signals), risk estimates, cost estimates, constraints.
Output: target portfolio that approximately balances forecast strength, diversification, and costs.

You do not need to implement a full-blown enterprise optimization system inside the engine; instead, you can design a clean interface and plug in existing solvers where needed. Let us sketch the core ingredients at a conceptual level.

Basic Ingredients of a Portfolio Optimizer

In words, a typical optimizer tries to:

- reward assets with strong positive forecasts and penalize those with negative forecasts;
- penalize total portfolio risk, as measured by a risk model;
- penalize trading costs associated with moving from the current portfolio to a new one;
- satisfy all hard constraints (for example, leverage limits, sector caps, bounds).

You can think of it as trading off three forces:

1. **Forecast strength**: push weights in the direction suggested by signals.
2. **Diversification and risk control**: pull weights toward a diversified, low-risk configuration.
3. **Cost discipline**: discourage big jumps from current positions unless the forecast benefit is large.

The exact mathematical formulation is beyond the scope of this introductory section, but most common approaches boil down to setting up an objective function that encodes these trade-offs and then solving for the weights that perform best under that objective subject to constraint rules.

Backtest-Friendly Optimizer Design

When integrating optimization into a backtest engine, some principles are especially important:

Deterministic inputs and settings. Given the same inputs and configuration, the optimizer should always return the same target portfolio. This means:

- fixed seeds if any randomness is involved;
- fixed tolerances and stopping criteria;
- consistent handling of tie situations.

Well-defined failure behaviour. Numerical solvers sometimes fail to converge or find a feasible solution. Your engine should define:

- how to detect such failures;
- what fallback to use (for example, revert to the previous portfolio, or fall back to a simpler heuristic);
- how to log and surface these events.

Stable formulations. Optimizations should be formulated in a way that is stable over time and across small changes in inputs. For example, overly aggressive use of tiny forecast differences may lead to unstable portfolios that flip frequently between similar configurations. Introducing modest regularization or step constraints can improve stability.

Versioning and audit trails. As with other components, optimizer configurations—choices of objective terms, penalties, and constraints—should be versioned. Backtest runs should record which optimizer version and settings were used.

By treating the optimizer as a versioned, deterministic component, you preserve the reproducibility of the overall engine even when some internal steps are mathematically complex.

Avoiding Over-Optimization

A common danger is to give the optimizer too much freedom to fit historical data, especially when backtesting. If you allow a rich objective with many adjustable parameters and a large set of constraints, it becomes easy—consciously or not—to overfit to the past. The backtest may look excellent, but performance may not carry forward.

To keep the backtest informative rather than misleading, it is helpful to follow some guardrails:

- **Keep objectives simple.** Focus on a small number of well-motivated terms (for example, forecast reward, risk penalty, cost penalty). Avoid dozens of tuning knobs.
- **Prefer robust constraints.** Use constraints to express structural requirements (like leverage caps or sector limits), not to micromanage individual positions in ways tailored to a particular sample.
- **Test alternative constructions.** Compare results using a simple heuristic portfolio construction method and a more advanced optimization-based method. If results differ wildly, understand why before trusting the more complex approach.
- **Document assumptions.** Make explicit what you are assuming about risk, costs, and correlations when constructing portfolios. Treat these as part of the model, not as background details.

The overarching idea is that portfolio construction, like any other model component, should be parsimonious enough that its behaviour can be understood and stress-tested, not a black box that magically reconciles all objectives.

Determinism and Swappability

One of the themes of this book is modularity: you should be able to change parts of the simulation (for example, the execution model) without rewriting everything else. Portfolio construction is no exception.

To support this, design the engine so that:

- There is a clear API between the sizing layer and portfolio construction: typically, a set of per-asset proposed targets plus risk and cost metadata.
- Portfolio construction itself can be configured to use either a simple heuristic method or an optimization-based method, without changing callers.
- The outputs—target portfolios—have the same format regardless of the internal method used.

This makes it possible to:

- start with a simple, transparent construction method while building and validating the rest of the engine;
- later introduce more advanced portfolio construction for certain strategies, while preserving comparability against earlier results;
- run controlled experiments: same signals and data, different portfolio construction methods, to isolate their effects.

As always, the key is that both methods be deterministic and versioned, so that switching between them is a controlled, documented change.

In this section we have moved from asset-level sizing to portfolio-level construction. The main messages are:

- Even if you have per-asset target positions from signals and sizing, there is value in a separate portfolio construction layer that combines them into a coherent, diversified, and cost-aware portfolio.
- Simple heuristic methods—proportional to signals, risk-parity overlays, sector and factor neutralization, turnover-aware rebalancing—often capture most of what you need and are easy to debug.
- When constraints and trade-offs become complex, small-scale optimization can be used, but it must be integrated in a deterministic, versioned, and backtest-friendly way.

- Over-optimization is a real danger; keeping formulations simple and assumptions explicit helps preserve the informational value of backtests.
- A clean interface and modular design allow you to swap portfolio construction methods without disturbing upstream (signals, sizing) or downstream (execution, costs) components.

With a clear view of portfolio construction in place, we are ready to move further along the simulation pipeline and consider how these target portfolios are translated into actual orders, how different order types interact with market microstructure, and how the backtest engine should model execution and slippage.

4.5 Order Types & Microstructure

Up to this point our focus has been on the *desired* portfolio: features produce signals, signals are mapped to target positions, and portfolio construction blends them into a coherent set of exposures. None of this yet says *how* the portfolio changes hands in the market.

In live trading you do not trade weights or signals; you submit *orders* to an exchange or other venue, and those orders interact with other participants through the market's microstructure. A backtest that ignores these details can be seriously misleading: it might assume fills at mid-price with no delay, or unlimited liquidity, or no interaction between your own orders and the book.

This section introduces a minimal but robust microstructure model for backtesting. Our goal is not to emulate every quirk of every venue, but to:

- represent common order types in a uniform way;
- model an order's lifecycle through states: new, queued, partially filled, filled, cancelled, expired;
- capture how orders interact with the bid–ask spread, available depth, and priority rules (such as price–time priority);

- do all of this with deterministic, parameterized rules that can be shared across backtests.

We will work step by step from order types, to order states, to a stylized order book and priority model, and then to how this all fits into the backtest engine.

Why Microstructure Matters for Backtesting

At first glance, order–level microstructure may seem like a detail you can sweep under a simple "execution cost" or "slippage" term. For some high–level, low–frequency strategies that may be acceptable. However, even there, you need to know *what* that cost is tied to.

Several aspects of performance are tightly linked to microstructure:

- **Realistic fills**: a large market order cannot be filled entirely at the best quote if the top of book has limited depth.
- **Spread costs**: a market buy will typically pay the ask; a limit buy that posts at the bid may avoid the spread, but risks non–execution.
- **Queue position**: a passive limit order at the best bid only fills when incoming sells exhaust prior resting bids at that price.
- **Order interaction**: placing an aggressive order can move the price and change the conditions encountered by subsequent orders.

If the backtest engine always treats any target position as instantly achievable at a single synthetic price, it implicitly assumes a particular and usually optimistic microstructure. Making that microstructure explicit is the purpose of this section.

Canonical Order Types

We begin by defining the main order types that our backtest engine should support in a standardized way. Real venues offer many variants, but most can be expressed as combinations or parameterizations of a few basics:

- **Market orders**: instructions to buy or sell immediately at the best available prices in the book.
- **Limit orders**: instructions to buy or sell at a specified limit price or better, possibly resting in the book until filled or cancelled.
- **Stop orders**: orders that become active only when the market trades at or through a trigger price.
- **Stop–limit orders**: stop orders that, once triggered, place a limit order rather than a market order.
- **Pegged or relative orders**: orders whose price is tied to some reference, such as the current best bid, best ask, or midprice.

For backtesting, we can define a canonical order schema that includes:

- side (buy or sell),
- quantity (in shares or contracts),
- type (market, limit, stop, stop–limit, pegged),
- limit price (if applicable),
- stop price (if applicable),
- time–in–force (for example, good–till–cancelled, day, immediate–or–cancel),
- creation time, and any additional flags (such as whether the order may add liquidity only).

This schema is rich enough to express most strategy orders you will need in a backtest. We then need a lifecycle model that tells us how these orders evolve over time in response to market events.

Order Lifecycle: From New to Final State

Every order progresses through a sequence of states between creation and termination. A minimal but useful state machine includes:

- **New**: the order has been created in the strategy or engine and is about to be routed to a venue.
- **Queued**: the order rests in the book, waiting to be matched.
- **Partially filled**: some quantity has traded, but there is remaining open quantity.
- **Filled**: the order is fully executed; no open quantity remains.
- **Cancelled**: the strategy or risk system has removed the remaining open quantity from the book.
- **Expired**: the order's time–in–force has run out without being fully executed.

In a real exchange, additional internal states exist, but for modeling purposes these are sufficient. The key point is that at any simulated time, each order has exactly one state and a well–defined remaining quantity.

Right after enumerating these states, it is useful to visualize the lifecycle and its interaction with a stylized order book.

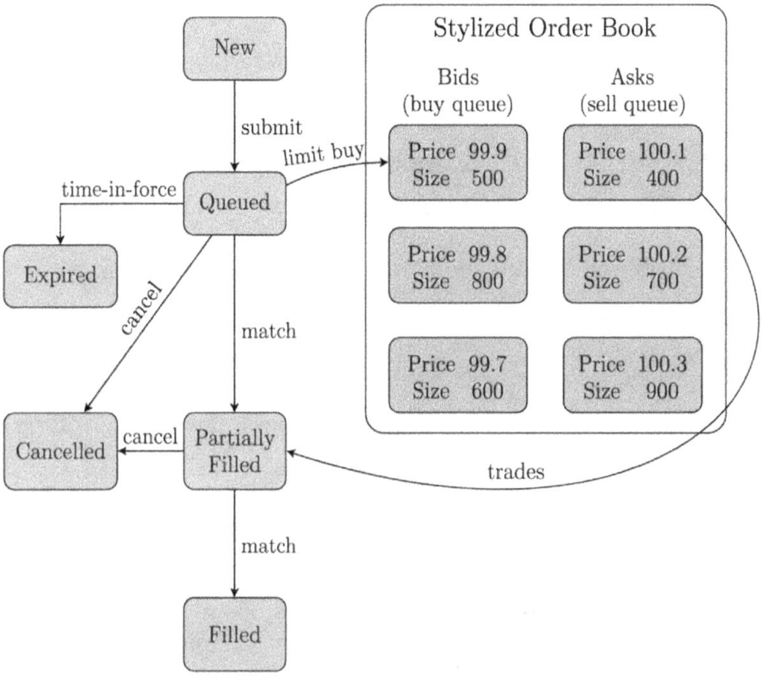

A Stylized Order Book

To model how orders fill, we need a representation of the order book, or at least of the parts of it that our orders interact with. The full order book is a time–varying set of buy and sell limit orders at various prices and quantities. For backtesting we usually simplify this in two ways:

- Focus on a small number of price levels: typically the best bid and best ask, and optionally a few levels of depth behind them.
- Represent the state at discrete times aligned with your market

data bars, rather than tick by tick, unless you are running a high–frequency simulation.

At each simulation time step and for each instrument, the engine maintains or infers:

- the best bid price and available size,
- the best ask price and available size,
- possibly additional depth at higher bids and lower asks,
- a priority ordering within each price level (for example, first–in, first–out).

You can parameterize this stylized book in several ways, depending on available data:

- If you have quote data with sizes, you can treat those as the top of book.
- If you only have bars (open, high, low, close, volume), you may need to infer spreads and depths using a simple model calibrated to typical market conditions.

The goal is not to reconstruct the exact historical book, but to have a consistent, repeatable approximation of the prices and sizes that an order would have seen.

Price–Time Priority and Matching Logic

Most modern limit order markets use price–time priority to decide which orders are matched first:

- Orders at better prices are filled before orders at worse prices (for example, higher bids before lower bids).
- Among orders at the same price, earlier orders are filled before later ones.

Our simulated matching logic should capture this basic structure. Conceptually, matching works as follows:

- An aggressive order (for example, a market buy) will trade against resting orders on the opposite side of the book starting from the best price and moving outward until its quantity is exhausted or the book is depleted.
- A passive limit order (for example, a buy at a price below the current ask) will either rest in the book (if its limit is inside or at the current best bid) or be immediately executed if it crosses existing orders (for example, a limit buy above the best ask is effectively a market order up to its limit).

In the backtest engine, you can implement price–time priority in a stylized way:

- For each price level, maintain a total available size and treat your orders as arriving either before or after the "crowd" depending on your assumptions.
- When simulating a trade, consume the quantity at the best price up to the available size, then move to the next level if needed.
- If multiple of your own simulated orders would trade at the same level, use a deterministic tie–breaking rule (for example, by order creation time or a fixed ordering of strategies).

For backtesting, it is usually enough to track *how much* of your orders would have filled at each price, rather than modeling every counterparty order explicitly.

Modeling Spreads and Depth with Bar Data

Many backtests, especially those covering long histories or broad universes, are based on bar data (for example, daily or intraday bars) rather than full order book histories. In that case, you need to infer spreads and depths.

A simple and commonly used approach is:

- Estimate an effective spread for each bar, perhaps as a fixed number of ticks or a small fraction of price, possibly varying by instrument and liquidity.
- Assume that the best bid is midprice minus half the spread, and the best ask is midprice plus half the spread.
- Model available depth at the best levels as a fraction of total bar volume (for example, assume some percentage of volume traded at the top of book).

This gives you a synthetic order book state consistent with the bar's prices and volume. You can then test how your simulated orders would have interacted with that synthetic book, honoring spread and depth limitations:

- A market buy pays the synthetic ask, and if its size exceeds assumed depth, it may push into worse prices (modeled as additional impact).
- A passive limit buy at the synthetic bid only fills up to the assumed depth, and only if the bar's trade range includes that bid level.

The specific parameters (typical spread, depth fraction) become part of your microstructure model's configuration and should be versioned. Different parameter sets can be used to run scenario tests (for example, tighter or wider spreads, more or less depth) while holding the rest of the strategy fixed.

Order Types in the Stylized Book

With a basic order book and matching logic in place, we can define how each order type behaves in the simulation.

Market orders. A market order seeks immediate execution and is matched against the best available prices:

- A market buy consumes asks starting from the best ask.

- A market sell consumes bids starting from the best bid.

The backtest engine should:

- determine, for the current bar, which prices and quantities are available at each level under your depth model;
- allocate fills across levels according to price–time priority;
- record the volume–weighted average price achieved and any unfilled quantity if the market is assumed to be too shallow.

Limit orders. A limit order specifies the worst acceptable price. In our stylized model:

- A limit buy with a price below the current best bid is added to the bid queue and may or may not fill in this bar depending on whether the simulated trade range includes that price and whether sufficient sell volume is modeled.
- A limit buy with a price at or above the best ask is treated as a crossing order: it executes immediately up to the volume available at prices up to its limit.

To determine whether and how a resting limit order fills during a bar, the engine can use simple rules tied to the bar's high and low:

- If the bar's low is above the limit price for a buy, the order does not trade.
- If the bar's low is at or below the limit, and the high is above, the order may trade; you allocate fills based on assumed participation in volume and priority assumptions.

These rules are crude but give a consistent mapping from bar data to likely fill events.

Stop and stop–limit orders. Stop orders become active when the market trades at or through their trigger price. In a bar–based simulation:

- For a stop buy, if the bar's high is at or above the stop price, the order triggers at some point during the bar.
- Once triggered, the order becomes a market or limit order and is handled accordingly within the same bar, subject to decisions about intra–bar timing.

This introduces subtle timing questions (for example, did the stop trigger before or after some other event?), which we will handle in a deterministic way in the execution model. For now, it is enough to note that stop orders require the microstructure layer to reason about intra–bar price paths, not just open and close.

Pegged or relative orders. Pegged orders, such as "buy at best bid" or "sell at best ask," track a reference price over time. In a stylized model, you can treat them as limit orders whose price is reset whenever the reference changes, subject to rules about when repricing is allowed.

For backtesting, it is often sufficient to:

- re–evaluate the pegged price at each bar or sub–bar step;
- treat the resulting limit as a normal limit order for matching purposes.

Time, Latency, and Event Ordering

Microstructure is fundamentally about timing: who gets to the book first, and which prices were available when. In a backtest driven by discrete bars, you must decide where your own decisions and orders sit within each bar.

A simple but explicit convention might be:

- At the end of bar t, your strategy sees features and signals based on data up to that bar.
- It decides on new target positions and generates orders.
- Those orders have a latency (for example, one bar) before they can affect the book, so they are assumed to arrive at the market during bar $t + 1$.

Given such a convention, microstructure modeling respects *causality*: orders cannot trade at prices that were not yet known when they were decided. This is aligned with the leakage–free feature design from earlier chapters.

Within each bar where orders are active, you may need a deterministic rule for event ordering:

- Do you assume that your orders arrive before the bar's price extremes or after?
- How do you interleave multiple orders from your own strategy?

The engine should choose simple, fixed rules (for example, assume orders encounter the bar's average book state, or that they execute roughly at the bar's volume–weighted price, subject to spread and depth). Whatever you choose, encode it as configuration, not as unspoken assumptions.

Venue Differences and Trading Sessions

Not all venues are alike. Differences include:

- trading hours and calendars;
- auction mechanisms at open and close;
- specific order types and priority rules;
- minimum tick sizes and lot sizes.

A practical backtest engine need not model every venue idiosyncrasy, but it should capture:

- **Sessions**: when trading is possible. Orders submitted outside a session should queue until the next open or be rejected, depending on time–in–force.
- **Tick size**: prices must be rounded to allowed price increments, which affects where limit orders can be placed and what spreads are feasible.

- **Basic priority rules**: for example, price–time priority versus pro–rata matching in some derivatives markets.

You can represent each venue as an object with its own calendar and tick rules. Instruments are then associated with venues, and orders inherit venue behaviour. During simulation, the engine maintains a time–indexed state per venue, so that if you replay a backtest, orders encounter the same modeled conditions at the same timestamps.

Determinism and Configuration of Microstructure

As with other layers, microstructure modeling should be deterministic and configurable:

- **Deterministic**: given the same bar data, order stream, and configuration, the simulated fills are identical.
- **Configurable**: spreads, depths, latency, and priority assumptions can be changed by swapping configuration sets, not by rewriting engine code.
- **Versioned**: each configuration set (for example, "Equities US 1" or "Futures FX 2") has a version identifier that is recorded in backtests.

This lets you run scenario analyses such as:

- "What if spreads had been twice as wide?"
- "What if we had access to a deeper, more liquid venue?"
- "How sensitive is performance to our assumptions about top–of–book depth?"

Because the microstructure model is explicit and deterministic, these questions can be answered by re–running the same strategy under different configurations and comparing the outcomes.

In this section we have walked from abstract order types to a concrete, if simplified, microstructure model suitable for backtesting. The key ideas are:

- Orders have a lifecycle through states (new, queued, partially filled, filled, cancelled, expired) that must be modeled explicitly.
- A stylized order book with bid–ask, depth, and price–time priority gives structure to how orders fill.
- Different order types—market, limit, stop, stop–limit, pegged—interact with the book according to consistent, parameterized rules.
- When only bar data are available, spreads and depth can be inferred via simple models, but those models must be explicit and versioned.
- Venue characteristics and trading sessions shape when and how orders can trade.
- Above all, microstructure modeling must be deterministic and configurable, so that backtests remain reproducible and microstructure assumptions can be stress–tested.

These microstructure foundations set the stage for the next step in the strategy pipeline: an *execution model* that takes target portfolios and, using the order and microstructure framework described here, simulates how trades are sliced, scheduled, and filled over time, and how slippage and impact arise from that interaction.

4.6 Execution Model & Slippage

The previous sections brought us from features to signals, from signals to target positions, and from targets to concrete orders that interact with a stylized order book. We now focus on the final leg: how these orders turn into *fills* and how the backtest accounts for the difference between the prices we would like to trade at and the prices we actually obtain.

This is the role of the *execution model.* Within a backtest engine, the execution model is a deterministic policy layer that:

- takes target portfolios and current positions as inputs;

- decides what orders to send, in what size and schedule;
- simulates how those orders interact with the modeled order book and microstructure;
- outputs fills: quantities and prices for each trade;
- attributes the gap between midprice and execution price to spread, impact, and residual slippage.

Our goal is not to create a perfect high–fidelity exchange simulator, but to build a model that is realistic *enough* to keep backtest results honest, while remaining simple, transparent, and reproducible.

From Target Portfolios to Orders

Execution begins with a discrepancy between the *current* portfolio and a *target* portfolio produced by the sizing and portfolio construction layers. Conceptually, the desired change is straightforward:

- If the target weight of an asset is higher than its current weight, we need to buy.
- If the target weight is lower, we need to sell.

A naive backtest might assume that we instantly jump from current to target, effectively trading at a single synthetic price (often the bar's close). A more realistic engine introduces an explicit policy that determines:

- **Participation rate**: what fraction of market volume we are willing to be each period.
- **Execution style**: aggressive (market–like), passive (limit–like), or mixed.
- **Time slicing**: whether we spread trades over multiple bars (for example, a VWAP–like schedule) or try to fill within one.

This policy converts the desired position change into a sequence of child orders over time. Each child order then goes through the microstructure layer described earlier, and yields simulated fills.

For example, suppose we want to buy 100,000 shares of a stock over the next day. An execution policy might decide to:

- split the trade into 10 equal slices of 10,000 shares;
- submit one slice every bar during the next 10 bars;
- use a mix of aggressive and passive orders depending on intra–bar price moves.

In the backtest, these decisions are made by deterministic rules based on known quantities such as target size, recent volatility, and liquidity estimates.

Latency: Decision Time vs Arrival at the Book

In live trading there is always latency between the moment the strategy decides to trade and the moment its orders affect the book. This latency includes:

- computation time (feature calculation, signal generation, risk checks);
- communication delays (routing orders to the venue);
- exchange processing time.

Ignoring latency can introduce subtle look–ahead bias: you might be simulating trades at prices that would not have been observable or reachable when the decision was made.

To avoid this, the execution model incorporates a simple but explicit latency convention. For example:

- Decisions are made at the end of bar t using data up to that bar.

- Orders generated from those decisions are assumed to arrive and start trading during bar $t + 1$.

Latency can be parameterized:

- as a fixed number of bars,
- or as a time duration relative to bar length (for example, half a bar).

Once latency is encoded, the backtest engine enforces it uniformly: no matter how the strategy changes, orders derived from decisions at time t cannot interact with the book earlier than prescribed. This keeps causal ordering consistent with our leakage–free design.

Execution Styles

Different strategies use different execution styles depending on their urgency, alpha horizon, and sensitivity to costs. The execution model should support a handful of standard styles:

Aggressive (market–like) execution. Here, the trader prioritizes speed over cost, submitting orders that are likely to fill quickly, often by crossing the spread. In our stylized microstructure:

- Aggressive buy orders trade against the current asks, possibly walking up the book.
- Aggressive sell orders trade against the current bids, possibly walking down the book.

This tends to incur higher spread and impact costs but reduces execution risk (the risk of not getting filled).

Passive (limit–like) execution. Here, the trader posts orders that are more likely to capture the spread at the cost of possibly not executing. For example:

- A passive buy posts at the bid or slightly below.

- A passive sell posts at the ask or slightly above.

In the backtest, passive orders may or may not fill during a bar, depending on modeled depth, volume, and price path.

Schedule–based execution. For large orders, it is common to use pre–defined schedules such as:

- VWAP–like execution: slice the order proportionally to expected or realized volume over a window.
- TWAP–like execution: trade equal amounts in each time slice.

These schedules can be combined with aggressive or passive tactics at each slice. The schedule itself is part of the execution policy and should be deterministic given its parameters.

Participation–rate execution. Another widely used style caps our participation as a fraction of market volume (for example, never more than 10% of volume in any bar). This reduces market impact and lowers the chance of revealing our full intentions.

In the backtest, this means that if the desired slice is larger than the allowed participation rate times the bar's volume, the engine either:

- reduces the executed size to the cap and leaves the remainder to be executed later, or
- flags part of the order as unfilled according to the policy.

All of these styles can be expressed as fixed rules operating on the same inputs: target size, bar volume, volatility, and time remaining until a horizon. This keeps the execution model modular and testable.

Decomposing Slippage

Whenever we trade, the execution price will typically differ from a reference price such as the midprice at decision or arrival time. The difference is often called *slippage*.

For modeling and diagnosis, it is useful to decompose total slippage into three components:

- **Spread cost**: the half–spread paid when crossing from mid-price to bid or ask.

- **Impact**: additional price movement caused (or attributed) to our own trading, which tends to increase with participation rate and order size.

- **Residual slippage**: the remaining difference, capturing un-modeled effects and random noise.

Conceptually:

- The midprice is the average of best bid and ask at some reference time (decision or arrival).

- If we buy at the ask, we immediately incur half the spread as a structural cost.

- If we are a large fraction of volume, our trades may move the price further in our disfavor, which is attributed to impact.

- Whatever remains after accounting for these two is residual, often modeled as mean–zero noise.

This decomposition is central because it separates costs driven by structural microstructure features (spread, depth) from those driven by our own behavior (participation, urgency), and from purely unpredictable variations.

Right after introducing this decomposition, it is helpful to visualize how these components add up across different participation rates.

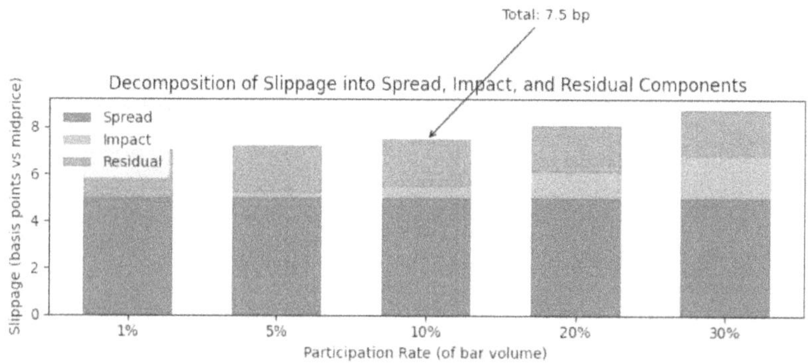

Modeling Spread Cost

Spread cost is the simplest component. At a given time and for a given instrument, the model knows or infers:

- the best bid and ask prices;
- the midprice (their average);
- the bid–ask spread.

If an order crosses the spread:

- a buy filled at the ask incurs a spread cost equal to half the spread;
- a sell filled at the bid incurs the same cost (in absolute terms).

If your execution style uses passive orders that rest at or inside the spread, the model may assign zero or reduced spread cost when those orders fill, reflecting that you earned the spread rather than paid it.

In bar–based simulations where you infer spreads from midprices, this component is deterministic once you have chosen a spread model. For example, you might define a baseline spread per instrument (in ticks or basis points), optionally scaling with volatility or price level.

Modeling Impact as a Function of Participation

Impact represents the idea that larger, faster trades tend to move prices against you. While true impact is complex and path–dependent, a backtest–friendly model can capture its main shape with a simple relation between impact cost and participation rate.

A common assumption is that impact cost:

- is negligible at very low participation rates;
- grows more than linearly with participation (for example, proportional to a power of participation between one and two);
- depends on daily or bar volume and volatility.

In words, this means that trading 1% of volume usually has little impact, 10% has noticeable impact, and 30% or more can be very expensive.

In the backtest engine, impact can be encoded as a deterministic formula that:

- takes as input: order size, bar volume, volatility, and an instrument–specific impact coefficient;
- outputs an incremental cost per share (or per contract) beyond spread;
- is symmetric by side but opposite in sign (buys push up, sells push down).

Impact coefficients can be calibrated from historical trade and quote data, from broker estimates, or chosen conservatively for scenario analysis. Once set, they remain fixed within a backtest run, ensuring reproducibility.

Residual Slippage: Noise, Not a Knob

Even with spread and impact modeled, real executions will vary. Sometimes your fills are slightly better than expected, sometimes worse, even at the same participation rate. This variation can be treated as residual slippage.

In the strictest deterministic sense, you could set residual slippage to zero and accept that all randomness is in the market data itself. However, to better reflect the variability of realized prices relative to coarse bar data, some engines introduce a small residual term.

If you do so, two rules help maintain discipline:

- **Do not use residual as a free performance knob.** The residual term should have mean zero and represent randomness or modeling error, not an adjustable bias that improves backtest Sharpe.
- **Keep its design simple.** For example, residual could be a small random draw from a distribution with zero mean and a standard deviation tied to volatility and spread.

However, randomness conflicts with strict determinism. If reproducibility is paramount, you can either:

- use a pseudorandom generator with a fixed, recorded seed so that the same backtest can be exactly replayed; or
- avoid randomness, using a fixed, deterministic residual function (for example, a small systematic penalty).

In this book we prefer the second approach for core backtests and reserve randomized residuals for separate robustness tests where exact replication is less critical.

Queue Priority and Limited Liquidity

The microstructure section introduced price–time priority and depth limits. The execution model must respect these when assigning fills.

Two scenarios are particularly important:

Competing for queue position. For passive limit orders at the best price, we are not the only participants. How much of our resting order fills depends on:

- how much other volume is ahead of us in the queue;
- how much incoming marketable volume arrives.

In a stylized backtest, we typically lack full queue histories. Instead, we can adopt conservative assumptions, such as:

- assume we are last in queue at that price level;
- only count fills if simulated incoming volume at that price exceeds a threshold large enough to reach our place in the queue.

This tends to underestimate fills for limit orders, which is a safer bias than overestimation.

Demand exceeding available liquidity. When our simulated orders attempt to trade more than the modeled depth at a given price level, the execution model must:

- cap the filled quantity at available depth, leaving residual as unfilled; or
- allow the order to walk up (or down) the book into more expensive levels, incurring additional impact.

Both behaviours can be configured. The important point is that whenever our simulated demand exceeds modeled supply, there is an explicit and deterministic rule for how the excess is handled.

Bar–Level vs More Granular Execution Models

A major design choice is time granularity:

- **Bar–level execution**: treat each bar (for example, a day or minute) as a single interval in which orders interact with aggregate volume and price statistics.
- **Tick– or event–level execution**: simulate order interactions on a finer time grid, potentially at each trade or quote update.

Bar–level models are faster and integrate naturally with daily or intraday strategies that make decisions at bar boundaries. They require approximations about intra–bar price paths (for example, assuming trades occur near VWAP or within high–low ranges).

More granular models are useful for high–frequency strategies or when you have detailed order book data. They can handle more realistic order scheduling, partial fills, and dynamic adaptation during a bar, but are much more demanding in terms of data and computation.

A flexible backtest engine should support at least:

- a standard bar–level execution model as the default;
- an optional plug–in interface for finer–grained execution models where needed.

Crucially, the interface between portfolio construction and execution should be stable: both models accept the same target portfolios and produce fills in the same format. This allows you to swap execution models for a given strategy without rewriting the rest of the pipeline.

Determinism, Calibration, and Overfitting

Like any model, the execution model can be overfit. If you choose parameters (spreads, impact coefficients, participation rules) by maximizing backtest performance, you risk building an unrealistically benign execution environment.

To avoid this, it is helpful to follow a few principles:

- **Calibrate from external data.** Use live or sample execution data, broker cost estimates, or independent studies, rather than optimizing parameters for your own backtest.
- **Use coarse parameter grids.** Choose a small set of plausible parameter values (for example, low, medium, high impact) and treat them as scenarios, not tunable knobs.
- **Keep the model structure simple.** Prefer a small number of interpretable parameters over a complicated function that can match historical quirks.

- **Version configurations.** Each distinct execution parameter set should have an identifier. Backtest runs must record which set was used, so you can compare results across configurations.

Determinism is preserved by:

- using fixed formulas and parameter values within each run;
- avoiding hidden heuristics that depend on global state in unpredictable ways;
- treating any randomness (if used) through controlled pseudorandom generators with recorded seeds.

Putting It All Together

Let us summarize how the execution model fits into the broader backtest architecture:

1. Features are computed in a deterministic, leakage–free way.
2. Signals are generated with clear semantics of size, horizon, and decay.
3. Position sizing and portfolio construction turn signals into target portfolios subject to risk and constraint policies.
4. Order generation translates differences between current and target portfolios into child orders, parameterized by execution style and schedule.
5. The microstructure layer provides a stylized order book with spreads, depth, and priority rules.
6. The execution model applies latency rules, sends orders to the microstructure, and simulates fills.
7. Slippage between midprice and execution price is decomposed into spread, impact, and residual components, each tracked explicitly.

At every step, the emphasis is on deterministic policies and versioned configurations. This ensures that if you re–run a backtest with the same inputs and settings, you obtain the same fills and the same P&L, and that any change in performance can be traced back to a specific change in model, data, or parameters.

In the following sections we will connect these execution outcomes to a comprehensive transaction cost and fee model, and then to compliance and risk controls, closing the loop between strategy intent, simulated market interaction, and realized portfolio accounting.

4.7 Transaction Cost & Fee Model

By now we have a complete path from features to signals, from signals to target portfolios, and from targets to simulated executions with realistic slippage. The next question is: *what did all of that cost us?*

Trading and holding positions incurs a wide variety of monetary frictions: explicit broker commissions, exchange fees and rebates, spread and impact costs from interacting with the book, borrow fees on short positions, and financing charges or income on cash and margin. If these are handled informally, it becomes difficult to say where performance is really coming from and whether a strategy would survive in the real world.

This section formalizes a *transaction cost and fee model* for the backtest engine. The objectives are:

- to apply a fully specified cost model to every trade and position;
- to make every P&L component traceable to explicit parameters and data;
- to ensure the model is deterministic and versioned, so that changing fee assumptions is a controlled, auditable operation.

We proceed from per–trade costs, to position–level carrying costs, to a ledger view that supports detailed P&L attribution.

Why a Structured Cost Model Matters

It is tempting to treat costs as a single haircut—for example, "assume 10 basis points per trade." While this may be acceptable for toy examples, it conflates very different sources of friction and hides important sensitivities.

A structured cost model helps in several ways:

- **Realism**: explicit treatment of commissions, spread, impact, borrow, and financing keeps the backtest closer to live conditions.
- **Attribution**: you can later ask, "How much of the performance was eaten by commissions? How much by impact?" rather than having only a blended number.
- **Scenario testing**: you can easily re–run a backtest under different fee schedules (for example, higher borrow rates or lower commissions) and see how results change.
- **Risk control**: for some strategies, cost risk (for example, sudden borrow fee spikes) is a major driver of outcomes; modeling it explicitly is essential.

In a disciplined engine, transaction costs are not an afterthought; they are a first–class, parameterized layer that consumes execution data (fills) and position data, and produces cost entries.

Per–Trade Explicit Costs: Commissions and Exchange Fees

We begin with the costs that are directly attached to each trade as it occurs.

Broker commissions. Brokers may charge:

- **Per–share or per–contract fees**: a fixed amount per unit traded, possibly with tiered schedules.
- **Ad–valorem fees**: a percentage of traded notional.

- **Minimums per order or per ticket**: for small orders, a minimum commission may apply.

In the backtest, each fill record (instrument, side, quantity, price, time, venue) passes through a commission module that applies the relevant schedule. That schedule is part of the cost model configuration and may depend on:

- instrument class (equity, future, option, FX);
- region or venue;
- trade direction (buy/sell, opening/closing);
- strategy or account (if fees differ across them).

The commission for a fill is a deterministic function of these inputs and the configured schedule. It is recorded as a cost line in the ledger, with clear identifiers.

Exchange and venue fees/rebates. Exchanges may charge or pay fees depending on whether you add or remove liquidity and on the venue's fee model. For example:

- Removing liquidity (marketable orders) may incur a fee per share.
- Adding liquidity (resting limit orders) may earn a small rebate.

Our execution model already knows whether a simulated fill came from an aggressive (liquidity–taking) or passive (liquidity–providing) order. Coupled with venue metadata, the fee module can:

- look up the correct fee or rebate per unit;
- compute the total for the fill;
- record it as a distinct cost or income entry.

In some markets, these fees are large enough to change the sign of net trading costs for certain styles (for example, high–frequency market making). Modeling them explicitly is therefore important for some strategies.

Spread and Impact: Consistency with Execution

The execution model already incorporates spread and impact costs into the simulated execution prices. We must ensure that the cost model is consistent with that, and that we do not double–count.

A clean approach is:

- Treat the execution price as the *all–in* price that already includes spread and impact.
- Use the midprice (at a defined reference time) as the neutral reference.
- Record, for each fill, a decomposition of the difference between execution price and midprice into:

- spread cost component;
- impact cost component;
- residual component (if modeled).

These components were defined in the execution section. The cost model now simply turns them into monetary amounts:

- multiply per–unit spread cost by traded quantity to get total spread cost;
- do the same for impact and residual components.

The important points are:

- **No double counting**: if spread and impact are baked into execution prices, you should not add an extra ad hoc "slippage" fee on top.
- **Traceability**: by storing spread and impact costs as separate ledger lines, you can later understand how much each contributed.

In some setups, you may wish to *not* adjust execution prices, and instead keep them at midprice and account for spread and impact only as separate cost lines. That is also possible, but you must choose one convention and follow it consistently.

Borrow Costs for Short Positions

When you are short an asset, you often pay a *borrow fee* (stock loan fee) for the right to borrow and sell it. This fee:

- is usually quoted as an annualized rate;
- can vary widely across instruments and over time, especially for hard–to–borrow names;
- accrues while the short position is open.

In the backtest, for each short position and each day (or bar) it is held, the borrow module:

- looks up the appropriate borrow rate (from historical data, vendor feeds, or a proxy model);
- computes the daily or per–bar borrow cost based on position notional and rate;
- records this as a cost entry attributed to that position and time.

The borrow rate itself may have different sources:

- If you have historical stock loan data, you can use the point–in–time rate per instrument.
- If not, you can use proxies, such as:

- a typical borrow rate by market cap or sector;
- an elevated rate for names flagged as hard to borrow;
- a base rate plus a small premium for all shorts.

Regardless of the source, the rate choice becomes part of the cost model configuration. You can later vary it as a scenario (for example, stress tests with higher borrow costs).

Financing and Cash: Margin and Interest

Portfolios rarely sit entirely in cash. Long positions are financed, short positions generate cash, and margin rules prescribe how much leverage is allowed. The financing and cash module accounts for:

- **Interest on cash balances**: positive balances may earn interest; negative balances (borrowing cash) incur interest.
- **Margin financing**: some assets may be financed at specific rates, possibly different from the risk–free rate.
- **Collateralization**: certain instruments (such as futures) may require posting margin that earns or pays interest at particular rates.

At each time step, given the current portfolio state and a set of interest rate curves, the financing module:

- computes net cash (or credit) balances;
- applies the applicable overnight or per–bar rate, using a clear day–count and compounding convention;
- records financing income or expense as a separate line.

Important modeling details include:

- **Day–count convention**: for example, actual/360 or actual/365. This defines how annualized rates convert to per–day accruals.
- **Calendar**: weekends and holidays may or may not accrue interest depending on market practice and instrument type.

- **Multiple rate curves**: you may have different rates for cash, margin loans, and collateral accounts.

As with other components, all of these conventions and curves are part of the configurable cost model, and should be versioned.

Other Carry Components

Beyond borrow and basic financing, some strategies are sensitive to additional carry components tied to specific instruments. Examples include:

- **Dividend and coupon accruals**: long stock positions may receive dividends; long bond positions receive coupon interest; these are positive cash flows, partially offsetting financing costs. Short positions typically owe these amounts.
- **Funding in FX**: holding foreign currency exposures can lead to gains or losses related to interest rate differentials (the FX carry).
- **Roll costs in futures**: maintaining a continuous futures exposure requires rolling contracts, which may incur roll yield gains or losses depending on the shape of the futures curve.

Some of these effects may already be embedded in price data (for example, total–return indices), in which case they should not be separately modeled to avoid double counting. Others, such as net cash effects of discrete dividends or the economics of futures roll, can and should be captured explicitly.

A structured cost model identifies which carry components are:

- captured in the price series;
- modeled explicitly as cash flows;
- ignored or approximated.

This documentation is critical for interpreting P&L attribution correctly.

Accrual Conventions and Calendars

Any cost that accrues over time (borrow, interest, financing) must use clear conventions:

- **Accrual period**: per calendar day, per trading day, or per bar.
- **Day–count**: how to convert annualized rates into per–period rates.
- **Holiday treatment**: whether weekends and holidays accrue at the same rate as trading days.

For example, a simple convention for daily backtests might be:

- Rates are annualized on an actual/360 basis.
- Accrual occurs on all calendar days, including weekends.
- Interest is applied once per trading day, but covers the elapsed calendar days since the last trading day.

Intraday backtests may use per–bar accrual for simplicity, but still refer back to an underlying daily or annual rate.

These conventions have noticeable effects over long horizons, particularly for leveraged or carry strategies. They should therefore be treated as part of the model specification, not left implicit.

Ledger Representation of Costs

To make every P&L component traceable, the engine maintains a *ledger* of cost entries. Each entry records:

- time (and possibly exact timestamp);
- instrument or portfolio–level context;
- type of cost or income (commission, exchange fee, spread, impact, borrow, financing, dividend, etc.);

- sign (costs as negative, incomes as positive);
- amount (in base currency);
- any additional attributes (strategy, venue, order ID, position ID).

You can think of this ledger as parallel to the trade and position records. For every fill or time step that generates a cost, a corresponding line is written. This serves several purposes:

- **Reconciliation**: summing all cost entries over time and adding them to price–driven P&L should match total portfolio P&L.
- **Attribution**: you can group and analyze costs by type, instrument, sector, or strategy.
- **Scenario analysis**: by re–running the backtest with altered cost parameters, you can compare ledgers and see exactly which components changed.

In implementation terms, a ledger entry is just another event in the engine's event stream, but one whose semantics are purely monetary rather than positional.

Separating Price P&L and Cost P&L

For analysis and risk management, it is often helpful to separate:

- **Price P&L**: gains and losses due to changes in market prices (holding everything else constant).
- **Cost P&L**: the cumulative effect of all explicit and implicit costs and fees as recorded in the ledger.

You can then express total P&L as:

Total P&L = Price P&L + Cost P&L.

In a sample path:

- Price P&L is computed from position holdings and price changes, ignoring costs.
- Cost P&L is the sum of all ledger entries over the same period.

This decomposition is invaluable when diagnosing underperformance. For instance, a strategy might have strong raw alpha (positive price P&L) but be unprofitable net of costs because turnover is too high or borrow expenses are excessive.

Determinism and Versioning of the Cost Model

As with other components of the backtest engine, the cost and fee model must be:

- **Deterministic**: given a sequence of fills, positions, and a specific cost configuration, the ledger entries are uniquely determined.
- **Versioned**: any change to fee schedules, rate curves, or accrual conventions creates a new cost model version.
- **Documented**: each version includes a clear description of its assumptions and parameter values.

In practice, you might:

- store all cost parameters and rules in a configuration object with a unique identifier;
- record that identifier in every backtest run;
- provide tools that, given a run identifier, can reconstruct exactly which cost model was applied.

This makes it possible to compare different cost scenarios fairly and to replicate historical analyses when cost structures change (for example, when commissions fall over time or when regulatory fees are introduced).

Scenario Testing and Robustness

Once the cost model is structured and parameterized, it becomes straightforward to conduct scenario analyses. Some useful exercises include:

- **Higher transaction costs**: increase commissions or widen spreads to test how fragile the strategy is to cost deterioration.
- **Borrow stress**: raise borrow rates or mark some names as hard–to–borrow to see how short strategies behave in stressed conditions.
- **Leverage cost increases**: increase financing rates to test leveraged strategies.
- **Fee–free scenario**: set commissions and exchange fees to zero to estimate the "pure alpha" before explicit frictions.

Because the cost model is separate from the execution model and pricing, you can often perform these tests by rerunning the cost layer on previously generated fills and positions, without needing to recompute everything else. This is computationally efficient and keeps the logic modular.

Integration with Risk and Compliance

Although the primary purpose of the cost model is P&L accounting, it also feeds into risk and compliance:

- **Cost limits**: some mandates place limits on turnover or cost budgets (for example, maximum annual commissions per unit of capital). The ledger provides the data to monitor these.
- **Hard constraints**: if certain assets become prohibitively expensive to borrow, risk or compliance rules may prohibit or cap shorts in those names. The cost model provides the input rates.
- **Ex–ante cost estimates**: by combining the cost model with planned trades, risk systems can estimate expected costs before execution, helping to decide whether trades are worthwhile.

For reproducibility, any such policies should refer explicitly to the same cost parameters used in the backtest, rather than relying on disconnected assumptions.

In this section we have turned the output of the execution model into a structured accounting of transaction costs and fees. The key ideas are:

- Costs come from multiple sources: commissions, exchange fees/rebates, spread and impact, borrow fees, financing, and other carry components.
- Each source is modeled with explicit parameters and rules, applied deterministically to trades and positions.
- A ledger of cost entries allows detailed P&L attribution and reconciliation with price–driven gains and losses.
- Accrual conventions, calendars, and rate curves are part of the model specification and must be versioned.
- Scenario analysis becomes straightforward: you can reapply different cost models to the same execution history to test robustness.

Together with the feature, signal, sizing, portfolio construction, microstructure, and execution layers, a rigorous transaction cost and fee model completes the chain from raw data to realistic net performance. In the final section of this chapter, we will see how compliance rules and risk controls can be woven into this chain as deterministic checks, ensuring that simulated strategies never violate the operational or regulatory constraints under which they would actually be traded.

4.8 Compliance, Limits & Risk Controls

The previous sections have focused on what your strategy *wants* to do: which positions it prefers, how it constructs a portfolio, and how it trades that portfolio through a stylized market with realistic costs. In practice, however, there are many things your strategy is *not allowed* to do.

Some restrictions are legal or regulatory: you may be barred from trading certain instruments, shorting particular securities, or exceeding leverage limits specified by regulators or fund documents. Others are internal risk and governance guardrails: concentration caps, liquidity constraints, limits on turnover, or rules such as "no new positions after a certain time of day."

This section explains how to represent these constraints as first-class citizens in the backtest engine. Instead of being encoded informally in scattered strategy code, they become explicit, deterministic checks that act at well-defined points in the simulation loop. The goals are:

- to ensure that simulated strategies never take positions that would be impossible or forbidden in production;
- to make the effect of limits and risk controls reproducible and auditable;
- to support experiments under alternative rule sets simply by swapping configurations.

We will move from a high-level view of constraint types to concrete patterns for integrating them into sizing and order generation.

Why Encode Controls as First-Class Checks

It is common in early research code to "bake in" constraints directly:

- zero out signals for restricted names;
- cap position sizes within sizing functions;
- skip trades for illiquid instruments.

This may work at small scale, but it has several drawbacks:

- The logic is scattered across many files and is hard to audit.
- Changing a rule (for example, updating a restricted list) may require code changes.

- It is difficult to answer questions like "How much performance did we lose because of leverage caps?" because their impact is not isolated.

By contrast, a structured compliance and risk layer:

- centralizes guardrails in a configuration and policy engine;
- applies them as declarative checks at known stages of the pipeline;
- logs whenever a rule fires, what it changed, and which version of the rule set was active.

This mirrors how professional trading firms and asset managers operate: strategy logic is separated from the risk and compliance framework that governs it.

Types of Guardrails

We can group common controls into three broad categories:

Portfolio-level limits. These constrain aggregate exposures and portfolio behavior. Examples include:

- maximum gross leverage (sum of long and short exposure);
- bounds on net exposure (overall long/short tilt);
- sector, country, or factor exposure caps;
- portfolio-level turnover limits over a day or month;
- liquidity rules based on average daily volume (ADV) or modeled depth.

Instrument-level and list-based controls. These apply to specific assets or groups of assets:

- hard bans on restricted securities (legal, ethical, or sanctions lists);

- "no short" or "long-only" flags;
- limits on maximum position size per instrument (in weight, dollars, or notional);
- trading halts or suspensions (for example, during an exchange halt).

Behavioral and process controls. These govern how and when the strategy trades:

- no trading outside of approved hours or sessions;
- no new positions after a specified cut-off (for example, near the close);
- limits on order size relative to volume (participation caps);
- restrictions on specific order types (for example, no market orders in illiquid names).

Each of these can be expressed as either:

- a *predicate*: a rule that is either satisfied or violated by a proposed action;
- a *transform*: a rule that modifies proposed positions or orders to bring them into compliance.

The backtest engine applies these predicates and transforms systematically.

Where Controls Live in the Simulation Loop

The strategy pipeline has several natural checkpoints where controls can be applied:

1. **Before sizing**: constraints that alter which signals are allowed to influence positions, such as restricted lists or asset-level bans.

2. **During sizing and portfolio construction**: constraints that shape target positions, such as leverage caps, sector limits, or liquidity-based size adjustments.

3. **Before order submission**: controls on trading behavior, such as order type restrictions, participation caps, or time-of-day rules.

4. **End-of-day or periodic checks**: reconciliations that enforce overnight policies (for example, no overnight positions, or tight leverage bounds at the close).

It is not necessary to implement every rule at every stage. The key is that for each control you declare:

- when in the loop it is evaluated;
- what inputs it sees (signals, current positions, target portfolio, orders, market data);
- what outputs or adjustments it may produce (blocked trades, scaled positions, warnings).

By fixing these interfaces, you make the effect of each control understandable and reproducible.

Portfolio-Level Limits in Sizing and Construction

Earlier sections introduced position sizing and portfolio construction under risk constraints. Many of those constraints—gross and net exposure boundaries, sector caps, name-level limits—double as risk controls. The difference in this section is that we treat them explicitly as *policy objects* with compliance semantics.

For example, consider a gross leverage cap:

- Policy: "Total gross exposure must not exceed 200% of capital."
- Implementation: after computing unconstrained target weights, the sizing layer:

1. computes implied gross exposure;
2. if it exceeds 200%, scales all positions proportionally until the cap is met;
3. records that the leverage cap fired and by what factor it scaled.

Treating this as a compliance control means:

- the cap value (200%) is part of a named, versioned rule set;
- every time the rule triggers, a log entry is created linking it to the affected target portfolio;
- different backtests can use different rule sets (for example, 150% vs 200% caps) while keeping the rest of the pipeline unchanged.

A similar pattern applies to:

- sector or factor caps (identified by group exposure measures);
- concentration limits (caps on single-name exposures);
- liquidity-based size rules (for example, positions not exceeding a percentage of ADV or book depth).

In each case, the policy lives in the compliance layer, and sizing/portfolio construction consult it as a deterministic mapping from proposed targets to allowed targets.

Liquidity Rules and ADV-Based Constraints

Liquidity constraints deserve special attention because they rely on market data and may be path-dependent. Typical forms include:

- Maximum position size per name as a fraction of recent ADV (say, no more than 10% of 20-day ADV).
- Maximum daily trading volume per name as a fraction of ADV (participation caps).

- Eligibility filters: only trade instruments whose ADV exceeds a threshold.

In the backtest:

- ADV and related liquidity metrics are computed in the feature pipeline, with leakage-free alignment.
- Compliance rules read these features at sizing and order-generation time.

For example, a size rule could be:

> "If the target weight for stock X would correspond to more than 10% of its 20-day ADV, reduce the target so that it equals exactly 10%."

This is implemented as a transform on the target portfolio:

1. translate proposed target weights to shares or notional at current prices;
2. compare to allowed maximum based on ADV;
3. clip positions that exceed the limit;
4. recompute resulting weights and exposures.

Participation caps at the order level are treated similarly, but applied to desired trade sizes instead of positions, often at each bar.

These rules provide a bridge between high-level risk appetite and the detailed execution model: they ensure the strategy does not require more liquidity than the simulated market reasonably offers.

Restricted Lists and Instrument-Level Bans

Compliance often maintains lists of instruments that are off-limits for legal, regulatory, or ethical reasons. Examples include:

- securities issued by sanctioned entities;
- companies under internal research blackout;
- names restricted by client mandate (for example, no defense stocks).

In the backtest engine, a *restricted list* is a time-varying set of instrument identifiers, each entry with an effective period. The compliance layer exposes a predicate:

> "Is instrument i tradable at time t?"

This predicate is checked at:

- the sizing level: signals or targets for restricted instruments are forced to zero (no desired exposure);
- the order level: any attempted order in a restricted instrument is rejected or zeroed out.

Both actions should produce log entries that include:

- the instrument, time, and attempted action;
- the rule that caused it to be blocked;
- optional metadata (for example, a restriction code or reason).

Similar treatment applies to "no short" or "long-only" flags. These can be encoded as instrument attributes and enforced by:

- clipping negative targets to zero for long-only instruments;
- blocking sell orders that would create or increase shorts when not allowed.

Because these rules are deterministic and versioned, you can run backtests under different restriction universes (for example, different client mandates) simply by swapping lists and reapplying the same strategy.

Behavioral Controls on Trading

Behavioral controls govern the *how* and *when* of trading. Common examples include:

- no trading in the first or last N minutes of the session, to avoid volatile auctions or thin liquidity;
- no new positions after a specified time (but reductions or liquidations allowed);
- restrictions on order types (for example, no market orders in small-cap names);
- maximum order size per slice relative to bar volume (participation thresholds).

In the engine, these controls operate on the set of proposed child orders produced by the execution policy:

1. The strategy proposes orders based on targets and execution style.
2. The compliance layer inspects each proposed order together with time, instrument, and market context.
3. It either passes the order through, modifies it, or blocks it entirely.

For example, a participation-rate control might say:

> "If a proposed buy order in stock Y at time t exceeds 15% of the bar's expected volume, scale the order down to exactly 15%."

In a backtest using historical volume, expected volume can be approximated by recent ADV or intra-day profiles. The rule then acts as a deterministic transform on the order quantity.

Time-of-day rules read the bar timestamp and session schedule. For instance, a rule could:

- block any new opening trades in the last bar of the day;
- allow only closing trades needed to reduce existing risk.

By encoding these behaviors as compliance policies, you ensure that no future researcher subtly circumvents risk guidelines by changing strategy code.

End-of-Day and Periodic Risk Checks

Some risk controls are evaluated not continuously, but at the end of a day or other period. Typical examples include:

- end-of-day leverage limits tighter than intraday limits;
- "no overnight positions" rules for intraday strategies;
- VaR or stress-test limits that, if breached, require position reductions.

In the backtest, an end-of-day risk check can be modeled as:

1. At the end of each day, after all intraday executions, compute risk metrics from current positions and prices.
2. Evaluate each periodic control against these metrics.
3. If a control is violated, apply a deterministic remediation policy (for example, proportionally scale down all positions to restore leverage within bounds).
4. Record both the violation and remedial adjustments in logs and in the event history.

This approach simulates how a real risk committee or automated risk system might enforce firm-wide limits. It ensures that backtests do not maintain overnight risk profiles that would not have been permitted operationally.

Logging, Overrides, and Auditability

A crucial benefit of treating compliance and risk controls as first-class citizens is that you can log their actions in detail. For every control, the engine should be capable of answering:

- when it fired;
- what inputs it saw (for example, proposed targets, orders, positions, market data);
- what changes it made (blocked trades, scaled positions, etc.);
- which exact rule version triggered the action.

This information supports:

- **Audit trails**: reconstruct why the strategy held a given position or did not trade a given opportunity.
- **Attribution**: assess how much performance is sacrificed to each category of constraint (for example, restricted lists, leverage caps, liquidity rules).
- **Policy tuning**: compare outcomes under alternative rule sets; for instance, tighter vs looser leverage limits.

In live trading, there is often a notion of *override*: a human may temporarily allow an exception to a rule under controlled circumstances. In backtesting, you generally avoid overrides, because they break determinism. If you must model them (for example, to replicate a historical episode), treat overrides as explicit events with their own identifiers and rules, so that a rerun with the same override record remains reproducible.

Determinism and Rule-Set Versioning

As with other layers of the engine, compliance and risk controls must be deterministic and versioned:

- **Deterministic**: given the same inputs—signals, positions, orders, market data—and the same set of rules, the resulting constrained targets and orders are identical.
- **Versioned**: any change to a rule, threshold, list, or schedule creates a new rule-set version.

A practical scheme is to:

- encapsulate all rules, thresholds, and lists into a configuration object with a unique version ID;
- record that ID in every backtest run;
- treat the configuration as data rather than code, so that non-programmers (for example, risk managers) can propose and review changes.

This separation lets you, for example, compare:

> "Strategy A under risk rule set R1" versus "Strategy A under risk rule set R2"

while holding everything else—features, signals, execution, cost model—constant. It also ensures that if regulators or clients ask "Which rules were in force when you simulated this strategy?", you can give a precise answer.

Interplay with Other Engine Layers

Compliance, limits, and risk controls do not exist in isolation; they sit on top of, and interact with, the rest of the engine:

- They consume features (liquidity, classification, risk estimates) produced by the feature pipeline.
- They see signals and targets generated by the strategy and sizing layers.

- They constrain orders that will be fed to the execution and microstructure models.
- They feed back into performance analysis and transaction cost attribution through logs and the P&L ledger.

By designing controls as a clear layer with well-defined interfaces, you keep these interactions manageable. For example:

- the execution model does not need to know *why* an order was scaled down, only that it now has a smaller size;
- the cost model does not need to know about compliance rules; it simply prices whatever fills occur;
- risk reporting tools, however, can combine position histories with control logs to understand how constraints shaped realized exposures.

In this section we have elevated compliance, limits, and risk controls to first-class components of the backtest architecture. The main ideas are:

- Guardrails span portfolio-level limits, instrument-level and list-based restrictions, and behavioral trading controls.
- These are implemented as deterministic predicates and transforms applied at well-defined checkpoints: before sizing, during portfolio construction, before order submission, and at periodic risk reviews.
- Liquidity and ADV-based rules tie desired exposures and trade sizes to realistic market capacity.
- Restricted lists, long-only flags, and time-of-day rules ensure that simulated trading adheres to legal, client, and internal policies.
- A structured logging mechanism records every time a control fires, what it changed, and which rule set was in force, enabling attribution and audit trails.

- Rule sets are versioned and treated as configuration, allowing backtests to be replayed or compared under different compliance and risk regimes.

Together with the feature pipeline, signal schema, sizing and portfolio construction logic, microstructure and execution models, and cost accounting, this compliance layer completes the design of a backtest engine that does not merely simulate a trading idea, but simulates it under the same operational and regulatory constraints that would apply in production.

Chapter 5

Portfolio Accounting & PnL

Backtests live or die on whether their portfolio accounting tells the truth. This chapter opens the engine room: how lots, cash, margin, shorts, and corporate actions actually move through time, and how those flows ultimately crystallize into returns you can trust-and reproduce.

5.1 Positions, Lots & Inventory

Portfolio accounting begins with a deceptively simple question: *what do we own, and at what economic terms?* Everything else in this chapter—PnL, returns, taxes, corporate actions, margin—rests on how your engine answers that question.

This section defines a precise representation of holdings at two levels:

- the **instrument-level position** (how many units of a symbol we are long or short at any instant), and
- the **lot-level inventory** (each individually identifiable "chunk"

of that position, with its own entry time, price, fees, and metadata).

We will see why net position alone is not enough, how every fill and partial fill becomes a lot event, and how careful inventory modeling creates a stable foundation for accurate PnL, tax logic, and corporate action handling.

Position vs. Exposure: The Top-Level View

At the highest level, a portfolio holds assets and liabilities. For a tradable instrument such as a stock, future, or currency pair, the engine usually summarizes this as a **position**:

- a *quantity* (positive for long, negative for short),
- some notion of *average price* or cost basis, and
- auxiliary state (e.g., unrealized PnL, market value).

This *position* is your net exposure to that instrument at a timestamp. If your position in XYZ is +1,000 shares, then small price changes in XYZ move your portfolio value roughly in proportion to 1,000 units.

For many high-level tasks—like computing portfolio beta or stress-testing a one-day shock—this net exposure is sufficient. But for detailed accounting it is inadequate. Consider:

- You buy 500 shares of XYZ at 100, and later another 500 at 120. Your position is 1,000 shares. What is your cost basis? Is it a simple average (110)? What if your tax rules use FIFO and you later sell only 400 shares?
- You hold 1,000 shares of XYZ across a split, a special dividend, and then a spin-off. Each event changes quantities and cost basis in subtle ways. How do you explain your realized PnL when you later sell?
- You run a strategy that opens multiple overlapping trade "episodes" in the same symbol (e.g., several intraday entries and exits). You want to attribute PnL to each episode.

In all of these, the single net position loses too much information. You need to remember *how* you got there.

Lots: Atoms of Inventory

A **lot** is a minimal piece of inventory created by a fill. Intuitively:

> A lot is a specific quantity of an instrument, acquired at a specific time and price, with specific fees and metadata, that can later be partially or fully closed.

If one order is filled in three partial fills, you get three lots. If you place two separate orders at different times, you get at least two lots, even if the final net position is the same.

At minimum, each lot should store:

- **Instrument identifier**: symbol or ID.
- **Side**: long or short.
- **Quantity opened**: signed or absolute; the sign convention just needs to be consistent.
- **Entry price**: the economic trade price.
- **Entry time**: the timestamp at which the lot becomes effective.
- **Fees and commissions**: costs directly attached to opening this lot.
- **Status**: open, partially closed, or closed.
- **Remaining quantity**: how much of the lot is still open.
- **Metadata**: order ID, strategy ID, venue, tags for experiments, etc.

Lots are the "ground truth" of your inventory. Positions, cost bases, realized PnL, and tax reports must be derivable from the collection of lots and their close-outs.

From Orders to Fills to Lots

Execution in realistic markets is rarely all-or-nothing. An order to buy 1,000 shares might be filled like this:

- 300 shares at 99.80,
- 400 shares at 100.00,
- 300 shares at 100.10.

Your backtest's execution model (defined elsewhere) produces these fills. The inventory engine's job is to transform each fill into a corresponding lot event.

Notice we do *not* let the execution model directly mutate positions. Instead:

1. The engine receives a fill event.
2. It creates or updates one or more lots.
3. It recomputes the instrument-level position by aggregating the lots.

This separation is crucial for reproducibility. It ensures that if you replay the same sequence of fills, you reconstruct the identical inventory state, independent of any higher-level logic.

Opening, Increasing, Reducing, and Flipping Positions

Every new lot changes the net position in one of a few canonical ways. It is useful to classify trades in terms of their *effect on the position*:

- **Opening** a position: going from zero to non-zero net quantity (e.g., buy 100 shares when you had none).
- **Increasing** a position: same sign, larger magnitude (e.g., long 100 to long 300).

- **Reducing** a position: same sign, smaller magnitude (e.g., long 300 to long 100).
- **Closing** a position: going from non-zero to zero (e.g., long 100 to flat).
- **Flipping** a position: crossing through zero and ending with opposite sign (e.g., long 100 to short 50).

At the lot level, these map to operations on your inventory:

- *Opening/increasing*: create new lots on the same side as the existing position.
- *Reducing/closing*: consume quantity from existing lots on the opposite side of the new trade.
- *Flipping*: first fully close the existing position (consuming all opposite-side lots), then open new lots for the residual quantity in the new direction.

For example, suppose you are long 100 shares in a single lot. You sell 150 shares. At the instrument level, you move from +100 to -50. At the lot level:

1. The first 100 of the sell closes the long lot (now marked closed).
2. The extra 50 creates a new short lot of 50 shares.

This decomposition is what makes realized PnL and cost basis unambiguous.

Partial Fills and Multiple Lots per Instrument

In realistic trading, each instrument will accumulate many lots over time. Your representation must handle:

- **Multiple lots open simultaneously** for the same instrument, potentially on the same side.

- **Partial closes** of one or several lots in response to a single new trade.
- **Non-tradable remainders** due to minimum order sizes or rounding.

Consider a simple sequence in a long-only context:

1. Buy 100 shares at 50 (Lot A).
2. Buy 100 shares at 55 (Lot B).
3. Sell 120 shares at 60.

Your closing trade of 120 needs to be matched against 200 shares of open long lots. The engine must choose exactly *which* 120 shares to treat as closed. That choice determines:

- the realized profit you book today,
- the remaining cost basis of your open position,
- any tax consequences that depend on holding period and gain size.

Lot Selection Rules and Realized PnL Paths

The policy that decides which lots to close when you trade in the opposite direction is the **lot selection rule**. Common rules include:

- **FIFO (First-In, First-Out)**: close the oldest open lots first.
- **LIFO (Last-In, First-Out)**: close the most recently opened lots first.
- **Specific identification**: close whichever lots the strategy, broker, or tax optimizer explicitly chooses.
- **Average cost**: conceptually pool all lots and treat them as a single blended-cost lot (often used in some mutual fund or non-US tax contexts).

Different rules can produce the same ending equity but very different *paths* of realized vs. unrealized PnL. For backtesting, this matters because:

- Realized PnL might feed another component (e.g., a risk limit or bonus allocation).
- Tax-sensitive strategies care about when gains and losses are realized.
- Some corporate actions (like spin-offs) require reallocation of basis per lot, and their later realization depends on which lot was closed.

Your engine should make the lot selection rule:

- *Explicit*: configured once and recorded.
- *Deterministic*: given the same trade and lot history, you always get the same matches.
- *Auditable*: you can reconstruct, for any realized PnL figure, precisely which opening and closing trades contributed.

We will not prescribe a particular rule here; instead, the point is that the rule must exist, be clear, and be implemented in the inventory engine rather than scattered across ad-hoc code.

Non-Tradable Remainders and Rounding

Many markets enforce minimum tradable quantities or lot sizes (for example, futures contracts or FX tickets). Even in equities, fractional shares may appear due to corporate actions (e.g., splits and spin-offs) and then be rounded or cashed out as "cash-in-lieu."

At the inventory level, this means:

- You may end up with tiny open lots (e.g., 0.3 shares) that are not directly tradable.

- Corporate actions may create fractional quantities per lot, which then must be rounded according to exchange or broker rules.
- Rounding may generate small realized PnL or cash adjustments that need to be recorded explicitly, not silently dropped.

Your engine should decide:

- the minimum quantity it will represent internally (e.g., track down to 1×10^{-6} units even if you cannot trade that size),
- how to convert between *internal* quantities and *executable* quantities (e.g., floor or round to the nearest lot size),
- how to book the PnL of these conversions (for example, the broker sells fractional remainders at a specific price).

Again, lots are the place where these rules show up concretely: every rounding step is a transformation of lot quantities and, potentially, a cash flow.

Inventory State Over Time: Ledgers and Snapshots

To support debugging and audit, the engine should provide three complementary views of inventory:

1. Trade Ledger

A chronological list of all fills and corporate-action-related quantity changes, including:

- time,
- instrument,
- signed quantity,
- price,
- fees,

- event type (e.g., trade, split, merge, cash-in-lieu adjustment).

This is the raw event stream that drives the inventory.

2. Position Timeline

For each instrument, a time series describing:

- position quantity at each event or bar,
- possibly average cost, unrealized PnL, and market value.

This is derived from the lots (and any corporate actions). It is what you usually plot on a chart or use for exposure calculations.

3. Position Snapshots

At any timestamp, a snapshot lists:

- all open lots for every instrument,
- their remaining quantities and cost bases,
- per-instrument aggregates (net position).

Snapshots are helpful for point-in-time debugging: given a surprising PnL move, you can inspect exactly which lots were open right before it happened.

Under the hood, you can implement these using:

- **Per-instrument ledgers**: each instrument keeps a small list or array of its lots, which is more cache-friendly than global maps for large universes.
- **Event-sourced views**: the primary data is the event stream (fills, corporate actions), and positions are recomputed by replaying events if needed.
- **Indices and maps**: maps from instrument ID to its current open lots, and from lot ID to its history.

The key is that all views are consistent: given the trade ledger and corporate actions, you can rebuild the lot inventory and positions exactly.

Maintaining Invariants: Quantity Conservation and Reconciliation

A reliable backtest engine treats inventory as a mini accounting system with strict invariants. The most important are:

Quantity Conservation

For each instrument, over any period:

> Net position change = sum of signed trade quantities and corporate-action-driven quantity changes.

If you start a day with 0 shares of XYZ, trade +100 then -40, and have a 2-for-1 split, your end-of-day position should be

$$(0 + 100 - 40) \times 2 = 120$$

shares, *and* the sum of lot quantities should match this exactly.

If an invariant like this breaks, something is wrong: a corporate action was applied twice, a trade was dropped, or a partial close miscounted its quantities.

Reconciliation Between Trade History and Position State

At any point in the backtest, the engine should be able to:

1. Start from an earlier known-good snapshot.
2. Replay every fill and corporate action event up to the current time.
3. Recover exactly the same positions and lot inventory.

This property is central to reproducibility. It means that bugs are localizable: if a position is wrong only after a specific event, you can inspect the transformation around that event.

To enforce this, you can:

- Periodically recompute positions from scratch and compare to the running state.

- Assert that the sum of open and closed quantities in lots equals the cumulative trade quantities, adjusted for corporate actions.
- Log sufficient identifiers (order ID, lot ID, event ID) so that inconsistencies can be traced.

Positions and Lots in the Broader Accounting Stack

Positions and lots do not exist in isolation. They are the bridge between:

- **Market data and execution**: prices, quotes, and fills determine when lots are opened, closed, and repriced.
- **Cash and margin**: each lot opening or closing is paired with a cash flow (or multiple flows, including fees).
- **Corporate actions**: splits, dividends, rights issues, and spin-offs transform the quantity and basis of existing lots without new trades.
- **PnL and returns**: realized PnL is computed from which lots were closed at what prices; unrealized PnL comes from repricing open lots.
- **Taxes and attribution**: holding periods, short vs. long-term classification, and strategy-level PnL attribution all depend on lot-level history.

Because of this centrality, the positions-and-lots layer must be stable. New features (e.g., borrow costs, multi-currency) should plug into this layer, not bypass it. For example:

- Borrow fees on shorts are computed on the market value of open short lots.
- Corporate actions adjust each lot's quantity and notional, preserving the link to its original cost basis.

- FX conversion can be handled by tagging each lot with its trade currency and applying appropriate exchange rates in the PnL engine.

With this architecture, every downstream quantity—from a daily return to a tax loss—can be traced back to a specific sequence of events on specific lots.

State Transitions: From No Position to Open and Closed Lots

We can summarize the life cycle of inventory with a state-transition view. Each instrument transitions through a few core states as trades occur:

- **No position**: no open lots; net quantity is zero.
- **Open lots**: one or more lots with non-zero remaining quantity (long or short).
- **Closed lots**: lots whose remaining quantity is zero; they still exist in the ledger for PnL and audit.

Trades cause transitions:

- A *buy* from no position creates new open long lots.
- A *sell* from a long position partially closes existing long lots; if more is sold than the current long quantity, the position flips to short and new short lots are created.
- Symmetrically, a *buy* from a short position partially closes short lots and may flip to long.

The following diagram encodes these transitions at a conceptual level.

The diagram emphasizes two ideas:

- The *position* at the instrument level is always the sum of open lots.

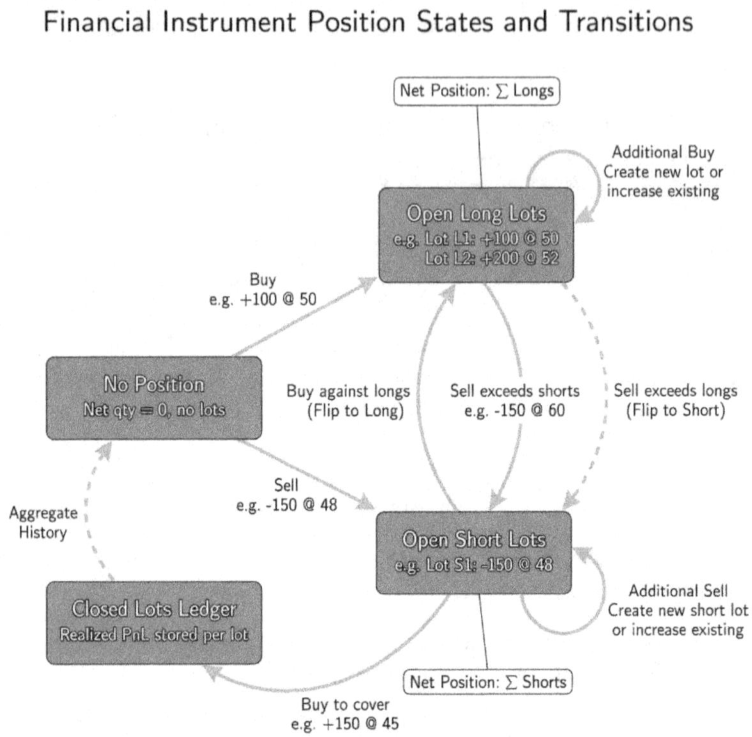

- Every trade is a transition that either creates, modifies, or closes lots, and closed lots move into a ledger that records realized PnL and history.

Design Principles for a Robust Inventory Model

We close with a few design guidelines that will pay dividends as the rest of the accounting system develops:

1. **Lots are first-class objects**. Treat them as persistent records, not ephemeral details. Never throw them away; closed lots are

essential for PnL and audit.

2. **Positions are derived, not primary**. Net position, average price, and similar aggregates should be computed from lots, not stored as independent truth that can diverge.

3. **Every state change is event-driven**. Trades, corporate actions, and adjustments all enter the system as events that act on lots. This makes replay and debugging straightforward.

4. **Invariants are enforced continuously**. Regularly check that per-instrument quantity conservation holds, and that replay from the event stream reproduces the current state.

5. **Configuration is explicit**. The lot selection rule, rounding conventions, and any tax-related choices should be part of the engine's configuration and recorded with the results.

With a clear, lot-based inventory model in place, we can now layer on the cash and margin engine, followed by shorting, corporate actions, and finally a full PnL and return pipeline. All of those later pieces will rely on the guarantee that the portfolio's holdings—down to each individual lot—are represented accurately and reproducibly over time.

5.2 Cash, Margin & Financing

In the previous section we concentrated on *what* the portfolio holds: positions and lots. We now turn to the other side of the balance sheet: *how those holdings are funded.* A realistic backtest must track cash balances, settlement timing, and margin usage as carefully as it tracks shares and contracts. Otherwise you can easily simulate trades that would have been impossible in live trading, or misstate PnL by ignoring financing costs.

This section builds an accounting model for:

- the **cash ledger**: every cash in and cash out,
- **settlement**: when cash from trades actually becomes usable,

- **margin**: how positions consume buying power and can trigger calls, and
- **financing**: interest on cash and borrowed funds, including product-specific flows.

The goal is a deterministic, auditable cash and margin engine that constrains what the strategy can do and feeds cleanly into your PnL.

The Cash Ledger: Every Flow, Explicitly Recorded

Just as lots are the atomic units of inventory, **cash ledger entries** are the atomic units of funding. You should think of the cash ledger as a chronological journal where every movement of money is recorded as a separate line.

Typical cash events include:

- **Trade-related flows**
- trade principals (debits for buys, credits for sells),
- commissions and exchange fees,
- taxes or transaction levies.
- **Corporate actions**
- cash dividends and special dividends,
- cash-in-lieu of fractional shares,
- merger consideration paid or received in cash.
- **Financing**
- interest earned on positive cash,
- interest paid on margin debt or short proceeds,
- borrow fees for hard-to-borrow securities (conceptually separate, but booked as cash flows).

- **External flows**
- initial capital,
- contributions and withdrawals,
- fund-level management and performance fees.

Each ledger entry should minimally include:

- a timestamp,
- a signed amount (positive for cash in, negative for cash out),
- a currency,
- a type or category (trade principal, commission, interest, dividend, etc.),
- references to related objects (order ID, lot ID, instrument).

The sum of all ledger entries up to a point in time defines the **gross cash balance** in each currency. Later we will refine this into *settled*, *unsettled*, and *available* balances.

From Trades to Cash: Basic Mechanics

When a trade is filled, you already know from the inventory engine:

- instrument,
- fill quantity,
- fill price,
- fees at the trade level.

The cash engine converts this into **cash debits and credits**.

For example, for a simple long equity trade in the base currency:

- Buying shares: you pay cash

- principal: cash outflow equal to quantity times price,
- commissions/fees: additional cash outflows.
- Selling shares: you receive cash
- principal: cash inflow,
- commissions/fees: cash outflows.

Even in this basic case, you should avoid directly modifying a "cash balance" variable inside the trade-handling code. Instead:

1. The fill handler creates one or more cash ledger entries.
2. An aggregation pass sums relevant cash entries to update your notion of current cash, equity, and buying power.

This mirrors the way positions are derived from lots. It keeps the cash side consistent, replayable, and easy to audit.

Settlement Conventions: Pending vs. Available Cash

In live trading you cannot always recycle cash from trades immediately. Many products settle on a delayed basis (such as T+1 or T+2), and brokers enforce separate metrics for *settled* and *unsettled* cash. A realistic backtest needs at least a simplified version of this.

Key concepts:

- **Trade date**: when the trade is executed.
- **Settlement date**: when the associated cash and security exchange is deemed final.
- **Pending cash**: cash flows that are known but not yet settled.
- **Available cash**: cash that is both known and settled, and can be used to meet new obligations without creating settlement violations.

A simple pattern is:

1. On trade date, create cash ledger entries marked with their future settlement date.
2. Maintain, per currency, separate running totals for:
   - total cash (all entries, settled or not),
   - settled cash (entries whose settlement date is at or before current date),
   - pending cash (total minus settled).
3. When checking whether a new order is allowed, use *settled* cash and other relevant balances, according to your brokerage rules.

You may choose to simplify by assuming T+0 (immediate settlement) in early prototypes. But even then, *keep the concept* of settlement date in your data model so that you can later plug in realistic conventions without redesigning everything.

In some markets, partial settlements and fails can arise (for instance, when a counterparty defaults or a transfer is delayed). A fully realistic simulation of those is complex. For most quant backtests, it is sufficient to assume that all trades settle on schedule and that settlement risk is negligible. The important step is merely to separate *known future cash* from *cash truly available to spend.*

Multiple Cash Buckets and Currencies

Institutional portfolios often have multiple distinct cash "buckets." Examples include:

- base currency operating cash,
- segregated collateral accounts for futures and options,
- cash locked up as margin at a prime broker,
- cash in different currencies.

From a modeling perspective, this suggests that a cash ledger entry should always specify *which bucket* and *which currency* it belongs to. Then at any point in time you can ask:

- How much cash is in each bucket and currency?
- What is total portfolio cash in base currency, after FX conversion?
- How much of that cash is truly free to fund new trades?

For example, variation margin on a futures contract is typically posted to a margin account, not your regular cash account. Your PnL engine therefore needs to know that the margin account balances are part of portfolio equity, even if they are not directly usable for a new equity trade.

From Cash and Positions to Equity

Cash balances do not exist in isolation. At each timestamp your engine should be able to compute **portfolio equity** as:

- the total market value of all positions (long and short), plus
- all cash and cash-like balances, net of any margin loans or other liabilities.

The exact formula will depend on product mix and brokerage rules, but conceptually you have a simple hierarchy:

- **Holdings value**: derived from open lots and current prices.
- **Cash and cash-equivalents**: derived from the cash ledger.
- **Liabilities**: margin loans, negative cash, short sale obligations, etc.

Your portfolio equity is the quantity that performance reporting, risk limits, and margin calculations all rely on. That makes it essential to connect your cash engine tightly to the inventory engine: if positions change without a corresponding cash adjustment, or vice versa, the equity computation will silently drift out of reality.

Introducing Margin: Borrowing Against the Portfolio

So far we have treated cash balances as the only funding source. In practice, many strategies rely on **margin**: borrowing from the broker, secured by the portfolio, in order to hold larger positions than cash alone would permit.

At a high level, the margin system answers two questions at each step:

1. Given my current holdings and cash, *what positions am I allowed to hold*? (Buying power.)
2. Given my current holdings and cash, *how much must I keep posted as collateral*? (Margin requirement.)

To model this, your engine should maintain, at each timestamp:

- **Portfolio equity**: as above.
- **Initial margin requirement**: the minimum equity required to open a new position.
- **Maintenance margin requirement**: the minimum equity required to keep an existing position open.
- **Excess or deficit**: equity minus the relevant requirement.

Different assets and positions contribute differently to the margin requirement:

- Long fully-paid equities in a cash account may have no margin requirement beyond the cost itself.
- Marginable equities in a margin account might require, say, 50% initial and 30% maintenance of the position's market value.
- Short positions often carry higher requirements than equivalent long positions.
- Futures and options typically use exchange- or broker-defined margin models.

In a backtest, you have to choose how much realism you want. A common approach is to implement a stylized margin model:

- assign each instrument a margin rate (e.g., 50% for long equity, 150% for some shorts),
- compute the total margin requirement by summing over positions,
- check that equity divided by requirement meets both initial and maintenance thresholds.

The critical property is determinism: given the same positions and prices, the margin engine always returns the same requirements and the same available buying power.

Buying Power: What the Strategy Is Allowed to Do

Buying power is the amount of additional exposure the portfolio is permitted to take on, given current equity, existing positions, and the margin model.

Conceptually:

- It is not just available cash.
- It includes the capacity to borrow more from the broker, up to margin limits.

For example, in a simplified long-only, 2:1 leverage regime:

- If you have $100 of equity and no positions, buying power might be $200 (you can borrow another $100).
- If you already hold $150 of long stock, you may have $50 of remaining buying power.

In your engine, checking a proposed new order should follow this pattern:

1. Simulate adding the order's fills to current positions and cash (using your execution model).

2. Recompute equity, margin requirement, and buying power under the hypothetical new state.

3. Approve or reject the order depending on whether constraints are satisfied (e.g., buying power stays non-negative, maintenance margin is respected).

This may happen at order-submission time or fill time, depending on how detailed your execution modeling is. For reproducibility, you should clearly document which convention you adopt and apply it consistently.

Visualizing the Flow: Trades, Cash, Margin, Equity

Before we dive into margin examples, it is helpful to visualize how a single trade propagates through the cash and margin machinery. The diagram below uses "swim lanes" for the trade events, cash ledger, margin engine, and portfolio equity.

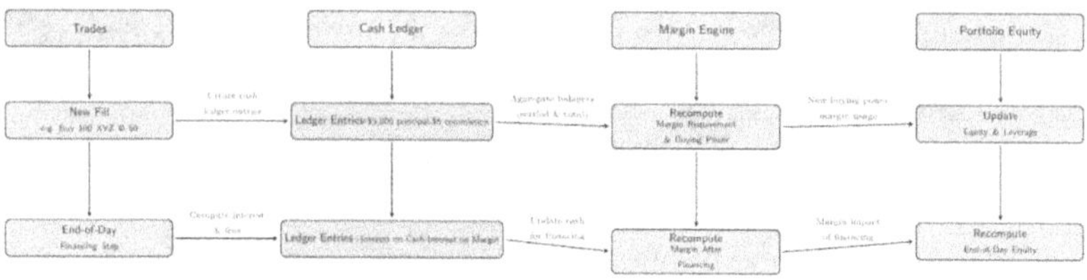

This flow emphasizes two points:

- Trades first become *cash entries*, then margin and equity are recomputed.

- Financing is treated as a separate step that also flows through the cash ledger, then into margin and equity.

Keeping these pathways explicit will later make it much easier to debug unexpected margin calls or financing PnL.

Margin Accounting in Practice: Long and Short Regimes

Let us now spell out how margin typically behaves for long and short positions, in a simplified but useful style.

Long Margin Accounts

In a basic equity margin account:

- Buying marginable securities is partly funded by your equity and partly by a loan from the broker.
- The broker specifies maximum leverage (for example, you may be allowed to hold long stock worth up to twice your equity).
- The unpaid portion effectively appears as a negative cash balance or margin loan.

In your engine, a long margin trade might look like this:

1. The buy order is filled. You create cash ledger entries for the full principal and fees, even if they exceed your current positive cash. The net result may be a negative total cash balance.
2. The margin engine interprets that negative cash as a margin loan, and charges interest on it during the financing step.
3. When you later sell some of the stock, the cash inflow reduces or eliminates the negative balance, reducing future interest.

The important modeling choice is to *never silently cap* the size of the margin loan. Instead, you rely on the margin engine's *constraints* (maintenance requirements and buying power) to prevent the strategy from drifting into impossible leverage.

Short Positions

Short selling introduces an additional twist:

- When you short a stock, you receive cash proceeds from selling borrowed shares.
- Those proceeds are usually held as collateral and may not behave like free cash.
- Brokers often pay little or no interest on short sale proceeds, and in some cases you may pay a borrow fee.

A simple way to handle this in the backtest is:

- tag cash from short sales as belonging to a special "short proceeds" bucket,
- treat that bucket as collateral backing the short, not as cash you can immediately spend,
- apply product-specific interest or borrow rules to that bucket during the financing step.

The margin requirement for short positions is usually higher than for comparable longs. In your margin engine, you may assign different margin rates and haircut assumptions to long and short lots of the same instrument.

Margin Calls as Explicit Events

In live trading, if portfolio equity falls below maintenance margin, the broker issues a **margin call**: you must deposit cash or reduce positions. Many backtests gloss over this by assuming margin calls never happen, or by implicitly assuming the strategy will magically reduce risk.

A more honest backtest:

- explicitly detects margin deficits,
- generates a margin call event,
- applies a deterministic rule for how the portfolio reacts.

For example, you could model a rule:

- If a margin deficit occurs at the end of day, liquidate positions in a fixed order until equity meets maintenance margin again.

In the engine, this means:

1. At each margin evaluation point, compute equity and maintenance requirement.
2. If equity is below requirement, create a margin call event with details of the shortfall.
3. Trigger a liquidation policy that generates a sequence of trades.
4. Those trades, in turn, create cash ledger entries and position changes, which you then feed back into the margin engine.

Even if you do not intend to trade so aggressively that margin calls are likely, having this mechanism in place provides a safety net for rare edge cases and makes the simulation more robust.

Financing Flows: Interest and Product-Specific Mechanics

Up to this point, we have mostly talked about *constraints*: buying power and margin requirements. But the cash and margin subsystem also generates **financing PnL**.

Common examples include:

- interest on positive cash balances (sometimes tiered or benchmarked to a reference rate),
- interest on negative cash or explicit margin loans,
- foregone or reduced interest on short sale proceeds,
- product-specific flows such as:

- daily variation margin on futures,
- option premiums at trade time and any residual cashflows at expiration or exercise.

A clear implementation pattern is:

1. At each financing step (for example, end of day), inspect each cash bucket:
    - If balance is positive, compute interest earned.
    - If balance is negative, compute interest owed.
2. Create cash ledger entries for these interest amounts, tagged as financing income or expense.
3. For products like futures, also process variation margin:
    - change in contract value over the day is settled in cash and recorded via ledger entries,
    - the futures position itself remains at a standard price (often marked to zero cost).
4. After all financing entries are added, recompute cash balances, margin, and equity.

By routing everything through the cash ledger, your PnL engine can later distinguish:

- price-driven PnL from changes in market values of lots,
- financing PnL from interest and margin effects.

This separation is important for attribution and for understanding whether a strategy's performance was driven by alpha, leverage, or cash management.

Determinism and Auditability in the Cash/Margin Subsystem

Like the inventory model, your cash and margin subsystem must be reproducible and explorable. A few guiding principles help:

1. **Ledger-first design**. All changes to cash and financing go through the cash ledger. Equity and margin are recomputed from it, not maintained as opaque state.
2. **Time-consistent updates**. For each event (trade fill, corporate action, financing step), define a strict order:
   (a) update positions and lots,
   (b) update the cash ledger,
   (c) recompute cash balances,
   (d) recompute margin and buying power,
   (e) recompute equity.
3. **Clear separation of levels**. Distinguish:
   - raw data (ledger entries, positions),
   - derived metrics (available cash, margin requirement, equity),
   - decisions (e.g., order rejections, margin call triggers).
4. **Assertion checks**. Periodically check invariants such as:
   - sum of all cash ledger entries matches reported cash balances,
   - equity change equals total PnL plus external flows,
   - margin requirements are non-negative and buying power is consistent with rules.

With these pieces in place, the cash, margin, and financing layer becomes a reliable foundation. In later sections we will add shorting specifics, corporate actions, and ultimately a full PnL pipeline. All of those will rely on the guarantee that when a trade is simulated, its funding, constraints, and financing consequences are captured accurately and reproducibly.

5.3 Shorting & Borrow Costs

So far we have assumed that the portfolio owns what it sells. Many equity and multi-asset strategies, however, rely on **short selling**: selling borrowed securities in the hope of buying them back later at a lower price. Shorting introduces new economic mechanics and new accounting requirements, but it should still fit cleanly into the positions, lots, and cash/margin framework developed earlier.

In this section we extend the model to describe:

- what it means, in the engine, to be short an instrument,
- how *locates* and availability constraints limit which shorts are allowed,
- how *borrow fees* are represented and accrued over time,
- how *recalls* and forced buy-ins alter exposure and PnL.

Our goal is not to mimic every detail of a prime broker, but to capture the essential economics: a short is an obligation as well as a position, and its costs and constraints must be modeled explicitly.

What It Means to Be Short in the Engine

From the portfolio engine's perspective, a short position has two key characteristics:

- The **position** in the instrument is negative: the lots representing that instrument have a net negative quantity.
- There is an implicit **obligation** to return borrowed shares, which may incur fees and can be subject to recall.

On the positions-and-lots side, nothing fundamentally new is needed:

- A **short lot** is simply a lot with negative quantity, created by a sell trade that exceeds any existing long quantity.

- Closing a short happens via buys that reduce or eliminate negative lots, according to your lot selection rule.

On the cash and margin side, however, shorts behave differently from longs:

- **Cash flows**: when you short a stock, you receive sale proceeds, but they may be restricted as collateral.
- **Margin**: short positions typically require higher margin and may consume buying power rapidly.
- **Financing**: you may pay a borrow fee, and you usually pay away dividends to the lender.

To handle all of this consistently, we treat short positions as a specialization of the existing accounting model: the same primitives (lots, cash ledger, margin rules) apply, but the parameters and flows differ.

Locates and Availability: When Shorting Is Allowed

In live markets, you cannot always short any stock in any quantity at will. Most equity shorts rely on borrowing shares from a lending pool controlled by a prime broker or lending agent. This introduces two constraints:

- **Availability**: is the instrument shortable at all, on the desired date?
- **Capacity**: up to what quantity can you borrow?

Operationally, brokers provide *locates*: an indication that shares can be borrowed to support a short sale. For backtesting, we need a simplified but explicit abstraction that answers, for each instrument and time:

1. Is shorting permitted?

2. If so, what is the maximum short size or additional borrowable quantity?
3. What borrow rate applies (we discuss this shortly)?

Depending on data availability and your goals, you may choose between several modeling regimes:

Always-shortable regime

This is the simplest assumption:

- every instrument is shortable at any time,
- borrow capacity is effectively unlimited,
- borrow fee is either zero or a flat rate.

This regime is easy to implement but potentially unrealistic, especially for small caps or special situations. It can be acceptable for strategies focused on liquid, large-cap universes where hard-to-borrow events are rare.

Rule-based availability

A more realistic middle ground introduces rules based on observable characteristics, for example:

- only instruments above a certain average daily volume or market capitalization are shortable,
- new IPOs or low-priced stocks are never shortable,
- maximum short size per instrument is a percentage of average daily volume or shares outstanding.

Your engine then checks these rules at order time or fill time: if a proposed short violates shortability or capacity limits, the trade is rejected or re-sized.

Data-driven availability

The most realistic approach uses historical data on short sale restrictions, hard-to-borrow lists, or borrow availability flags (if you have them). In this case you may integrate a separate data stream that, for each instrument and date, carries:

- a shortable flag,
- maximum borrowable size for your account type,
- an estimated borrow rate.

This stream becomes an input to the event engine, much like prices or corporate actions. Your shorting logic then uses it as a hard constraint.

Regardless of the regime, it is important that the rule or data be:

- **explicit**: defined in configuration or in a documented data source,
- **deterministic**: given the same inputs, generate the same accept/reject decisions,
- **aligned with fills**: the check should occur at the same logical moment you simulate the execution.

Short Lots, Cash, and Margin: Basic Mechanics

Once a short trade is allowed, it flows through the same machinery you already have:

1. The execution model emits a sell fill.
2. The inventory engine creates or increases short lots.
3. The cash engine records trade principal and fees in the cash ledger.
4. The margin engine updates margin requirements and buying power.

Two elements deserve emphasis.

Short sale proceeds and collateral

When you short, you receive cash equal to *price times quantity*. However, in many regimes:

- those proceeds are "locked" as collateral against the short,
- you may not be able to fully draw them down for other trades,
- the broker may pay reduced or zero interest on these funds.

In the backtest, it helps to represent these proceeds in a distinct cash bucket, for example:

> "short proceeds USD"

The cash ledger records the inflow into this bucket, and the margin engine treats it as part of your collateral but not as fully fungible cash. Depending on how granular you wish to be, you can either:

- implement explicit rules on how much of the short proceeds is usable for further buying, or
- take a simpler approach where short proceeds are part of total cash but are always included in the margin requirement with conservative haircuts.

Margin on shorts

As discussed previously, shorts often have higher margin requirements than longs. For example, a broker might require:

- 150% of short market value as margin, consisting of:
  - 100% from short sale proceeds,
  - 50% from the rest of your equity.

You do not need to replicate every detail of such formulas. It suffices to:

- assign higher margin rates per unit of market value to short lots,
- ensure margin requirements increase when short notional grows,
- ensure maintenance margin is computed consistently from these requirements.

The key is that, from the engine's point of view, shorts are fully integrated into the same margin pipeline: only the parameters differ.

Borrow Fees: Pricing the Right to Stay Short

The key distinctive cost of shorting is the **borrow fee** (also called stock loan fee, stock borrow, or rebate shortfall). Conceptually:

> You are paying an interest-like fee to the lender for the privilege of borrowing and selling the shares.

Borrow fees are usually expressed as an annualized percentage of the *short market value*. They can vary over time and across instruments, and can be extremely high for hard-to-borrow names.

To model borrow fees, you need:

- a borrow rate for each shorted instrument and time period,
- a rule for how often and how the fee is accrued and settled,
- a representation of fees as cash flows in your ledger, separate from commissions and price-driven PnL.

Borrow rate representation

You can store borrow rates in several ways:

- as a constant rate per instrument (simplest),
- as a time series of rates per instrument, if you have historical borrow data,
- as a function of observable attributes (e.g., volume, market cap, or a hard-to-borrow flag).

The engine should be able to answer, on any day you hold a short lot:

> What is the applicable borrow rate for this quantity and date?

Accrual and booking

Borrow fees are commonly accrued daily on the current short market value and settled periodically (often daily or monthly). In the backtest you might:

1. At each end-of-day (or financing step):
    - compute the market value of each open short lot,
    - apply the appropriate borrow rate to obtain a daily fee,
    - sum across lots to obtain total borrow fee per instrument or per currency.
2. Record a cash ledger entry:
    - a cash outflow in the appropriate bucket,
    - tagged as "borrow fee" or similar.
3. Recompute cash, margin, and equity with this new outflow included.

Conceptually, this is analogous to interest on a margin loan, but attached to the market value of short positions instead of a negative cash balance.

Separating borrow PnL from price PnL

One of the main reasons to model borrow explicitly is **PnL attribution**. For each shorted instrument you would like to distinguish:

- *Price-driven PnL*: from price moves between open and close of the short lots.
- *Borrow PnL*: from the running stream of borrow fees.

Your PnL engine can do this cleanly by:

- valuing short lots at market prices to compute price PnL,
- reading borrow fee entries from the cash ledger to compute financing PnL,
- reporting both components separately, and then aggregated as part of total PnL.

This separation is especially important in strategies that target crowded shorts or hard-to-borrow names, where borrow can dominate economics.

Dividends and Other Cash Flows on Borrowed Shares

A subtle but important feature of shorting is the treatment of **dividends**. When you are short a dividend-paying stock:

- the lender of the shares is still economically entitled to the dividend,
- you, as the borrower, typically must pay the equivalent amount to the lender,
- your cash account therefore experiences a cash outflow when dividends are paid.

Your corporate action engine already knows when cash dividends occur for each instrument and the amount per share. To extend it to shorts:

1. On each dividend event:
   - For long lots, credit cash ledger entries with dividend income.
   - For short lots, *debit* cash ledger entries with the same per-share dividend (a "dividend expense").
2. The inventory engine ensures that long and short quantities are derived from open lots at the dividend date.
3. The PnL engine later reports dividend income and expense, again separate from price-driven and borrow PnL.

Other cash flows—for example, payments in lieu or corporate action proceeds—can be handled similarly: apply the economic rule per share and sign it appropriately for longs versus shorts.

Recalls and Forced Buy-Ins

So far we have assumed that once a short is opened, you may hold it as long as you wish (subject to margin). In practice, lenders can **recall** shares:

- the lender no longer wishes to lend those specific shares,
- your broker must find replacement borrows or ask you to close part or all of the short,
- if replacement cannot be found, a **forced buy-in** may occur at current market prices.

To make the backtest robust, it is helpful to model at least a stylized version of recalls and buy-ins.

Modeling recalls

Create a separate event stream representing recalls. At each recall event, specify:

- the instrument,
- the quantity being recalled,
- timing (for example, effective date or deadline).

When the event triggers:

1. Determine which short lots will be affected (e.g., using FIFO, LIFO, or specific-lot rules).
2. Either:
    - automatically generate buy orders to close the recalled quantity,
    - or mark the recalled lots with a deadline by which the strategy must close them, else a forced buy-in occurs.

Forced buy-ins

If a recall cannot be satisfied voluntarily (for example, the strategy chooses not to close, or liquidity is insufficient), a forced buy-in event simulates the broker closing the position at a price and time you specify. In the engine this is just another trade, but with the following properties:

- the order is system-generated, not strategy-generated,
- it may execute at an unfavorable price (for instance, worst price of the day),
- it creates or closes lots and cash flows exactly like any other trade.

Modeling forced buy-ins serves two purposes:

- It honors the economic risk of relying on fragile borrow.
- It avoids impossible scenarios where the backtest stays short in a stock that was, in reality, unshortable for long periods.

In most strategies you might treat recalls and buy-ins as relatively rare, driven by simple heuristics (e.g., high borrow rate plus drop in short availability). But even a simple model, applied consistently, is superior to ignoring the risk altogether.

Integrating Shorting into the Broader Accounting Stack

The key design choice is to keep short-specific logic *orthogonal but coupled* to your core accounting systems:

- **Positions and lots**: shorts are just negative lots with the same lifecycle as longs.
- **Cash ledger**: short sale proceeds, borrow fees, and dividend expenses are all normal cash entries with their own tags.
- **Margin engine**: shorts use the same margin computation but with different rates and possibly different treatment of collateral buckets.
- **Corporate actions**: dividends, splits, and other corporate actions act symmetrically on long and short quantities, but with sign-adjusted cash flows and PnL impacts.

- **PnL attribution**: price, borrow, dividend, and other financing components are separated by reading from lots and cash entries with appropriate categories.

This modularity allows you to:

- run the same strategy with shorting disabled (for a long-only backtest) simply by forbidding negative positions and borrow events, without changing the rest of the engine,
- plug in more realistic borrow and availability data over time, without refactoring core accounting logic,
- debug issues by following a short's history through inventories, cash flows, and margin snapshots.

Design Guidelines for Shorting and Borrow Modeling

We close with practical guidelines that will help keep the shorting model robust and transparent:

1. **Explicit availability model**. Never silently assume an instrument is shortable. Encode your assumptions as a configuration or data stream and log rejections when shorts are not allowed.
2. **Per-lot borrow tracking**. Tag each short lot with the borrow rate and any availability metadata applicable at open time, and update if your model allows rate changes over time.
3. **Daily accrual discipline**. Accrue borrow fees and dividend expenses at well-defined, repeatable times (for example, end of each trading day) and through the cash ledger.
4. **Audit-ready PnL decomposition**. Design PnL reports that clearly separate, for each short:
    - realized and unrealized price PnL,
    - borrow fees,

- dividend and other corporate-action-related cashflows.

5. **Deterministic recall handling**. If you simulate recalls and buy-ins, make the rules deterministic and log each event, with the affected lots and resulting trades.

6. **Conservative defaults**. In the absence of rich data, choose defaults that *penalize* shorts rather than making them artificially cheap or unconstrained. It is better to underestimate performance than to rely on impossible borrow.

With these extensions, your backtest engine can support strategies that use shorting in a way that is economically meaningful, constrained by realistic borrowing limits, and fully reconciled with the rest of the portfolio accounting and PnL system.

5.4 Corporate Actions Processing & Effects

Up to this point, we have assumed that quantities and prices change only because we trade or because the market moves. Real markets introduce a third source of change: **corporate actions**. Splits, dividends, rights issues, spin-offs, mergers, and similar events can alter quantities, prices, and cash flows even if the portfolio never trades.

In a backtest, corporate actions are dangerous because they are both common and quiet. If you ignore them, or model them inconsistently, you will:

- misstate PnL around event dates,
- mix pre- and post-adjustment data, creating hidden look-ahead bias,
- distort cost basis and tax-relevant information,
- break the link between positions, prices, and cash.

In this section we show how to apply the main types of corporate actions to positions and cash so that the portfolio remains economically correct at every timestamp. We assume the positions, lots, and cash/-margin structures from earlier sections are in place.

A Taxonomy of Corporate Actions

Corporate actions come in many flavors, but for accounting purposes it is helpful to group them into a few families:

- **Quantity-changing but value-neutral actions**
- stock splits and reverse splits,
- stock dividends.
- **Cash-distributing actions**
- regular and special cash dividends,
- return of capital distributions.
- **Participation rights**
- rights issues and subscriptions,
- optional dividends (cash or stock choice).
- **Reorganizations**
- spin-offs,
- mergers and acquisitions,
- symbol changes and re-domiciliations.

Each category has a characteristic pattern:

- How do quantities of each lot change?
- How does cost basis (per share and total) change?
- What happens to cash?

- Are there new instruments created or old ones retired?

Your engine should represent each corporate action as a separate event, with a clear *effective time*. The event stream then drives adjustments to lots and cash, just as fills drive trades.

Splits and Reverse Splits: Rescaling Quantity and Price

A **stock split** multiplies the number of shares and divides the price per share, leaving the overall value of the position unchanged (ignoring small rounding). For example:

- In a 2-for-1 split, each share becomes two shares, and price roughly halves.
- In a 3-for-2 split, each 2 shares become 3 shares, and price scales down accordingly.

A **reverse split** does the opposite: it reduces the number of shares and increases the price per share.

From the engine's perspective, splits and reverse splits are purely mechanical rescalings. There is no cashflow and, under ideal conditions, no gain or loss at the moment of the split.

At the *lot* level, a split event must:

- multiply the quantity of each open lot by the split ratio,
- divide the per-share cost basis by the same ratio,
- keep the total cost of each lot unchanged (quantity times cost per share).

For reverse splits, the ratio is less than one (for example, 1-for-10 means dividing quantities by 10 and multiplying per-share cost by 10). The same rules apply.

There are two subtle points to handle:

Fractional shares

If the split ratio does not divide your share count evenly, you can end up with fractional shares. For example, a 3-for-2 split applied to 100 shares yields 150 shares exactly, but applied to 101 shares yields 151.5 shares.

Brokers typically handle fractional shares in one of three ways:

- allow fractional holdings,
- round quantities to the nearest share and adjust cost basis accordingly,
- round down and pay *cash-in-lieu* for the fraction.

Your engine must choose a convention:

- If you allow fractional shares in the inventory model, you simply track them as decimal quantities and rely on later events (like a cash-in-lieu payout) if your corporate action feed includes them.
- If you require integer quantities, you must implement a rounding rule and recognize any residual value as realized PnL or a cash adjustment.

Point-in-time consistency

In the data you consume, prices may be provided in either raw (unadjusted) or split-adjusted form. To avoid look-ahead bias and discontinuities in your PnL:

- if you use *unadjusted* prices for simulation, you must apply split events to lots and quantities exactly when the market does, so that the market value before and after the split aligns,
- if you use *adjusted* prices for signals (for example, continuous adjusted close), you must ensure that inventory and PnL calculations are aligned with an unadjusted or appropriately synchronized view to avoid phantom gains or losses.

A robust approach is to treat corporate actions as part of the simulation event stream and keep your internal book in unadjusted units, applying corporate actions explicitly.

Cash Dividends: Income Without Quantity Change

A **cash dividend** distributes cash to shareholders without changing the number of shares held. Economically:

- on the ex-dividend date, the stock price typically falls by roughly the dividend amount,
- holders of record receive cash on the pay date.

In your engine, you need to decide how to handle the timing:

- Many backtests simplify by crediting the dividend on ex-date, because that is when new buyers are no longer entitled to it and the price drop occurs.
- Others faithfully separate ex-date (when price adjusts) and pay date (when cash arrives).

Whichever you choose, apply the following:

1. For each open *long* lot in the instrument on the dividend event date:
   - compute the dividend amount as shares held times dividend per share,
   - create a positive cash ledger entry for that amount, categorized as dividend income.
2. For each open *short* lot, do the opposite:
   - compute the same notional amount,
   - create a negative cash ledger entry, representing the dividend you must pay to the lender.

You do *not* change share counts. Cost basis per share is also typically unaffected by regular cash dividends (though tax jurisdictions differ in their detailed treatment). The immediate economic effect is:

- a decrease in stock price (a mark-to-market loss for longs, gain for shorts),
- an offsetting cash inflow (for longs) or outflow (for shorts).

If your modeling is consistent, holding a stock through a dividend should generate approximately zero PnL on ex-date, aside from market noise and taxes: the price drop is offset by the cash.

Worked Example: Split Followed by Dividend

To make these ideas concrete, consider a simple example in which a position goes through both a split and a cash dividend. We start with a single long lot and track how quantity, price, cost basis, and cash evolve.

Diagrammatic representation:

Date	Event	Quantity	Price	Cost Basis	Cash Balance	
Jan 2	Buy 100 shares	100	$100	$100 / $10,000	–$10,000	
Mar 30	Pre-split close	100	$120	$100 / $10,000	–$10,000	Value Conserved
Mar 31	**2-for-1 Split**	**200**	**$60**	$50 / $10,000	–$10,000	(Qty × 2, Price ÷ 2)
Apr 1	Post-split trade	200	$62	$50 / $10,000	–$10,000	Cash Inflow
Apr 15	**Dividend $1/sh**	200	$61	$50 / $10,000	–$9,800	(+$200)

In this illustrative ledger:

- The split doubles quantity and halves per-share cost; total cost remains $10,000.
- The dividend pays $1 per share on 200 shares, increasing cash by $200.
- Prices adjust around events, but if markets behave ideally, the combined effect of split and dividend is value-neutral at the moment of each event.

This kind of worked example is useful both for validating your implementation and for explaining behavior to non-technical stakeholders.

Stock Dividends and Rights Issues: Quantity and Choice

Stock dividends

A **stock dividend** grants additional shares instead of cash. For example, a 10% stock dividend gives you 10 extra shares for every 100 you own.

Mechanically:

- quantity of each open long lot increases by the stock dividend ratio,
- total cost basis is usually unchanged (in many jurisdictions),
- per-share cost basis decreases because the same total cost is spread over more shares,
- there is no immediate cashflow.

This is similar to a split, but with different ratios and possibly different tax treatment.

Rights issues

A **rights issue** gives existing shareholders the right (but not the obligation) to buy more shares at a specified subscription price, often at a discount to the market. In a backtest, you must choose a policy for exercising rights:

- *Automatic exercise*: always exercise rights if you have enough cash and the terms are favorable.
- *Never exercise*: ignore rights, treating them as worthless.
- *Rule-based*: exercise only if the discount exceeds a threshold and cash/margin allow.

At the accounting level, exercising rights involves:

1. Creating new lots (or increasing existing ones) with quantity equal to rights exercised, at the subscription price.

2. Creating a cash ledger entry for the subscription cost, debiting your cash.
3. Possibly updating cost basis of existing shares if your model or jurisdiction requires allocating cost between old and new shares.

If rights are tradable and you choose to sell them instead of exercise, you treat that as a separate instrument with its own trades, lots, and cash flows.

Spin-Offs and Mergers: New Instruments and Basis Allocation

Spin-offs and **mergers** create or retire instruments altogether. These are the most complex corporate actions because they alter not just quantities and prices, but also the mapping between instruments.

Spin-offs

In a spin-off, a company distributes shares of a new company (the "child") to holders of the parent company. For example:

- for each share of ParentCo, you receive 0.5 shares of ChildCo,
- ParentCo's price typically drops because part of its business has been carved out,
- your total economic value (ParentCo plus ChildCo) should be roughly unchanged at the moment of the spin-off.

To model a spin-off:

1. For each open lot of ParentCo, create a new lot in ChildCo with quantity equal to the spin-off ratio times the parent quantity.
2. Allocate cost basis between ParentCo and ChildCo lots according to a specified rule, often based on relative market values immediately after the spin-off.
3. Do *not* create any cash flow unless the spin-off includes cash components.

It is essential to have a deterministic rule for cost allocation. A typical pattern:

- Compute the combined market value of ParentCo and ChildCo immediately after the spin.
- Allocate the original cost basis proportionally:
  - parent cost = original cost times (post-spin parent value divided by combined value),
  - child cost = original cost times (post-spin child value divided by combined value).

If you lack detailed price data at the event, you may use an external adjustment factor from your corporate action feed.

Mergers and acquisitions

Mergers often involve one company (the acquirer) absorbing another (the target), with target shareholders receiving:

- cash,
- stock in the acquirer,
- or a mix of both.

In your engine:

1. On the effective date, close all open lots in the target:
   - If the consideration is cash, create corresponding cash ledger entries and realize PnL by comparing proceeds with cost basis.
   - If the consideration is stock, create new lots in the acquirer with quantities and cost basis determined by the exchange ratio and any cash component.
2. Retire the target symbol from further trading.

As with spin-offs, cost basis allocation between cash and stock components must follow a clear, deterministic rule, ideally aligned with tax- or accounting-standard methods when available.

Corporate Action Event Streams and Engine Integration

To keep your simulation clean, corporate actions should be fed into the engine as a separate, time-stamped event stream, alongside:

- market data (prices, volumes),
- trades and fills,
- cash and financing events.

At each step the event engine processes all events at a given timestamp in a consistent order. A typical sequence per instrument might be:

1. Apply corporate actions effective at this time to lots and, if needed, cash.
2. Process trades and update lots and cash.
3. Revalue positions at new prices.
4. Recompute cash, margin, and equity.

The ordering rule should be documented and fixed, so that re-running the same event stream always reproduces the same portfolio state.

Invariants and Sanity Checks Around Corporate Actions

Because corporate actions can be complex, it is important to enforce invariants that catch inconsistencies early. Useful checks include:

Economic value continuity

For actions that are supposed to be value-neutral (splits, stock dividends, spin-offs under ideal pricing), check that:

- total market value of affected positions plus cash immediately before and after the event is approximately unchanged, allowing for small price drift or rounding.

If this continuity fails for many events, you may be misaligning your price data and action dates.

Quantity and basis consistency

After processing an action:

- the sum of lot quantities for the instrument(s) should match your intended ratio or exchange rule,
- total cost basis across all related lots (parent and child, or target and acquirer) should match the pre-event total, except where cash components explicitly realize gains or losses.

Replayability

As with trades, you should be able to start from an earlier snapshot, replay all corporate action and trade events, and recover the same positions, lots, and cash. If replay diverges, the processing might be order-dependent or non-deterministic.

Aligning Corporate Actions with Adjusted Data in the Signal Layer

Many quant workflows use *adjusted* price series for signal generation, where past prices are restated to remove the jumps caused by splits and dividends. If your simulation also uses these adjusted prices directly for PnL, you risk double-counting:

- once via explicit corporate action processing,
- and again via the adjustment embedded in prices.

To avoid this:

- Use unadjusted (or minimally adjusted) prices for simulation and PnL, applying corporate actions explicitly to positions and cash.
- If you use adjusted prices for signal calculation, keep them logically separate from the prices used in the accounting engine.

- Make sure that any adjusted series and corporate action series come from consistent sources, so that implied adjustments and explicit events agree.

The critical goal is that, for a portfolio that simply buys and holds, corporate actions do not create fake alpha: total return over time should be driven by genuine price and cash returns, not data quirks.

Design Principles for Corporate Action Handling

To summarize, a robust corporate action subsystem should:

1. **Treat actions as first-class events.** Store them in a dedicated event stream with clear timestamps, types, and parameters.
2. **Operate at the lot level.** Apply quantity and basis adjustments to each lot, not just net positions, so that realized PnL and tax-relevant data remain accurate.
3. **Route all cash through the ledger.** Dividends, cash-in-lieu, merger proceeds, and rights subscriptions should all appear as explicit cash entries.
4. **Preserve economic value where appropriate.** For splits and similar actions, enforce approximate continuity of total value around the event.
5. **Be deterministic and replayable.** Given the same input series of corporate actions, trades, and prices, your engine must produce identical inventory and PnL.
6. **Remain conservative under uncertainty.** When in doubt (for example, about exact tax or cost-basis treatments), choose conventions that do not inflate performance or hide risks.

With these principles in place, the portfolio's evolution across even complex corporate histories remains transparent and economically sound. This, in turn, allows the final PnL and return calculations to rest on a foundation you can trace, explain, and defend.

5.5 Return Definitions & Compounding

By now we have a detailed picture of how the portfolio's holdings, cash, and financing evolve over time. The next step is to translate those evolving levels and flows into **returns**: numbers that summarize performance over days, months, and years; across assets; and for different audiences.

Return definitions are often treated as a mere reporting detail, but in a backtest engine they are structural. If you define returns ambiguously or inconsistently, you will:

- find that multi-period returns do not reconcile with the PnL ledger,
- miscompare strategies that use different leverage or cash usage,
- generate results that cannot be reproduced once you change frequency or sampling.

In this section we clarify:

- how to distinguish *levels* from *flows*,
- how to define basic period returns from them,
- the difference between **arithmetic** and **log** returns,
- **time-weighted** versus **money-weighted** performance,
- how to aggregate returns over time and across assets,
- how to keep all of this internally consistent with the PnL engine.

We avoid formulas where possible and instead focus on intuition and implementation patterns.

Levels vs. Flows: The Raw Ingredients of Returns

The accounting stack you have built produces two broad kinds of quantities:

- **Levels**: snapshots of "how much we have" at a point in time.
- portfolio equity,
- instrument or sector values,
- NAV (net asset value) per share, for a fund.
- **Flows**: transactions that move value in or out of the portfolio, without being driven by price changes.
- external flows: contributions, withdrawals, fund-level fees,
- internal flows: dividends, coupons, borrow fees, interest on cash, which are PnL components but also literal cash movements in your ledger.

For performance measurement, it is helpful to make a conceptual distinction:

- **Performance returns** should measure how much value changed because of *investment results*: price changes, income, and costs like financing and fees.
- **External flows** such as contributions or withdrawals should not be counted as performance. Instead, they adjust the baseline capital on which you measure returns.

Your return engine will therefore use:

- a time series of *equity snapshots*,
- a list of *external cash flows* between those snapshots.

Everything else (positions, lots, corporate actions) has already been absorbed into equity and PnL by the accounting layer.

Single-Period Returns: Basic Definitions

Consider two consecutive valuation times, "start" and "end." At each time you know the portfolio's equity. Between them you may also have external flows, for example, a capital contribution in the middle.

To define a **single-period return**, you conceptually ask:

> If I strip out external flows and just look at how much value the portfolio created or destroyed, relative to the capital at risk, what is the percentage change over this period?

In the simplest case, with *no* external flows during the period, the basic idea is straightforward:

- A positive return means equity increased.
- A negative return means equity decreased.
- A return of 0 means equity is unchanged.

In practice you will choose a specific return formula (arithmetic or log) and a convention for handling flows. But all of them follow this intuition: normalization of performance relative to starting capital.

At the *instrument* level, you may define returns in terms of prices plus accrued income (for example, including dividends). At the *portfolio* level, you use equity snapshots and external flows.

Arithmetic vs. Log Returns: Additivity vs. Intuition

Two return definitions dominate in practice: **arithmetic returns** and **logarithmic (log) returns**.

Arithmetic returns

Arithmetic returns are what most investors think of when they hear "percentage return." Over a period, you ask:

> By what percentage did my value change?

Arithmetic returns are intuitive:

- A 10% return means your value is 10% larger than at the start.
- A -10% return means your value is 10% smaller than at the start.

They are easy to explain and easy to interpret. However, there is an important caveat: *arithmetic returns do not add over time.* If you gain 10% one day and lose 10% the next, your overall return is not 0; it is slightly negative because the second 10% is applied to a larger or smaller base.

For multi-period performance, you must therefore *compound* arithmetic returns (by chaining them multiplicatively) rather than summing them.

Log returns

Log returns transform percentage changes into a form that *does* add over time. Intuitively, they measure:

> The continuous rate of growth that, when applied steadily, would produce the observed change.

The key property is:

- Over multiple periods, the sum of log returns equals the log of the total growth factor.

This additivity is extremely convenient in theory and some modeling tasks. It makes long-horizon growth easy to compute and works naturally with certain statistical assumptions.

However, log returns have quirks:

- For large negative moves, they are less intuitive than arithmetic percentages.
- They are undefined for returns of -100% (complete losses).

Which to use in the backtest engine?

For the engine's core accounting outputs, arithmetic returns are usually more practical:

- They align with the way most reports (such as monthly performance) are presented.
- They make it easy to interpret daily PnL relative to capital.

You can always derive log returns later from arithmetic returns if a downstream analysis needs them.

The important point is to *choose* and *record* your convention. Avoid mixing arithmetic and log definitions in different parts of the system without clear labeling.

Time-Weighted vs. Money-Weighted Returns

So far we have talked about single-period returns as if external flows did not exist. In reality, clients add and withdraw cash, and fund-level fees may be charged. How you treat these flows leads to two major performance concepts:

- **Time-weighted returns (TWR)**:
- measure the strategy's ability to grow capital, independent of the timing and size of external flows.
- are constructed by breaking the history into subperiods around each external flow, computing returns for those subperiods, and then chaining them.
- **Money-weighted returns (MWR)**:
- measure the actual investor's experience, accounting for when cash was invested or withdrawn,
- conceptually, they answer: "What single constant return would equate all my in- and outflows to the final value?"

Time-weighted returns (TWR)

In a backtest, TWR is often the main object you care about, because it isolates the skill of the strategy from the whims of cash timing. Conceptually, you proceed as follows:

1. Break the history into segments so that within each segment there are *no external flows*. For example:
   - from month end to a mid-month deposit,
   - from that deposit to a later withdrawal,
   - from the withdrawal to the next month end.
2. For each segment, compute an arithmetic return using only the starting and ending equity, ignoring flows (because by construction there are none inside the segment).
3. Chain these segment returns multiplicatively to get a longer-horizon return (for example, monthly, yearly, or over the full backtest).

The result is a pure measure of portfolio performance between valuation points, unaffected by how much capital was invested at each time.

In an automated engine:

- You already know every external cash flow from the cash ledger.
- You already compute equity snapshots at chosen evaluation times (for example, daily or monthly).
- The return engine can therefore segment the timeline automatically, compute subperiod returns, and compound them.

Money-weighted returns (MWR)

Money-weighted returns (often implemented as internal rate of return, IRR) give more weight to periods where more capital was at work. They are sensitive to when flows occur:

- Adding significant capital before strong performance will increase MWR.

- Adding capital before a drawdown will decrease MWR, even if TWR remains favorable.

MWR is important in some contexts (for example, to measure an individual investor's experience in a strategy or fund). However, it is more cumbersome to compute and less suitable as a *strategy* performance metric in a backtest, because you often control the flow pattern artificially.

In your engine:

- Use TWR as the default for strategy evaluation.
- Optionally provide MWR as a secondary report, computed on demand from the equity and flow history.

Above all, do not mix them; label clearly which convention is used in each performance figure.

Irregular Time Steps: Event-Driven vs. Bar-Based Engines

Many academic treatments of returns assume regular time steps (daily, monthly). Backtest engines often work differently:

- Event-driven engines update portfolio state on every fill, price tick, or corporate action.
- Bar-based engines update on each bar, which may itself be irregular across instruments or markets.

Your return engine should not depend on the granularity of these internal updates. Instead, you should define a set of **valuation times** at which you want performance measured (for example, end of each trading day), and then:

- sample the portfolio equity at those times,
- aggregate any external flows appropriately between them,

- compute returns from these sampled values and flows.

Internally, the accounting engine may handle thousands of intermediate events within a day. The return engine sees only:

- start-of-day equity,
- end-of-day equity,
- the list of external flows during that day.

This separation has two advantages:

- You can change the internal event resolution (for example, introduce intraday fills or corporate actions) without changing the return series definition.
- You can calculate performance at multiple horizons (daily, weekly, monthly) from the same underlying equity and flow series.

Per-Asset and Portfolio Returns

So far we have spoken of "portfolio returns" as if there were a single time series. In practice, you will often need:

- per-asset returns,
- contributions of each asset or factor to total portfolio return.

Conceptually:

- An **asset return** describes how that asset's price and income changed, relative to its own starting value.
- A **contribution** describes how much that asset's performance *mattered* to the portfolio, given its weight in the portfolio.

In a backtest, you can compute per-asset returns directly from market data (prices plus accrued income) using the same arithmetic return logic. Contributions follow a simple idea:

> Contribution over a period = asset's return over the period, weighted by its average share of portfolio value.

You do not have to be exact about weighting conventions at first (for example, start-of-period weights versus dollar-day weights), as long as you are consistent and document them. The important part is:

- For each period, the sum of all asset contributions (plus any residual such as cash and fees) should equal the portfolio's overall return.

This reconciliability makes the contribution and attribution reports trustworthy and debuggable.

Compounding Over Time: From Daily to Monthly to Inception-to-Date

Once you have a series of single-period returns (for example, daily arithmetic TWRs), you often want:

- cumulative returns over a longer horizon (for example, month or year),
- inception-to-date performance,
- rolling-window metrics (3-month, 1-year).

The guiding rule is:

- **Never** add arithmetic returns across periods as if they were linear.
- **Always** chain them multiplicatively to obtain the correct cumulative effect.

For example:

- To get a monthly return from daily returns, sequentially apply each day's growth factor to an initial value of 1, and then compute the net percentage change.
- To get inception-to-date return, do the same but use the full history.

If you are using log returns internally, you can sum them and then convert back to a growth factor. But the rules are the same: be consistent in your compounding and in your chosen return definition.

A practical design pattern in the engine:

1. Maintain a table of single-period returns at the base frequency (for example, daily).
2. Provide utility functions to compound them over arbitrary ranges.
3. Ensure that:
    - the compounded return over a set of periods matches the direct return computed from start and end equity snapshots and flows,
    - rounding and numerical issues are controlled (for example, by using sufficient precision).

These cross-checks give you high confidence that reported performance is not an artifact of the compounding logic.

Currency and FX: Local vs. Base-Currency Returns

In multi-currency portfolios, returns have an extra layer:

- Assets may be priced in their local currency (for example, EUR or JPY).

- Portfolio equity is often measured in a base currency (for example, USD).
- FX rates introduce an additional source of gains and losses.

You can think of each asset's performance as decomposing into:

- local-currency return (price and income in its own currency),
- FX return (change in exchange rate between local and base currency),
- combined base-currency return (relevant for total portfolio).

Your engine should, at minimum:

- compute local-currency returns for each asset from its own price and income data,
- convert asset values and flows into base currency using appropriate FX rates at each valuation time,
- compute portfolio-level returns in base currency from base-currency equity and external flows.

If you want to go further, you can attribute performance into local and FX components. But even a simple base-currency return series must be consistent: if you revalue positions and cash using FX data in the accounting engine, your return engine should use the same conversions.

Designing a Return API: Inputs, Outputs, and Contracts

To keep the return layer modular and reproducible, it is useful to design it as an API that takes in clean inputs from the accounting engine and produces standardized outputs.

Inputs

At a chosen set of valuation times (for example, each trading day close), the return engine needs:

- portfolio equity in base currency,
- per-asset values (if you want contributions),
- the list of external flows between this time and the previous one (amounts, signs, and timestamps),
- optional FX rates and flags for special flows (for example, management fees).

These should come from the PnL and cash subsystems, not recomputed from raw trades in the return layer.

Outputs

For each period between valuation times, the return engine should produce:

- arithmetic time-weighted portfolio return,
- optionally, log return,
- asset-level returns and contributions,
- cumulative returns over higher horizons (on demand),
- optional money-weighted return over user-selected intervals.

All outputs should:

- be labeled with the return convention (arithmetic vs. log, TWR vs. MWR),
- be reproducible: rerunning the engine with the same inputs produces identical return series.

Contracts and invariants

A few invariants should always hold:

- Aggregating PnL: change in equity over a period equals total PnL (from the PnL engine) plus net external flows.

- Aggregating contributions: sum of asset contributions plus any residuals equals portfolio return for each period.
- Aggregating across time: compounded single-period returns over a range equals the direct return from start to end equity and flows.

Embedding checks for these invariants in the engine makes it much easier to catch bugs where, for example, a flow is misclassified or a sign is flipped.

Choosing and Documenting Conventions

Finally, the most important design decision is simply to *choose conventions and document them*. Many disagreements about performance numbers arise because different tools or teams use:

- different return formulas (arithmetic vs. log),
- different treatments of flows (TWR vs. MWR, and different segmentation),
- different valuation times and calendars.

In your backtest engine:

- decide what the *default* portfolio return is (typically daily arithmetic time-weighted in base currency),
- encode this definition in code and configuration,
- ensure that every report and export clearly states the convention used,
- keep the mapping from equity and flows to returns as simple and transparent as possible.

Done well, return definitions and compounding become a dependable bridge between the low-level accounting engine and the high-level evaluation of strategies. Anyone reading your performance tables should be able to recreate them from the underlying data, and you yourself should be able to explain every number: what it measures, how it was computed, and what assumptions it encodes.

5.6 PnL & Return Calculation

We now have all the building blocks of portfolio accounting: positions and lots, cash and margin, shorting and borrow, corporate actions, and return conventions. The final step is to integrate them into a single **PnL and return engine** that:

- produces a clear breakdown of PnL by source,
- reconciles exactly with changes in portfolio equity,
- feeds consistently into your chosen return definitions,
- is deterministic and easy to debug.

This section lays out:

- a taxonomy of PnL components,
- a step-by-step daily (or per-event) PnL pipeline,
- how to connect PnL to returns and attribution,
- design patterns for reproducibility and extensibility.

Framing the PnL Pipeline

To keep the discussion concrete, we focus on a daily cycle. The same logic applies if your engine runs at bar or event level; you simply repeat the steps more frequently.

At a high level, each new day starts with a prior-day closing state:

- open lots and their cost bases,

- cash balances in each bucket,
- outstanding short positions and borrow state,
- any unsettled cash or pending corporate actions.

During the day, events occur:

- trades and fills,
- corporate actions,
- price moves,
- financing flows (interest, borrow, margin adjustments).

At the end of the day, you want:

- updated positions and cash,
- per-component PnL,
- portfolio equity,
- period returns consistent with the PnL.

Before detailing each step, it is useful to see the pipeline as a whole.

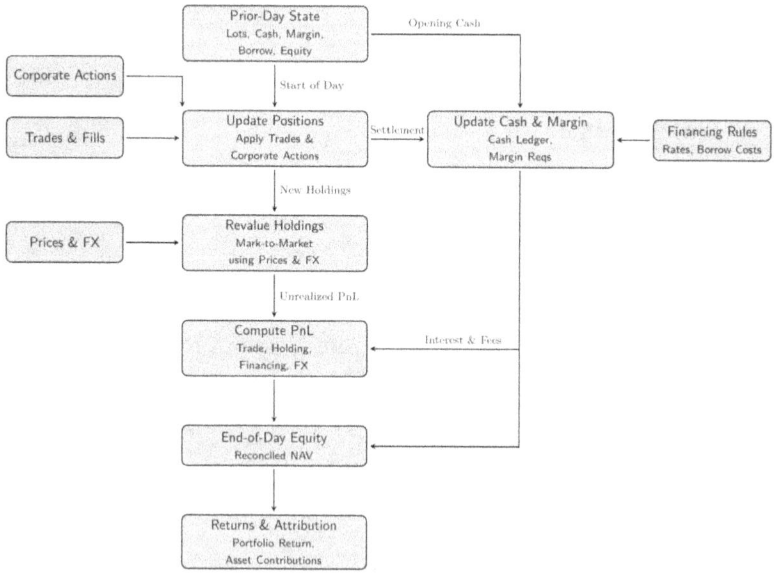

This diagram highlights three ideas:

- Inputs (prior state and events) flow through state updates (positions, cash, valuation).
- PnL is decomposed into components using those updated states.
- Equity and returns are derived outputs, not independent state variables.

A Clean Taxonomy of PnL Components

Before we describe the pipeline step by step, we need a clear vocabulary. A useful breakdown of PnL is:

- **Trade PnL**:
  - realized gains and losses from closing lots via trades,

  - driven by price differences between opening and closing trades,
  - includes slippage and execution effects if modeled.

- **Holding PnL**:
  - mark-to-market gains and losses on open lots due to price changes between valuation points,
  - unrealized until those lots are closed.

- **Fees and commissions**:
  - explicit transaction costs (commissions, exchange fees),
  - possibly taxes or stamp duties if applicable.

- **Financing and borrow costs**:
  - interest on positive and negative cash balances,
  - margin interest on loans,
  - borrow fees on shorts,
  - any rebates or interest on short sale proceeds.

- **Corporate-action-related flows**:
  - cash dividends and distributions,
  - payments in lieu on shorts,
  - merger cash consideration,
  - cash-in-lieu for fractional shares.

- **FX gains and losses**:
  - changes in value from currency movements,
  - applies both to foreign-currency positions and cash balances.

- **Other costs and adjustments** (optional buckets):
  - fund-level management and performance fees,
  - operational costs, if you choose to model them.

The exact granularity of buckets is up to you. The important thing is consistency: every change in equity must belong to *exactly one* PnL or external-flow category.

Step-by-Step Daily PnL Pipeline

Assume you measure performance once per day at market close. A robust pipeline for day D could be:

1. Start from prior-day closing state

Carry forward from day $D-1$:

- lots (open and closed) with their quantities and cost bases,
- cash balances in each bucket,
- margin state (e.g., margin loans, collateral),
- borrow state (short lots and their borrow rates),
- prior-day equity.

This state is your baseline; PnL for day D is defined relative to it.

2. Apply corporate actions effective on day D

Before you process trades or prices, adjust positions and lots for any corporate actions that take effect at or before the day's valuation time:

- split and reverse split: rescale quantities and cost basis per lot,
- stock dividends: increase quantities and adjust per-share cost basis,
- spin-offs: create new lots in child instruments and allocate basis,
- mergers: close lots in target instrument, possibly create lots in acquirer and/or add cash,
- cash dividends: create dividend cash flows for long and short holdings (depending on whether you model them at ex-date or pay date).

Each adjustment is implemented as a transformation on lots and, where applicable, cash ledger entries. Ideally, you also track a *corporate action PnL* bucket to record any minor value leak from rounding or approximations.

3. Process trades and fills for day D

Next, handle all trades that occur during the day:

1. For each fill:
    - update lots: create or close lots as described in the positions section,
    - write trade-related cash ledger entries:
        - principal outflows or inflows,
        - commissions and fees,
        - any taxes or levies.
2. Track **realized trade PnL** at the lot level:
    - whenever a lot is fully or partially closed, record the difference between closing trade price and lot cost basis, scaled by the closed quantity,
    - store this in a trade PnL bucket, keyed by instrument, strategy, or other tags if desired.

At this stage, realized PnL from active trading is fully determined, but unrealized PnL still depends on end-of-day prices.

4. Update cash and margin

Aggregate all cash ledger entries that occurred during the day so far (trades and corporate actions) to update:

- cash balances per bucket and currency,
- settled vs. unsettled cash (if you model settlement lags),
- margin loans and short-sale proceeds (for margin accounts),
- any reserved amounts for collateral.

Then run the margin engine:

- recompute margin requirements based on the updated positions and current prices (for intraday checks, you may use intraday prices; for end-of-day checks, closing prices),

- update buying power,
- detect any margin deficits and, if your model includes them, trigger margin calls and forced liquidations.

Trades generated by margin call liquidation then loop back through the same process: they update lots, cash, and realized PnL.

5. Revalue positions at end-of-day prices and FX

Now mark all open lots to end-of-day prices and exchange rates:

- For each lot:
  - compute its market value in its local currency,
  - if needed, convert that value to base currency using the appropriate FX rate.
- Sum across lots and instruments to obtain:
  - total holdings value,
  - holdings value per instrument, sector, or strategy.

By comparing today's market values with yesterday's (after adjusting for trades and corporate actions), you can compute **holding PnL**:

- the component due purely to price changes in local currency,
- the component due to FX rate changes (if you choose to separate them).

You can store these separately as *price PnL* and *FX PnL* in your PnL buckets.

6. Accrue financing, borrow, and other cost flows

At the end of the day, apply financing rules to cash balances and short positions:

- interest on positive or negative cash balances,
- margin interest on loans,

- borrow fees on short positions (accrued on their market value),
- any rebates or interest on short proceeds.

Mechanically:

1. For each cash bucket:
    - compute interest earned or owed over the day,
    - create a cash ledger entry with the appropriate sign, categorized as financing PnL.
2. For short lots:
    - compute daily borrow fee using the borrow rate and market value,
    - create a negative cash ledger entry in the relevant currency and tag it as borrow cost.

After adding these entries, recompute cash balances and, if needed, update margin one last time (for example, if financing materially changes equity).

7. Compute total PnL and reconcile with equity

At this point you have:

- prior-day equity,
- updated positions, cash, and margin,
- per-bucket PnL figures: trade, holding, fees, financing, borrow, corporate actions, FX, and others,
- external flows: contributions, withdrawals, fund-level fees.

Now:

1. Compute **end-of-day equity** as:
    - holdings value (sum of marked-to-market lot values) plus

   - cash and cash-like balances, net of loans and liabilities.

2. Sum all PnL buckets for the day into a total PnL figure.
3. Verify the central reconciliation identity:

   End-of-day equity = Prior-day equity + Total PnL + Net external flows.

If this identity fails, you have a bug or a missing component. Embedding an assertion for this reconciliation is one of the most important safeguards in the engine.

Mapping PnL to Returns

Once daily PnL and equity are known, computing returns is conceptually straightforward, as described in the previous section.

For each day:

- Let net external flows for the day represent contributions, withdrawals, and any other capital movements that are *not* part of performance.
- Define the daily time-weighted return based on:
  - starting equity for the day,
  - ending equity for the day,
  - net external flows between them.

Because PnL already aggregates all performance-related components (price moves, income, costs), and because you have enforced the equity reconciliation, you can be confident that:

- the daily return derived from equity and flows is consistent with the daily total PnL,
- chaining daily returns over a horizon matches the direct return from start and end equity and flows.

You can then compute:

- cumulative returns over longer windows by compounding daily returns,
- per-asset or per-strategy contributions by mapping each PnL bucket to the relevant asset or group and normalizing by starting equity.

Per-Asset and Factor-Level Attribution

A robust PnL engine should not only tell you *how much* you made or lost, but also *where* it came from. Attribution breaks total PnL and returns into contributions by:

- asset (instrument-level),
- sector, country, or style bucket,
- strategy sleeve or signal,
- PnL type (trade versus holding, financing versus price).

The lot-level and ledger-level design from earlier sections makes this relatively straightforward:

- Each lot is tagged with instrument, strategy, and any other relevant metadata.
- Each cash ledger entry is tagged with a type (commission, dividend, borrow fee, etc.) and often an instrument or strategy.
- The PnL engine can therefore:
  - allocate realized trade PnL to the instrument(s) and strategy that created the closed lots,
  - allocate holding PnL using lot or position weights at the start or end of the period,
  - allocate financing and corporate action flows to the instruments or portfolios that generated them.

Attribution reports then become an aggregation problem: summing per-lot and per-ledger PnL across categories. You can generate, for example:

- daily PnL by instrument and bucket,
- cumulative PnL by strategy sleeve,
- factor-level contributions based on pre-defined instrument-to-factor mappings.

The important constraint is that *all* these breakdowns sum back to the same total PnL and returns that the engine reports at the portfolio level.

Determinism, Idempotence, and Debug Views

Complex accounting logic is only useful if you can trust it. Three properties are especially important:

Determinism

Running the engine twice on the same inputs should produce the same outputs, bit for bit. To achieve this:

- define a strict ordering of events (trades, corporate actions, price marks, financing) within each day,
- avoid randomness in accounting computations, or control it via fixed random seeds where necessary (for example, in simulated slippage),
- avoid hidden side effects that depend on processing order.

Idempotence

Recomputing PnL for a given day from its starting state and events should not double-count anything. If you re-run the daily PnL routine, it should:

- either start from a known prior-day snapshot and re-derive all PnL, discarding the previous day's calculations,

- or be able to detect that PnL entries already exist for that day and overwrite them in a controlled way.

This makes it safe to change parts of the data or logic and recompute PnL history without accumulating errors.

Debug views

When numbers do not look right, you need tools to inspect intermediate quantities. Useful debug views include:

- per-day tables showing:
  - starting equity and positions,
  - PnL components (trade, holding, fees, financing, corporate, FX),
  - external flows,
  - ending equity and returns.
- per-instrument PnL trails:
  - lot histories (open, partial closes, full closes),
  - associated cash flows (commissions, borrow fees, dividends),
  - realized and unrealized PnL over time.
- per-strategy or per-book summaries:
  - daily PnL by bucket,
  - exposure and leverage metrics.

You can also log key invariants daily (such as equity reconciliation) and stop the simulation immediately when they are violated.

Extensibility: Adding New Cost Types and Asset Classes

A good PnL and return engine is not frozen at design time. Over a strategy's life, you may need to:

- introduce new cost types (for example, stock borrow taxes, regulatory levies),
- handle new asset classes (credit, structured products, crypto),
- refine existing models (more accurate financing for futures, new corporate action types).

To make such extensions safe:

- Keep the **core data model** (lots, cash ledger, PnL buckets) stable and generic.
- Add new components as:
  - new event types in the event stream,
  - new columns or categories in the cash ledger,
  - new PnL buckets derived from these events.
- Ensure the equity reconciliation identity still holds with the new components.
- Write migration tools so that historical PnL can be recomputed under the new logic without changing past input data.

When done well, adding a new feature (say, futures transaction taxes) becomes:

- augment the execution model to emit tax cash entries,
- add a "tax" PnL bucket that sums those entries,
- verify that total PnL and equity still reconcile.

You do *not* need to change the fundamental mechanics of how positions or returns are computed.

The PnL and return engine sits at the top of the accounting stack, integrating:

- positions and lots (what you hold and at what cost),

- cash and margin (how holdings are funded and constrained),
- shorting and borrow (obligations and associated fees),
- corporate actions (silent changes in quantities and cash),
- market prices and FX (mark-to-market valuation),
- external flows (capital movements in and out of the portfolio).

By routing all changes through explicit events, lots, and cash ledger entries; by decomposing PnL into clear buckets; and by enforcing reconciliation with equity and returns, you build a system where every reported number can be traced back to concrete economic events. This is the hallmark of a backtest engine whose results you can trust, explain, and defend.

Chapter 6

Validation & Statistical Evaluation

Backtests lie easily-and often without your noticing. This chapter turns your backtest from a persuasive story into a falsifiable statistical object: we will separate in-sample seduction from out-of-sample reality, quantify what we do not know, and build guardrails so that only genuinely robust edges survive the journey from simulation to live trading.

6.1 Train/Test Splits & Walk-Forward

Up to this point we have treated a backtest as a single reconstruction of history under carefully specified data, accounting, and execution assumptions. That is necessary, but it is not sufficient for deciding whether a strategy is likely to work in the future. The central question of validation is: given the outcomes we observe on historical data, how much of that performance is due to genuine structure in markets, and how much is due to luck and overfitting?

To answer that question, we must turn a single historical record into a sequence of realistic experiments. Each experiment should mimic the lifecycle of a live strategy: calibrate on the past, lock the model, run it on unseen data, and then evaluate the outcome. This section shows how to do that systematically with time-aware train/test splits, walk-forward schemes, purged cross-validation, embargo periods, and disciplined hyperparameter tuning. The goal is that any reported "out-of-sample" performance from your backtest engine is truly predictive, not wishful thinking.

Why Random Splits Fail for Financial Data

In many machine learning domains, it is common to take all available data, shuffle it, and then carve out random subsets for training and testing. This relies on an assumption that observations are independent and identically distributed: the order does not matter, yesterday looks like today, and tomorrow will look like both. Under that assumption, a random split can approximate how the model might behave on future samples drawn from the same distribution.

Financial data breaks this picture in several ways:

- **Time order matters.** Prices and returns form time series. A decision at time t uses only information available strictly before or at t. If your split mixes future observations into the training set for decisions in the past, you implicitly give the model access to the future.
- **Dependence over time.** Returns show autocorrelation, volatility clustering, and regime structure. A random split interleaves quiet and stressed periods in a way that never occurs in real time, blurring the true dynamics.
- **Regime shifts.** The relationship between signals and returns can change over years. A model trained on recent data might work on the next year but fail on data from a decade earlier, even if that earlier data looks "similar" in simple statistics.

If you ignore these features and rely on random splits, you will routinely obtain over-optimistic estimates. The model learns from patterns that, in reality, would not have been available at decision time.

This is a variant of look-ahead bias, but now embedded in the validation scheme itself rather than in the raw data.

For a backtest engine that aims at reproducible and honest science, random, order-agnostic splitting should be treated as a red flag. Validation must respect the arrow of time.

Basic Time-Ordered Train/Test Splits

The simplest time-aware split is a chronological cut:

- Use data from a start date up to a split date for training (model fitting, feature selection, and hyperparameter tuning).
- Use data strictly after the split date for testing (fixed model, no further tuning).

For example, you might train on 2010–2017 and test on 2018–2020. This arrangement respects causality: the test period always comes after the train period. It also mimics the real-world scenario of building a strategy today and then running it for the next few years.

This simple split has two major strengths:

- **Clarity.** It is easy to explain and audit. All design decisions were made on data up to the split date; everything after is a clean evaluation.
- **Protection against leakage.** As long as your data fields are themselves free of look-ahead, the split ensures that the model never saw test-period information during training.

However, a single split has limitations:

- **Sensitivity to split date.** If your split happens to cut in the middle of an unusual regime, your estimate of future performance may be unrepresentative.
- **Waste of data.** If you reserve a large chunk as test, you restrict the data available for model design. If you reserve a small chunk, your test results will be noisy.

- **No view of stability over time.** You get one number for out-of-sample Sharpe or drawdown, not a picture of how performance might evolve as the strategy is recalibrated and redeployed.

To address these limitations, we need to turn the single split into a structured sequence of time-ordered experiments: walk-forward validation.

From Single Split to Walk-Forward Experiments

Walk-forward validation is the practice of repeatedly training on a past window and testing on a future window, sliding these windows across the historical record. Conceptually, it simulates the process of a team that periodically retrains its model on recent data and then trades it going forward.

There are two main flavors:

Expanding windows. You begin with an initial training period, say 2010–2014, and test on the next period, 2015. Then you expand the training set to include the previous test year, train on 2010–2015, and test on 2016, and so on. The training set grows over time, always using all data up to the current date.

Rolling windows. Instead of letting the training set grow indefinitely, you fix a window length. For instance, train on the most recent three years, test on the next year, then roll the training window forward by a year. So you might train on 2010–2012, test on 2013; then train on 2011–2013, test on 2014; and so forth.

Expanding windows assume that older data remains relevant indefinitely and that more data is always better. Rolling windows acknowledge that markets have limited memory: data from a decade ago may be less informative about today's regime than data from last year.

In both cases, the key idea is the same: turn your backtest into a sequence of train/test episodes that preserve time order. For each episode, you obtain an out-of-sample performance slice. By stitching these slices together, you can form a pseudo-live equity curve that reflects repeated recalibration and re-deployment.

This sequence of experiments is far more informative than a single split. It tells you:

- How performance changes across regimes.
- Whether the strategy degrades when retrained in different periods.
- How sensitive results are to the exact placement of the split boundaries.

However, even well-designed walk-forward schemes can be misleading if they ignore overlapping information in the data. That leads us to purging and embargoes.

Purged Cross-Validation and Embargo Periods

Financial labels and returns often span multiple periods. For example:

- A trade might be entered today and held for five days; its profit and loss depends on prices over that entire holding period.
- A target variable could be an n-day forward return, so the "label" for day t uses prices from $t + 1$ through $t + n$.

If you train a model on examples whose labels depend on future prices that overlap with your test window, you have an information leak. The model has effectively seen part of the test outcomes during training, even though the raw timestamps may look properly separated.

To handle this, we introduce two concepts:

Purging. When you define a train/test split, you remove from the training set any observations whose label horizon overlaps the test period. If an example's label uses future returns from day $t + 1$ to $t + 5$, and your test period begins on $t+3$, then that example is excluded from training because it "peeks" into the test horizon.

Embargo. Around each test window, you insert a buffer period—an embargo—on both sides, during which no observations are used for training. This protects against more subtle forms of leakage, including overlapping positions, delayed market impact, and feature constructions that blend data across neighboring days.

In practice, you might specify the embargo as a fraction of the test window length or as a fixed number of days. The precise value should be grounded in domain knowledge: typical holding periods, speed of signal decay, and the horizon over which your features and labels interact.

Purged cross-validation combines these ideas with walk-forward or other time-based folds. For each fold:

1. Select a contiguous test window.
2. Apply an embargo around this window.
3. Purge from the training set all examples whose label horizons intersect the embargoed region or the test window.
4. Train on the remaining data and evaluate on the test window.

This procedure limits information leakage even when labels and positions span multiple periods. It is more conservative than simple time splits, but in finance conservatism is a virtue: if a strategy only looks good when you allow a bit of future information to slip into training, it is unlikely to survive live trading.

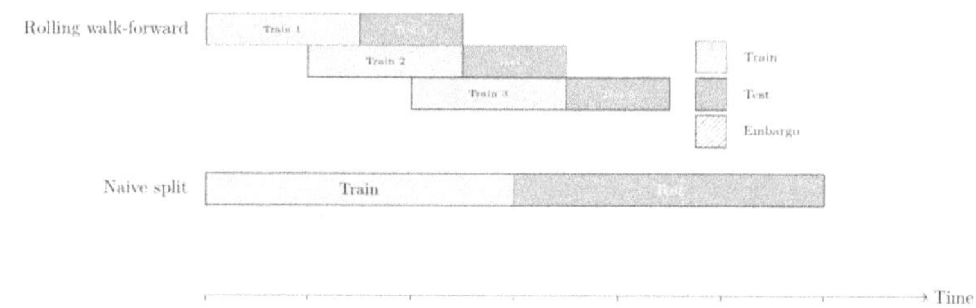

Hyperparameter Tuning as a Nested Process

Choosing model hyperparameters—such as regularization strength, tree depth, learning rates, or lookback windows—is a form of optimization. If you tune these hyperparameters by examining performance on a given test period, you are leaking information from that test back into training. The test set becomes part of the training process, and its performance no longer represents a true out-of-sample estimate.

To avoid this, hyperparameter tuning must be organized as a nested process:

- **Outer loop:** defines train/test splits used purely for performance estimation.
- **Inner loop:** operates only within the training portion of each outer split to select hyperparameters.

For each outer fold:

1. Take the designated training window (already purified and embargoed, as needed).
2. Within that training window, construct inner validation splits (for example, additional time-based folds).
3. For each candidate hyperparameter configuration, train on the inner-training slices and evaluate on the inner-validation slices.
4. Select the configuration that gives the best inner-validation performance.
5. Refit the model on the full outer training window using the chosen configuration.
6. Evaluate the refit model on the outer test window exactly once, without further tuning.

This structure ensures that the outer test windows remain untouched by the model-selection process. Their results are therefore a fairer approximation of what would happen when you deploy the model, tune it on historical data only, and then let it run on future data.

From an engine-design perspective, this nesting has several implications:

- **Configuration.** The engine must allow researchers to specify both outer and inner splitting schemes. These should be first-class configuration objects, not ad hoc scripts.
- **Reproducibility.** Every outer fold and inner tuning run should be logged with identifiers for:
  - Train/test window boundaries.
  - Embargo lengths and purging rules.
  - Hyperparameter settings tried.
  - Random seeds used (for any stochastic model components).
- **Cost-awareness.** Nested validation is computationally expensive. The engine should support caching intermediate results, parallel execution of independent folds, and resumption of long-running jobs.

The extra complexity is worth it: nested time-based validation greatly reduces the risk that an apparent edge is merely a byproduct of aggressive hyperparameter search on a fixed test set.

Generating Window Schedules in the Engine

Behind every validation scheme lies a concrete schedule of windows: which timestamps belong to training, which to testing, which to embargo, and which to purge. In an industrial backtest engine, this schedule should not be hand-crafted in notebooks; it should be generated, stored, and audited by the core system.

A practical design is to treat the schedule as a data structure that maps:

- A validation run identifier.
- A fold index (outer and, optionally, inner).
- A timestamp or bar index.

to a label such as TRAIN, TEST, EMBARGO, or PURGED. Once generated, this schedule is immutable for that run. The simulation layer simply respects it:

- During model fitting, it only consumes examples marked TRAIN.
- During evaluation, it only generates metrics on TEST.
- No examples from EMBARGO or PURGED are used to inform model parameters.

Key implementation considerations include:

Calendar awareness. Schedules must be built on the same trading calendar and bar definitions used by the data engine. If your data includes multiple time zones, asset classes, or irregular sessions, the schedule generator must operate on a canonical index that the rest of the system understands.

Parameterization. Users should be able to specify high-level parameters: initial train length, test window length, step size between windows, rolling vs. expanding behavior, label horizon (for purging), and embargo length. The engine translates these into precise boundaries.

Determinism. When randomization is necessary (for example, in more complex cross-validation patterns), the random seeds and any stochastic choices must be recorded. Two runs with the same configuration and data version should generate identical schedules.

Versioning and lineage. Schedules are part of the experiment lineage alongside data versions, feature sets, and execution assumptions. When you revisit an old result, you should be able to reconstruct the exact train/test assignment that produced it.

By elevating window schedules to first-class citizens, you reduce the risk of silent errors such as off-by-one boundaries, misplaced embargoes, or misaligned calendars. These are common sources of "mysterious" performance gains in ad hoc research code.

From Windowed Results to Predictive Insight

Once your engine produces performance statistics for each outer test window, the final task is to interpret them correctly. It is tempting to aggregate all out-of-sample trades into one big sample and compute a single Sharpe ratio or drawdown. That is useful, but you can do more.

A structured analysis of windowed results can answer questions like:

- **Stability.** Does performance remain roughly similar across different windows, or does it depend heavily on particular years or regimes?
- **Adaptivity.** Does retraining help? Compare walk-forward schemes that retrain frequently to a baseline where the model is trained once and then frozen.
- **Sensitivity to design choices.** How much do results change when you vary train/test lengths, rolling vs. expanding windows, or embargo durations?

Because each window is a self-contained experiment, you can also attach confidence intervals and uncertainty measures to each slice (using resampling methods from later sections). This reinforces the idea that a backtest is not a single number but a distribution of possible outcomes.

Finally, it is crucial that the reporting layer keeps a strict boundary between:

- **In-sample results:** metrics computed on data used directly or indirectly for model tuning.
- **Out-of-sample results:** metrics computed on outer test windows untouched by model selection.

The latter are the only numbers that deserve to be interpreted as forecasts of future performance. Everything else is exploratory: useful for understanding, but not for promising returns to investors or risk managers.

Putting It All Together

Turning historical data into a sequence of realistic experiments requires several ingredients to work in concert:

1. Respect the arrow of time by abandoning random, order-agnostic splits in favor of chronological train/test divisions.
2. Use walk-forward schemes—expanding or rolling windows—to simulate repeated cycles of calibration and deployment.
3. Apply purging and embargoes to prevent labels and positions that span multiple periods from leaking information into training.
4. Treat hyperparameter tuning as a nested process, with inner validation operating strictly within each outer training window.
5. Implement window schedule generation, storage, and auditing as core engine features, bound to the same calendars and data versions as the rest of the system.
6. Analyze windowed results as a panel of experiments, focusing on stability, regime dependence, and robustness rather than a single headline number.

When these practices are embedded in your backtest engine, they become default guardrails: every new strategy, no matter who develops it, benefits from the same disciplined validation. The result is a research environment where out-of-sample performance estimates are hard-earned, defensible, and genuinely informative about how a strategy might behave when it finally leaves the backtest and meets the future.

6.2 Backtest Biases & Guardrails

In the previous section we focused on *how* to slice history into train and test windows so that our performance estimates are meaningfully out-of-sample. Even with perfect windowing, however, a backtest can still deceive you. Data may quietly include information from the future, missing assets may be silently dropped, latencies may be ignored, and strategy choices may be made after peeking at too many results.

This section catalogues the main ways backtests go wrong and, more importantly, the *engine-level guardrails* that can prevent these errors from appearing in performance reports. You should view these guardrails the way engineers view circuit breakers: they are not optional features; they are structural protections without which the system is unsafe.

We will organize the discussion around several recurring bias families:

- Look-ahead bias
- Survivorship and backfill bias
- Selection and data-snooping bias
- Latency, microstructure, and execution realism bias
- Miscellaneous structural biases (such as unrealistic funding, fees, or corporate actions)

For each, we will explain *how* it arises, *what symptoms* it produces in performance metrics, and *what concrete checks* your backtest engine should enforce.

Look-Ahead Bias: When the Future Leaks Into the Past

Look-ahead bias occurs whenever a strategy uses information that would not have been known at the time the decision was made. It is conceptually simple yet astonishingly common in practice.

Common sources of look-ahead

- **End-of-day versus intraday decisions.** Using the full day's close price or volume to decide on a trade that is timestamped earlier in the same day. If your event engine triggers an order at 10:00 but uses features computed with that day's closing price, it has seen into the future.

- **Corporate actions and fundamentals.** Adjusted prices, split factors, dividends, index membership flags, and financial statement values often become *effective* in your data before they were actually known in real time. For example, a quarterly earnings figure might be included in the database from the period end date, whereas in the real world it was published weeks later.
- **Benchmarks and factors.** Using returns of a benchmark index or style factor that are known only after market close as inputs into intraday signals.
- **Target leakage.** When building predictive models, any feature constructed from the same window of data as the label (for example, using next month's volatility to forecast next month's return) will generally leak the outcome into the predictors.

How look-ahead bias shows up in results

Backtests infected with look-ahead bias usually look *too good to be true*. Tell-tale signs include:

- Extremely high hit rates or Sharpe ratios for simple signals.
- Strategies that trade near the close with uncanny accuracy.
- Perfectly timed entries around news events or reversals.

But by the time you see these symptoms, you are already late. The engine should prevent such biases before any strategy runs.

Guardrails against look-ahead

At the engine level, guardrails should include:

Effective timestamps for all data fields. Every data field—prices, volumes, fundamentals, index membership, risk factors—must be accompanied by an "as of" or effective timestamp: the time at which a trader could reasonably have known this value. The event engine must then enforce a rule: *a decision at time t may only use fields with effective times at or before t.*

Causality checks. The engine can implement invariant checks that trigger errors when:

- A feature references a data point whose effective time is later than the decision time.
- A model fit uses labels or targets with timestamps that are not strictly in the future of the features but then are later reused to drive decisions at those feature times.

These checks can be implemented as assertions in the data access layer and as audit logs of feature usage.

Intraday bar semantics. For intraday data, the engine should define clear semantics: for example, a bar labeled "10:00–10:05" might be interpreted as available only after 10:05. If a strategy wishes to trade based on that bar, its trade must occur no earlier than the bar's end time (or with a realistic latency). The engine should forbid placing trades that reference yet-unfinished bars.

Data field metadata. The data catalog should mark which fields are safe for same-period use (for example, open prices at the start of the bar) and which are end-of-period only (for example, close prices, volume). Any misuse of end-of-period fields before the period ends should trigger warnings or errors.

Survivorship and Backfill Bias: Over-Clean Histories

Survivorship bias arises when your historical universe includes only assets that survived to the end of the sample, omitting those that were delisted, merged, or went bankrupt. Backfill bias arises when historical data is filled in later, often only for assets that "made it" into some index or database.

How survivorship and backfill appear in practice

- **Index constituents.** If you backtest a stock strategy using the constituents of a broad index as of today and project them backward in time, you are implicitly ignoring companies that left the index along the way. These dropped names often performed poorly.

- **Database membership.** Some commercial databases only include securities or funds that meet certain criteria, such as a minimum history length or assets under management. They may load full histories only after those criteria are met, retroactively "backfilling" the time series.
- **Delisting data gaps.** If your data vendor omits the final, often abrupt decline of a security into bankruptcy, your backtest will never experience those losses.

The net effect is that your investable universe appears cleaner and more profitable than the one you would have faced in real time. This typically inflates returns and understates drawdowns, especially for long-only, high-capacity strategies.

Guardrails against survivorship and backfill

Engine-level protections include:

Universe definitions with effective dates. Rather than specifying the universe as "the S&P 500," define it as a time series of membership sets: for each date, which symbols are eligible? This can be stored as a mapping from dates to asset lists or as per-asset membership intervals. The engine then enforces that:

- A strategy can only trade assets that are in the eligible universe on that date.
- Entry and exit from the universe is treated as an event, possibly triggering forced liquidations or prohibiting new positions.

Delisting-aware price series. The market data layer should incorporate delisting events. When an asset delists, its final cash flows (including residual value or zero recovery) should be reflected in the return series. The accounting engine should then realize the full economic impact of such events.

Data provenance and flags. Data tables should carry metadata about their construction:

- Were series backfilled?

- Is the universe survivorship-free?
- Are there known gaps for delisted names?

If a user attempts to run a "production-grade" validation on data flagged as survivorship-biased, the engine should emit a prominent warning and require explicit override.

Universe snapshots stored with runs. For reproducibility and auditing, each backtest run should store a snapshot or reference to the exact universe definition used: which assets were eligible on each date. This allows later reviewers to verify that survivorship-free universes were applied.

Selection and Data-Snooping Bias: Too Many Shots on Goal

Selection bias arises when you focus on strategies that looked good in backtests, without properly accounting for the fact that you tried many others that did not. Data-snooping bias is the broader tendency to discover patterns by repeatedly probing the same dataset and then overestimating their persistence.

In modern quant research, this is perhaps the most pervasive bias. With flexible tooling and rich data, it is easy to try hundreds of ideas and only report the winners.

How selection and data-snooping bias creep in

- **Parameter over-search.** You run a grid search over thousands of hyperparameter combinations and pick the one with the best backtest. Even if no true edge exists, one configuration is likely to look great just by luck.
- **Unlogged experiments.** You casually try many variations in notebooks or scripts—different indicators, filters, risk rules—without logging them. Only the few that "work" get committed or presented.
- **Cherry-picked time periods.** You find that a strategy does especially well in a particular decade or market regime and empha-

size that period in presentations, quietly ignoring less flattering windows.

- **Peeking at the test set.** After seeing that out-of-sample performance is disappointing, you tweak the model or features and rerun the backtest on the same test period. Over time, the test set becomes part of your training loop.

The main symptom is an impressive-looking strategy that later fails to replicate in new data or live trading. Unfortunately, by the time this happens, much time and capital may already have been invested.

Guardrails against selection and data-snooping

Unlike look-ahead and survivorship, which can often be caught mechanically, selection bias is as much a process problem as a technical one. Still, the engine and its surrounding infrastructure can enforce discipline:

Experiment logging and identifiers. Every backtest run should be recorded with a unique identifier and associated metadata:

- Strategy code version and configuration.
- Data versions and universes used.
- Train/test window definitions and validation schemes.
- Hyperparameter search space and selection criteria.

A central experiment store allows you to count how many distinct strategies or parameter combinations were tried, even if most were abandoned. This is a precondition for adjusting for multiple testing later in the chapter.

Preregistration of evaluation criteria. Before running large searches, the research process should encourage (or require) you to declare:

- Which metrics will be used to judge success (for example, out-of-sample Sharpe above a threshold, maximum drawdown below a threshold).

- Which data period and universe constitute the final "confirmation" set.

The engine can support this by letting users flag certain splits as *holdout* or *confirmation* sets that are locked after first evaluation. Any attempt to rerun model selection using information from those sets can be blocked or at least logged as a protocol violation.

Separation of exploratory and confirmatory runs. It is useful to distinguish:

- *Exploratory runs*, where many ideas are tried and flexibility is high. Results from these runs are treated as hypothesis generators, not final evidence.
- *Confirmatory runs*, where a small set of pre-specified strategies are evaluated on untouched data. Only these runs should contribute to claims about future performance.

The engine can enforce separate namespaces or tags for exploratory versus confirmatory runs and restrict access to holdout data for exploratory runs.

Automatic reporting of search scope. When presenting performance for a chosen strategy, the reporting layer can automatically include context:

- How many parameter combinations were evaluated?
- Was this strategy the top performer among a larger set?
- Were multiple similar signals explored?

Even simple counts can dramatically change the interpretation of a p-value or t-statistic. Later sections on multiple testing will build on this information.

Latency, Microstructure, and Execution Realism

Many backtests assume that trades are immediately and fully executed at a convenient price: often the last traded price or the midquote of the bar. In real markets, latency, order queues, bid–ask spreads, and impact all intervene.

Sources of execution-related bias

- **Ignoring latency.** A strategy might observe a price move and react instantly in the backtest, whereas in live trading network and processing latency impose delays. If the signal is fast-moving, this difference can be decisive.
- **Unrealistic fills.** Assuming you can always trade at the bar's close price, or at the midquote, regardless of order size and market conditions. This often underestimates slippage and ignores the fact that your order may move the price.
- **Queue position.** For limit order strategies, backtests may assume you get filled as soon as price touches your limit, disregarding the existing queue of orders at that price and your place in it.
- **Ignoring partial fills and liquidity constraints.** Backtests may instantly resize large positions without testing whether sufficient volume traded at the chosen price.

These simplifications bias performance upward, especially for high-frequency or high-capacity strategies.

Guardrails for execution realism

An honest engine should:

Model latency explicitly. Let every strategy have an associated latency profile: time from observation to order submission, and from submission to potential fill. The event engine should schedule order effects accordingly. At a minimum, the engine should prevent a strategy from trading based on information that arrived in the same instant as the trade.

Separate quote and trade prices. Data models should distinguish:

- Best bid and ask (with spread).
- Last trade prices and sizes.

By default, the engine should use conservative assumptions: for market orders, fills at the bid when selling and at the ask when buying; for aggressive orders, additional slippage in illiquid or volatile markets. Using midquotes or last prices should be treated as an optimistic choice, clearly flagged in configuration and reports.

Liquidity and volume checks. The execution model should compare the strategy's order size to observed traded volume and, optionally, to estimates of depth at the best prices. If the order is too large to be filled at the assumed price without moving the market, the engine should:

- Limit the filled quantity.
- Apply price impact penalties.
- Or reject the backtest configuration as unrealistic for the chosen capacity.

Queue modeling for limit orders. At finer time scales, limit order backtests should approximate the order book queue. While detailed modeling may be complex, the engine can at least avoid the naive assumption that every limit order at the touch is instantly filled upon price touch.

Execution realism flags in reports. Every backtest report should summarize key execution assumptions:

- Average slippage model used.
- Latency assumptions.
- Volume utilization relative to market volume.

This makes unrealistic assumptions visible and open to challenge.

Other Structural Biases: Funding, Fees, and Corporate Actions

Several additional biases arise from simplifying the economic environment:

- **Ignoring transaction costs and fees.** Backtests that omit commissions, exchange fees, bid–ask spreads, and borrow costs for shorting will systematically overstate performance, especially for high-turnover or short-heavy strategies.
- **Unrealistic funding and leverage.** Using leverage without modeling margin requirements, financing rates, or capital constraints can make strategies appear more scalable than they are.
- **Misapplied corporate actions.** Failing to adjust for splits, dividends, and rights issues correctly can distort returns and make naïve buy-and-hold appear unusually profitable or unprofitable.

Guardrails here are largely about making sure that the accounting and data layers are complete and internally consistent:

Cost-aware accounting as default. The portfolio accounting engine should always include a realistic baseline of trading and funding costs, even if very simple. Setting costs to zero should require an explicit override and generate a visible warning.

Leverage and margin checks. The engine should enforce leverage limits, margin calls, and capital constraints as part of the simulation, not just as post-hoc metrics. Any breach of these constraints should be recorded and, by default, treated as a failure of the strategy configuration.

Verified corporate action processing. Data ingestion pipelines should apply corporate actions in a way that preserves economic equivalence: reinvesting dividends, adjusting prices and volumes for splits, and aligning these with the trading calendar. The engine can run invariants, such as checking that a buy-and-hold position's cumulative return matches the total-return index for the same asset, within tolerance.

Embedding Guardrails into the Development Process

It is not enough to define guardrails; they must be impossible to bypass accidentally. This is where integration with your broader development workflow matters.

Engine-level invariants and tests

Many of the checks described above can be encoded as automated tests:

- Unit tests for data access functions that ensure effective times are respected.
- Integration tests that run simple strategies on known datasets and verify that returns match expected values when corporate actions, fees, and slippage are applied.
- Regression tests that assert that survivorship-free universes remain so as data updates.

These tests should be part of your continuous integration (CI) pipeline. Any change in data models, accounting logic, or execution assumptions that violates them should fail the build.

Default-safe configurations

The engine should be configured so that:

- The default universe is survivorship-free where possible.
- The default data view includes realistic costs and latency.
- The default validation scheme is time-aware and includes basic purging/embargo rules when appropriate.

Researchers can still override these defaults when experimenting, but doing so should require explicit configuration changes that are visible in logs and reports.

Transparent reporting and auditability

Finally, every performance report should include a concise "assumptions summary":

- Data versions and any known biases (survivorship, backfill).
- Execution model and cost assumptions.

- Validation and splitting scheme.
- Number of strategies or parameter sets evaluated in the broader project.

Coupled with stored run metadata, this allows auditors—including your future self—to reconstruct the exact environment in which a result was produced and to judge its reliability.

From Deception to Discipline

Backtests are powerful because they let us explore an enormous design space cheaply. They are dangerous for the same reason: without guardrails, it is too easy to fool ourselves. Look-ahead, survivorship, selection pressure, unrealistic execution, and sloppy economics all push performance upward, just enough to be tempting and just enough to fail when real money is at stake.

The remedy is to bake discipline into the engine. Treat every source of bias as a potential system invariant: something the engine can detect, prevent, or at least surface conspicuously. When an apparent edge survives these filters—honest data, realistic execution, disciplined validation, and transparent accounting—it is still no guarantee of success, but it is far more likely to represent genuine structure in markets rather than a mirage of our own making.

In the next sections we will build on this foundation, quantifying uncertainty in backtest results through resampling and bootstrap methods, and addressing the statistical issues that arise when many strategies are tested in parallel.

6.3 Resampling & Bootstrap Methods

In the previous sections we were careful about *how* we carve history into train and test windows and how we avoid the main structural biases in backtesting. We now turn to a different question: even if a backtest has been designed correctly, *how much should we trust the numbers it produces?*

Any performance statistic—a Sharpe ratio, a maximum drawdown, a win rate—is computed from a finite sample of returns. If we had observed a different but equally plausible market history, the statistic would have taken a different value. This sampling variability is not a nuisance; it is an essential part of how we should interpret the backtest. A Sharpe ratio of 1.0 with a wide confidence interval is very different from a Sharpe of 1.0 with a narrow one.

Resampling and bootstrap methods give us a practical toolkit to quantify this variability. They let us construct confidence intervals and uncertainty bands for performance metrics by repeatedly recomputing them on synthetic samples that resemble the observed data. For financial returns, however, we must take special care: returns are not independent from one period to the next, and naïve resampling schemes that ignore this dependence can be badly misleading. That is where *block bootstrap* and its relatives come in.

Why Classical IID Bootstrap Fails for Returns

The basic bootstrap idea is simple. Suppose you have a sample of daily returns from a strategy. The naïve bootstrap would:

1. Treat these returns as independent observations from an underlying distribution.
2. Draw many resamples of the same length by picking returns at random, with replacement, from the original sample.
3. For each resample, recompute your statistic of interest (for example, the Sharpe ratio).
4. Use the distribution of these resampled statistics to form confidence intervals.

This works reasonably well in domains where the independence assumption is approximately true. In finance, that assumption is usually false:

- **Autocorrelation.** Returns may exhibit short-term momentum or mean reversion. Yesterday's move influences today's.

- **Volatility clustering.** Periods of high volatility tend to be followed by further high volatility; quiet periods cluster as well. The distribution of returns is not stable over time.
- **Regime switches.** Markets go through distinct phases: bull trends, crises, range-bound periods. The behavior of the strategy (and its risk) can be very different in each regime.
- **Strategy structure.** Many strategies hold positions for multiple days or weeks. The profit or loss from one day is not independent of the next; it is part of a longer trade.

If we resample individual days independently, we destroy this temporal structure. The synthetic paths mix high- and low-volatility days in unrealistic sequences. They break up runs of wins and losses that matter for drawdowns and behavioral risk. As a result, naïve bootstrap confidence intervals for things like maximum drawdown, tail loss, or even Sharpe ratio can be far too optimistic or simply inaccurate.

The central insight of block bootstrap methods is that while individual daily returns may not be independent, *blocks* of consecutive returns often behave more like self-contained units. By resampling blocks rather than single days, we can preserve important dependencies within blocks while still generating many alternative histories.

From Individual Days to Blocks of Returns

To see the logic, imagine a medium-speed equity strategy with a typical holding period of one week. Over any given week, its positions are relatively stable; from one week to the next, it may rotate or rebalance. The natural time unit for this strategy is not a single day but roughly a week.

If we carve the return series into overlapping or non-overlapping one-week blocks and resample those blocks, each block carries with it the within-week dependence structure: volatility, serial correlation, and any pattern of wins and losses over the holding period. By stitching such blocks together, we create alternative histories that:

- Respect the typical holding period.

- Preserve realistic clusters of volatility and performance.
- Shuffle the sequence of weeks in a way that reflects uncertainty about the order and combination of regimes.

Of course, real strategies may have more complex dynamics than a single fixed horizon. But the guiding principle remains: choose block lengths that reflect the time scales over which your strategy's returns are strongly dependent.

Fixed-Length Block Bootstrap

The simplest block bootstrap uses fixed-length blocks:

1. Choose a block length, for example 5 days, 20 days, or 60 days.
2. Form a set of consecutive blocks from the historical series. You can use:
    - Non-overlapping blocks (for example, days 1–5, 6–10, 11–15, and so on), or
    - Overlapping blocks (for example, 1–5, 2–6, 3–7, which produces more blocks).
3. To generate a bootstrap path of the same total length as the original, sample blocks with replacement and concatenate them until you reach or exceed the desired length (trimming excess at the end if necessary).
4. Compute cumulative returns and any performance metrics on this synthetic path.
5. Repeat many times to obtain a distribution of metrics.

Fixed-length blocks are easy to implement and interpret. They guarantee that within each block, the original time ordering and dependencies are preserved. Across blocks, you are deliberately shuffling regimes and transitions, which is precisely what we want when asking, "What would this strategy's performance look like across other plausible orderings of similar conditions?"

The key design choice is the block length. Short blocks (for example, 2–3 days) treat dependencies as very local; they may break up longer trades or volatility clusters. Long blocks (for example, 60 days) preserve longer patterns but provide fewer independent building blocks, which increases variability in the resampled statistics and can make confidence bands wider.

In practice, you can choose block lengths based on:

- The strategy's typical holding period.
- The time scale over which your signals decay.
- Empirical measures of how quickly autocorrelation in returns or squared returns decays.

There is no single correct choice, but it is better to err on the side of longer blocks than to ignore dependence altogether.

Moving Block and Stationary Bootstrap

Fixed-length blocks are a starting point. Two closely related variants provide additional flexibility:

Moving block bootstrap

In the moving block bootstrap, you consider all overlapping blocks of a given length. If your series has T days and blocks of length L, you obtain $T - L + 1$ blocks: days 1–L, 2–$L + 1$, and so on. You then resample from this richer set of blocks.

The advantage is that overlapping blocks give you more distinct patterns to choose from, especially when T is not much larger than L. They also smooth out edge effects that can arise when using non-overlapping blocks.

Stationary bootstrap

The stationary bootstrap goes one step further by randomizing block lengths:

- You choose an average block length, say L.

- To construct a synthetic path, you:

    1. Pick a random starting point in the original series.
    2. With a certain probability (related to $1/L$), you either extend the current block by one more day or restart a new block at another random position.
    3. Continue joining days in this way until you reach the desired path length.

This procedure results in an expected block length of L but with randomness around it. The synthetic path is "stationary" in the sense that any day from the original series is equally likely to appear at any position in the bootstrap sample, and dependence within blocks is preserved.

Randomizing block lengths can better mimic realistic variations in regime durations and holding periods. It also avoids the artificial periodicities that can occur when every block has exactly the same length.

What to Bootstrap: Returns, Trades, or Days?

So far we have spoken loosely about bootstrapping "returns." In a well-designed backtest engine, you have several levels at which you might apply bootstrap methods:

- **Daily (or bar-level) portfolio returns.** This is the most straightforward representation: a time series of portfolio-level returns. Bootstrapping at this level is appropriate when you care primarily about portfolio-level metrics such as Sharpe ratio, drawdown, or volatility.

- **Per-trade results.** For strategies with discrete trades of varying lengths, you can treat each completed trade as an observation with an entry date, exit date, and total return. Blocks may correspond to groups of trades. Bootstrapping trades is useful for assessing variability in measures such as average trade return, holding time, or trade-level profit factor.

- **Regime segments.** You may partition history into regimes based on exogenous indicators (for example, high versus low volatility environments, bull versus bear markets) and treat each regime as a block. Resampling regimes can help answer questions like, "What if the next decade resembled a random reordering of past regimes?"

The right choice depends on the question you're asking and on the structure of the strategy. The key is to ensure that the bootstrap units—days, trades, or regimes—are large enough to capture the important dependencies that affect your metrics.

Constructing Confidence Intervals and Uncertainty Bands

Once you have a block bootstrap mechanism in place, constructing confidence intervals for performance metrics follows a common pattern:

1. Run the original backtest and compute the "observed" value of the metric, such as a Sharpe ratio, a maximum drawdown, or a cumulative return over the test period.
2. Generate a large number of bootstrap resamples: for each one, create a synthetic return path by resampling blocks and then compute the metric for that path.
3. Collect all the bootstrap metric values and examine their empirical distribution.
4. Form confidence intervals by taking appropriate percentiles. For example, the interval between the 2.5th and 97.5th percentiles is a commonly used 95% confidence interval.

Interpreting these intervals is intuitive: they tell you the range of metric values you might reasonably expect to see if the underlying data-generating process were similar to what you observed, but history unfolded in a different way.

Beyond single-number intervals, bootstrapping is particularly powerful for constructing *uncertainty bands* around the entire equity curve:

1. For each bootstrap resample, construct the cumulative return path over time.
2. At each time point (for example, each day), collect the cumulative returns across all resamples.
3. For each time point, compute percentiles across resamples, such as the 5th, 50th (median), and 95th percentiles.
4. Plot the original equity curve together with, for example, the median curve and a shaded band between the 5th and 95th percentiles.

This visualization lets you see not just "How likely is this final cumulative return?" but "How wide is the range of plausible equity curves at each point in time?" Strategies with similar final performance may differ greatly in the width and shape of these uncertainty bands.

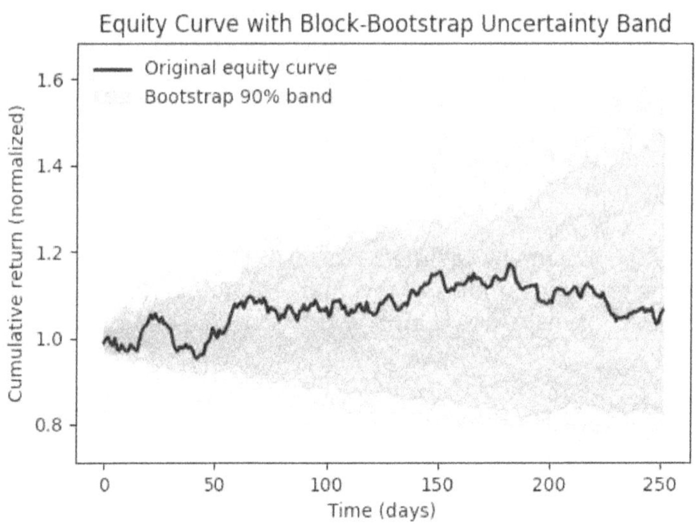

Choosing Block Length: Bias–Variance Trade-offs

The choice of block length is central to block bootstrap methods. It governs a trade-off between:

- **Bias.** If blocks are too short, important dependencies stretch across multiple blocks and are broken when you resample. This can bias your estimates by underrepresenting extended runs of good or bad performance.
- **Variance.** If blocks are too long, you have relatively few distinct blocks to resample. Synthetic paths will look very similar to the original, and your bootstrap distribution will be narrow, potentially understating uncertainty.

In addition to domain knowledge about holding periods and regimes, you can use empirical diagnostics:

- Plot autocorrelation of returns and squared returns. Blocks should be long enough that correlations beyond the block length are modest.
- Experiment with different block lengths and compare resulting confidence intervals. If intervals change dramatically when you shorten blocks slightly, your original choice may have been too aggressive.
- Consider using an average block length (as in the stationary bootstrap) rather than a fixed one, to smooth sensitivity.

A practical approach is to define a reasonable range of block lengths based on your understanding of the strategy and to report how sensitive your conclusions are to choices within that range.

Integrating Bootstrap Engines into the Backtest Framework

To make resampling and bootstrap analysis a routine part of validation rather than a one-off exercise, your backtest engine should treat bootstrap generation as a first-class component.

Key design considerations include:

Separation of concerns. The backtest engine should produce a clean, time-stamped series of portfolio returns (and possibly per-trade records) for each outer test window defined by your train/test splitting scheme. A separate *bootstrap engine* can then consume these series and generate resampled paths and metrics. This avoids entangling simulation with statistical analysis.

Configuration and reproducibility. Bootstrap runs should be fully configurable:

- Choice of bootstrap method (fixed-length blocks, moving blocks, stationary).
- Block length or average block length.
- Number of bootstrap resamples.
- Level of confidence intervals (for example, 90%, 95%).

All these parameters, together with random seeds, should be logged and stored with the experiment so that bootstrap results can be reproduced exactly later.

Random number management. Bootstrap procedures rely on pseudorandom draws. In a reproducible engine:

- Each bootstrap job should have a documented seed or seed sequence.
- Seeds should be managed centrally to avoid accidental correlations across parallel jobs.
- Where appropriate, you can use variance-reduction techniques (such as antithetic variates) to improve the stability of interval estimates without increasing the number of resamples.

Parallelization. Each bootstrap resample is independent of the others, making the workload embarrassingly parallel. The engine should exploit this by:

- Distributing resamples across cores or machines.
- Streaming results back to an aggregator that computes percentiles and intervals incrementally.

Storage of indices and paths. For audit purposes, you may wish to store:

- The sequence of block indices used to construct each bootstrap path.
- Or at least a compressed representation of bootstrap paths for selected runs.

This allows you to debug unusual results, verify that resampling respects time ordering and block boundaries, and, if necessary, recompute new metrics from the same resampled paths.

Using Bootstrap Results Responsibly

Bootstrap methods are powerful, but they have limits and should be interpreted with care:

- **They reflect the past.** Bootstrap resamples are built from historical data. If the future contains regimes that are qualitatively different from anything seen before, bootstrap-based intervals will not anticipate them.
- **They approximate, not guarantee.** Confidence intervals produced by block bootstrap methods are approximations whose accuracy depends on block choices, sample size, and the nature of dependencies. They should be viewed as informative ranges, not strict guarantees.
- **They interact with other biases.** If the original backtest suffers from look-ahead bias, survivorship bias, or unrealistic execution assumptions, the bootstrap will faithfully propagate those distortions. Bootstrap does not fix bad data or flawed models.
- **They can be misused.** It is tempting to report only the most favorable intervals or to ignore bootstrap results that contradict a preferred narrative. To prevent this, integrate bootstrap reporting into the standard performance summaries produced by the engine so that uncertainty measures appear alongside point estimates by default.

Despite these caveats, bootstrap and resampling methods represent a substantial improvement over treating backtest metrics as fixed numbers. They help shift thinking from "Our expected Sharpe is 1.0" to "Given what we have seen, a Sharpe of 1.0 is plausible, but values between, say, 0.4 and 1.6 are also reasonably consistent with the data."

Connecting Back to Validation and Guardrails

Conceptually, bootstrap methods complement the validation tools introduced earlier:

- Train/test splits and walk-forward schemes aim to reduce systematic over-optimism by enforcing strict separation between model design and evaluation.
- Guardrails against look-ahead, survivorship, and execution bias aim to remove structural distortions in how we simulate the strategy.
- Bootstrap methods quantify the *residual uncertainty* that remains even after these protections are in place.

In a mature backtest engine, these elements should work together:

1. Run the strategy under realistic data and execution assumptions, with proper temporal validation, to produce out-of-sample return series.
2. Feed these series into a bootstrap engine that respects the dependence structure of returns.
3. Report not just point estimates of performance but full distributions and confidence bands, with clear documentation of bootstrap settings.

This combination moves you from backtests as sales tools—sleek equity curves and single-number Sharpe ratios—to backtests as scientific instruments, capable of expressing both what you know and what you do not know about a strategy's behavior under uncertain future conditions.

In the next section, we will build on this foundation to address another source of over-optimism: the explosion of hypotheses in modern quant research and the need to control for multiple testing and false discoveries when searching for new alphas.

6.4 Multiple Testing & False Discovery

By now we have a backtest engine that respects time, defends against the most important structural biases, and quantifies sampling variability with resampling methods. Yet there is another, more subtle source of over-optimism that arises not from *how* we simulate a given strategy, but from *how many* strategies we simulate.

Modern research environments make it easy to try vast numbers of ideas: different signals, parameter grids, feature transforms, execution rules, and universes. If we then select only the best-looking results and ignore the rest, we are almost guaranteed to "discover" spurious edges that will not hold up in the future. This is the problem of multiple testing and false discovery.

This section explains how extensive strategy and parameter searches inflate false positives, and introduces tools such as Bonferroni and Holm corrections, along with false discovery rate (FDR) control, to keep our "discovered" alphas statistically honest. We will also discuss how to embed these ideas into the backtest engine so that they appear automatically in performance reports.

Why Many Backtests Guarantee Some "Success"

Suppose you have a single strategy idea and you backtest it once on a clean, out-of-sample dataset. You compute a performance statistic and a corresponding significance measure: for example, a t-statistic or p-value for the null hypothesis that the true Sharpe ratio is zero.

If that p-value is small (say below 5%), you might tentatively conclude that the strategy has a real edge rather than being pure noise. This classical line of thinking assumes that:

- You specified the strategy and its parameters *before* looking at the data.
- You tested it once.

In practice, this rarely holds. Instead, we often:

- Try many different indicators and feature combinations.
- Scan wide ranges of lookback windows and thresholds.
- Explore several execution styles and risk overlays.
- Vary universes and asset selections.

Each combination is, statistically speaking, a separate *hypothesis test*. If you run, say, 500 such tests and declare a discovery whenever the p-value is below 5%, you should expect about 25 seemingly "significant" results due to chance alone, even if none of the strategies has any true edge.

This is the core of the multiple testing problem: when we run many tests, the chance that at least one of them passes a naïve significance threshold by luck becomes very large. If we then present the best-looking backtest (or the top few) without adjusting for how many we tried, we are strongly biased toward false discoveries.

From the perspective of a backtest engine designed for reproducible research, this is unacceptable. We need mechanisms that:

- Keep track of how many distinct hypotheses have been tested.
- Adjust significance thresholds to account for this multiplicity.
- Provide interpretable summaries of how many of the discovered alphas are likely to be false.

Family-Wise Error Rate and False Discovery Rate

Two complementary concepts help us formalize what we want to control:

Family-wise error rate (FWER). This is the probability of making *at least one* false rejection (false positive) among a family of hypothesis tests. If we aim to keep FWER below 5%, we are saying: "Across all the strategy tests in this project, the probability that we incorrectly declare at least one non-existent edge to be significant should be at most 5%."

FWER control is conservative. It is suitable when false positives are very costly, for example when launching a large fund around a single flagship strategy.

False discovery rate (FDR). This is the expected *proportion* of false positives among all rejections. If FDR is set to 5%, we are willing to tolerate that, on average, up to 5% of the strategies we label as "significant" may actually be false edges.

FDR control is less stringent than FWER and more appropriate when testing many related hypotheses, such as a large pool of candidate alphas from which you might build a diversified portfolio. It acknowledges that some false positives are acceptable as long as they are a small minority.

In both cases, the starting point is the same: for each strategy or parameter configuration we compute a p-value (or an equivalent significance measure) based on an appropriate test statistic and sampling distribution. The difference lies in how we interpret and adjust those p-values across the whole set of tests.

Bonferroni and Holm: Controlling Family-Wise Error

The simplest, and historically first, approach to multiple testing is the Bonferroni correction.

Bonferroni correction

Assume you wish to control FWER at a level α (for example, 5%), and you have run m independent tests. Bonferroni says:

- Instead of declaring a strategy significant when its p-value is less than α,
- Declare it significant only when its p-value is less than α/m.

For example, if you run 100 tests and want FWER at 5%, you use a threshold of $0.05/100 = 0.0005$. Only p-values smaller than 0.0005 are deemed significant.

Intuitively, because each test has its own chance of producing a small p-value under the null, you must tighten the threshold as the number of tests increases. Bonferroni is easy to compute and applies regardless of dependencies among tests, but it is very conservative. In large search spaces it may declare nothing significant, even when some true edges exist.

Holm's step-down method

Holm's procedure is a refinement that controls FWER like Bonferroni but is less conservative:

1. Sort all m p-values in ascending order: $p_{(1)} \leq p_{(2)} \leq \cdots \leq p_{(m)}$.
2. Starting from the smallest p-value, compare $p_{(1)}$ to α/m, $p_{(2)}$ to $\alpha/(m-1)$, and so on.
3. Find the first p-value $p_{(k)}$ that exceeds its threshold. Reject all hypotheses with indices less than k (that is, $p_{(1)}, \ldots, p_{(k-1)}$), and accept the rest.

Holm's method adapts the threshold for each p-value in a way that still guarantees FWER control but gives more power, meaning it is more likely to detect true edges when they exist.

From the engine's point of view, implementing these corrections is straightforward once:

- You have a list of strategies or tests that belong to the same "family" (for example, all variations in a grid search, or all alphas tested in a research project).
- For each test you have a p-value derived from its out-of-sample performance.

The engine can then compute Bonferroni- or Holm-adjusted thresholds and mark which strategies remain significant. These adjusted results should be part of the standard reporting layer rather than an optional extra.

False Discovery Rate (FDR) Control

FWER control can be too harsh when m is large, which is common in quantitative research. If you test thousands of potential signals, insisting that the probability of even a single false positive be below 5% might leave you with no discoveries at all.

False discovery rate control offers a more forgiving alternative. The most widely used procedure is due to Benjamini and Hochberg (BH).

Benjamini-Hochberg procedure

To control FDR at level q (for example, 10%):

1. Sort the m p-values in ascending order: $p_{(1)} \leq \cdots \leq p_{(m)}$.
2. For each sorted p-value $p_{(i)}$, compute the threshold $q \cdot i/m$.
3. Find the largest index k such that $p_{(k)} \leq q \cdot k/m$.
4. Declare all hypotheses with indices 1 through k (the k smallest p-values) as discoveries; treat the rest as non-significant.

Intuitively, the BH procedure draws a line that increases with the rank of the p-value. The more p-values you consider, the higher the allowed threshold, but always scaled by q. Strategies whose p-values fall below this rising line are accepted as discoveries.

Compared to Bonferroni or Holm, BH allows more discoveries because it tolerates some false positives, but in a controlled proportion. If you accept 20 strategies under BH with $q = 10\%$, you should expect that, on average, about 2 of them might be false discoveries.

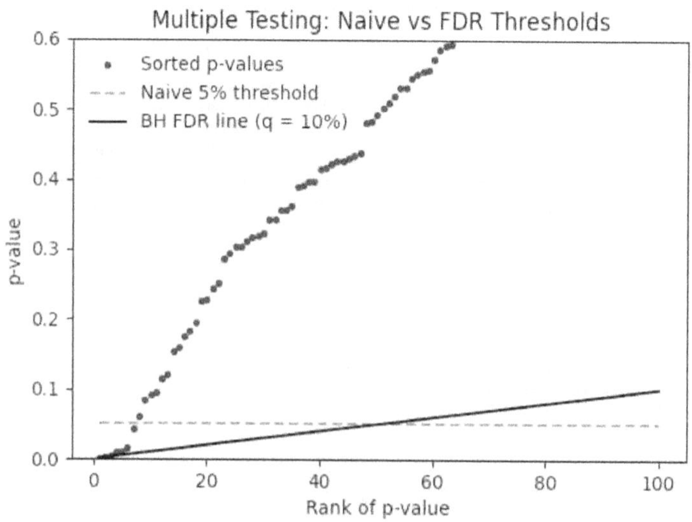

Visually, you can imagine plotting sorted p-values on the vertical axis against their rank on the horizontal axis, together with the BH line. Where the p-value curve lies below the BH line, discoveries are retained; where it rises above, they are rejected. This makes FDR control particularly amenable to graphical diagnosis and communication.

From P-Values to Engine-Level Metrics

So far, we have spoken abstractly about p-values. In a backtest engine, these must be computed in a concrete way, and then aggregated across tests.

Computing per-strategy p-values

For each strategy or parameter configuration, and for each outer test window (from your walk-forward validation), you can:

- Compute a test statistic that measures departure from the null hypothesis of no edge. Examples include:
  - Sharpe ratio-based t-statistics.
  - Mean return divided by its estimated standard error.
  - Nonparametric statistics derived from bootstrap distributions (for example, the percentile position of zero return in a bootstrapped distribution).
- Use either analytical approximations or resampling (e.g., block bootstrap) to convert that statistic into a p-value under the null.

It is important that these p-values reflect out-of-sample performance: they should be based on returns from outer test windows not used in model or parameter selection.

Defining test families

Multiple testing corrections require you to define which tests belong to the same "family." This should reflect the research question. Examples include:

- All parameter combinations explored for a given base strategy design.
- All distinct signals or alphas tested in a research campaign over a given asset class.
- All strategies considered for inclusion in a particular portfolio.

The backtest engine can support this by letting users tag experiments with family identifiers. When generating summary reports, the engine then:

- Gathers all p-values within each family.
- Applies Bonferroni, Holm, or BH FDR procedures as requested.
- Outputs adjusted significance labels and, where appropriate, estimates of the expected number of false discoveries.

Reporting adjusted significance

Rather than leaving users to interpret raw p-values in isolation, the reporting layer should include:

- The raw p-value for each strategy.
- The Bonferroni- or Holm-adjusted threshold for that family size.
- For FDR procedures, an indication of which strategies pass the BH criterion.
- Summary metrics such as:
  - Number of strategies tested in the family.
  - Number declared significant under each adjustment.
  - Expected number (or proportion) of false discoveries.

In other words, "significant at 5%" should no longer be a free-floating label; it must be interpreted in the context of how many other things were tried.

Designing Research Workflows Around Multiple Testing

Statistical adjustments alone are not enough. An honest validation framework also needs process discipline that works *with* these tools.

Logging all experiments. Earlier we stressed the importance of logging every backtest run, including those that "failed." That logging is essential for multiple testing control, because:

- It lets you count how many distinct hypotheses were tested, rather than only the winners.
- It guards against unconscious cherry-picking: if a result is not in the log, it did not happen.

The engine should make logging automatic and tamper-evident. Deleting failed runs to shrink the apparent number of tests should not be easy.

Separating exploratory and confirmatory phases. In an exploratory phase, you might run hundreds or thousands of tests, accepting that many will look promising by chance. FDR control is especially useful here: it lets you narrow down a manageable set of candidates while understanding how many may be false.

In a confirmatory phase, you then subject a much smaller number of pre-specified strategies to stricter evaluation:

- Using independent confirmation datasets or later time periods not touched during exploration.
- Applying stronger controls such as Holm or even Bonferroni, since m is now small.

The engine can help by enforcing that confirmation sets are only evaluated once, and by tagging which runs are exploratory versus confirmatory in its metadata.

Communicating uncertainty honestly. Finally, multiple testing adjustments should be visible in how results are communicated. For example:

- "We tested 300 variants and 8 passed FDR at 10%; we therefore expect fewer than one false discovery on average" is a very different message from "We found 8 significant strategies" without context.
- If only a single strategy remains significant under Holm at 5%, while many appear significant under naive thresholds, that should be front and center in any investment or risk discussion.

Embedding these summaries into standard reports reduces the temptation to selectively disclose only the most flattering numbers.

Beyond Classical Corrections: Shrinkage and Hierarchies

While Bonferroni, Holm, and BH are workhorses, the literature offers richer tools, many of which can be approximated or hinted at in practice even if not fully implemented in the engine:

Empirical Bayes and shrinkage. In large-scale testing, we may assume that each strategy has a true but unknown effect (for example, an unknown true Sharpe). Empirical Bayes methods estimate the distribution of these effects across the population of strategies and "shrink" individual estimates toward the overall mean. This has the effect of moderating extreme observed performances, which are often exaggerated by noise.

Even without full Bayesian machinery, you can adopt a shrinkage mindset: when a strategy looks exceptionally good compared to its peers, assume part of that is luck and temper your expectations accordingly.

Hierarchical testing. Sometimes strategies are grouped hierarchically: for example, by asset class, region, or style. You might first test whether any strategy in a group shows an effect, and only then drill down within that group. Hierarchical procedures adjust for multiple testing at each level, reducing the effective number of tests compared to treating all strategies as a flat list.

While implementing full hierarchical FDR in a backtest engine may be ambitious, supporting group tags and group-level summaries is a practical step in this direction.

From Many Tests to Honest Edges

Multiple testing and false discovery control close a crucial loop in validation:

- Train/test splits and walk-forward schemes protect against temporal overfitting.

- Guardrails eliminate structural biases that artificially boost performance.
- Resampling and bootstrap methods quantify sampling variability for a given strategy.
- Multiple testing corrections acknowledge the search process itself and adjust our confidence in discovered edges accordingly.

An engine that integrates all these elements changes the culture of research. Instead of treating a striking equity curve as proof, it encourages questions:

- How many cousins of this strategy were tried and discarded?
- How do its p-values look once we adjust for all those trials?
- Given FDR control, how many of our "winners" are we willing to accept as likely mirages?

When a strategy still looks promising after answering these questions—after rigorous temporal validation, realistic simulation, uncertainty quantification, and multiple testing adjustments—it earns a different level of trust. It is not guaranteed to succeed, but it is far less likely to be a product of chance and wishful thinking.

In the next section we will further refine our notion of "edge" by decomposing strategy performance into exposures to known risk factors and residual alpha, ensuring that even statistically robust results are not merely repackaged versions of familiar market risks.

6.5 Benchmarking & Factor Risk Models

The previous sections of this chapter have focused on making backtests statistically honest: respecting time, avoiding structural biases, quantifying sampling variability, and correcting for multiple testing. Even if a strategy survives all of those filters, one crucial question remains:

Relative to what is this strategy doing well?

A high Sharpe ratio or attractive equity curve is not, by itself, evidence of true "alpha." Many strategies that look impressive in isolation are, in fact, just cleverly repackaged exposure to familiar sources of risk: broad equity markets, value and momentum styles, carry trades, volatility premia, and so on. If markets continue to reward these risks, such strategies may do fine; if not, their performance can vanish suddenly.

This section shows how to decompose strategy returns into systematic factor exposures and residual alpha, using benchmarks and factor risk models. The goal is to make it hard for a strategy to claim credit for returns that can be explained by known risks.

Outperformance Relative to What?

Before we can talk about "outperformance," we must specify a yardstick. A benchmark is that yardstick: a reference portfolio representing the opportunities and risks that a strategy could have taken on with simpler, more transparent methods.

The choice of benchmark depends on the strategy family:

- **Long-only equity strategies.** A broad market index such as a total market or large-cap index, possibly adjusted for region or sector.
- **Sector or industry tilts.** Sector or industry-specific indices that match the sector exposure.
- **Style strategies.** Style benchmarks representing value, momentum, size, quality, or low-volatility tilts.
- **Multi-asset strategies.** A diversified basket of global equity, bond, and commodity indices reflecting the investable universe.
- **Market-neutral or hedged strategies.** A zero-beta benchmark, or a factor-neutral portfolio constructed to have minimal exposure to the main risk factors under consideration.

A good benchmark is:

- **Investable.** It should correspond to something one could actually hold, at least in principle (for example, an index ETF or a simple rules-based portfolio).
- **Relevant.** It should reflect risks that are natural for the strategy's mandate. A global equity benchmark is not helpful when evaluating a local bond-arbitrage strategy.
- **Transparent.** Its construction rules should be simple and documented, so that differences in performance can be interpreted.

At a minimum, your backtest engine should support attaching one or more benchmark return series to each strategy run and reporting performance relative to those benchmarks (for example, active return and active Sharpe). But benchmarks alone do not tell us which underlying risks are driving returns. For that, we need factor models.

From Benchmarks to Factor Models

A benchmark compares your strategy to a *single* reference portfolio. A factor model goes further: it treats strategy returns as potentially driven by exposures to *multiple* systematic sources of risk, called factors.

The intuition is straightforward:

- There exist broad, pervasive return patterns in markets (for example, the equity premium, value and momentum in stocks, term and credit premia in bonds).
- Many strategies can be understood as taking on some combination of these patterns, whether intentionally or not.
- Once we account for the returns "explained" by those factor exposures, whatever is left over is "residual alpha"—the part that cannot be attributed to known risks.

In practice, a factor model is often implemented as a regression of strategy returns on a set of factor returns:

- The dependent variable is the strategy's excess return over a risk-free rate (for example, daily or monthly).
- The independent variables are returns to chosen factor portfolios over the same periods.
- The regression coefficients (betas) estimate the strength and direction of the strategy's exposure to each factor.
- The intercept represents residual alpha after accounting for those exposures.

We avoid explicit equations here, but the conceptual picture is that each period's strategy return is approximated as:

> contribution from factor 1 + contribution from factor 2 + ...+ residual.

If most of the variation in returns is captured by factor contributions, and the residual is small and statistically indistinguishable from zero, your "alpha" strategy is essentially a factor strategy in disguise.

Choosing Factors

The choice of factors is domain-specific. Common examples in equity markets include:

- **Market.** Broad equity market excess return (market beta).
- **Size.** Small-cap versus large-cap performance.
- **Value.** Cheap versus expensive stocks by fundamentals such as book-to-price or earnings yield.
- **Momentum.** Past winners versus past losers over 6–12 month horizons.
- **Quality or profitability.** Companies with strong balance sheets and earnings versus weaker counterparts.
- **Low volatility.** Low-risk stocks versus high-risk stocks.

In fixed income, common factors might include:

- **Term.** Long-duration versus short-duration bonds.
- **Credit.** Investment grade versus high yield, or spreads over government bonds.
- **Curve shape.** Slope and curvature of the yield curve.

In multi-asset or cross-asset contexts, you might use:

- Broad equity, bond, and commodity indices.
- Currency carry, value, and momentum portfolios.
- Volatility and liquidity premia.

For backtest engine design, the key requirement is flexibility: the engine should not hard-wire a particular factor set, but instead allow users to:

- Register factor return series (with clear definitions and data sources).
- Group factors into named models (for example, "Equity 3-factor," "Style 6-factor").
- Attach one or more factor models to each backtest run for attribution.

Estimating Factor Exposures

Once factor returns are available alongside strategy returns, estimating exposures becomes a mechanical step. Conceptually:

1. Choose an estimation window, such as rolling 36-month returns for a monthly strategy or rolling 252-day returns for a daily one.
2. For each window:

- Collect the overlapping time series of strategy excess returns and factor returns.
- Fit a linear relationship between strategy returns and factor returns.
- Extract:
    - The estimated beta (exposure) to each factor.
    - The average residual return over the window (alpha).
    - Measures of fit (for example, fraction of variance explained).

3. Slide the window forward in time and repeat, building up a time series of factor exposures and alpha estimates.

Several practical issues arise:

Estimation window length. Short windows (for example, 6–12 months) adapt more quickly to changing exposures but produce noisier estimates. Long windows (for example, 3–5 years) are more stable but may miss regime shifts. A rolling approach, where you refresh estimates at each period using the last N observations, is typically suitable.

Overlap with validation splits. Factor regressions should respect the same temporal validation discipline as the backtest itself. When computing factor exposures for a given test window, you should use only information up to that point in time. Otherwise you risk "peeking into the future" when interpreting exposures.

Heteroskedasticity and autocorrelation. Residuals from factor regressions may exhibit changing volatility or serial correlation. Robust error estimation techniques (for example, using heteroskedasticity- and autocorrelation-consistent standard errors) can give more reliable inference about whether alpha is statistically different from zero. While the implementation details can live in a statistics library, the engine's reporting layer should be aware that not all t-statistics are created equal.

Multicollinearity. Factors can be correlated with one another (for example, value and quality may overlap). High correlation among factors makes it harder to disentangle their individual contributions. In practice:

- You may want to limit the number of factors in any given model.
- You should interpret highly correlated factors cautiously; their betas may be unstable over time.
- You can construct orthogonalized factor portfolios if needed, though that complicates interpretation.

Decomposing Performance: Factor Contributions vs. Alpha

The main payoff of factor modeling is a clearer decomposition of performance. For each period, you can attribute the strategy's return into:

- **Factor-contributed return.** The part explained by exposures to the chosen factors. For example, a positive beta to the market factor multiplied by the market's return in that period.
- **Residual (idiosyncratic) return.** The part left over, which we loosely call alpha.

Aggregating across time, you can compute:

- The average return contribution of each factor.
- The volatility (risk) contributed by each factor, which depends both on the factor's own volatility and the strategy's exposure to it.
- The residual alpha and its volatility.
- The proportion of total variance explained by the factor model versus residual.

From a validation perspective, several questions are then easy to answer:

- **Is the apparent edge just market beta?** If most performance is explained by exposure to the broad market factor, and the residual alpha is small and statistically insignificant, then the strategy is effectively a leveraged or tilted market bet.

- **Is the strategy a style tilt?** If performance loads heavily on a known style factor, such as value or momentum, the strategy may simply be a complicated way of accessing that style.
- **Is residual alpha stable across regimes?** Does alpha remain positive and statistically distinguishable from zero across multiple time periods, or is it concentrated in one particular regime?
- **How concentrated are the risks?** If one or two factors account for most of the variance, then diversifying across additional strategies that share those factors may not reduce risk as much as hoped.

Even when residual alpha is positive and statistically significant, the decomposition encourages humility: a strategy's edge may be smaller, and riskier, than a naïve Sharpe ratio suggests once systematic exposures are accounted for.

Integrating Factor Models into the Backtest Engine

To make factor-based attribution part of routine practice rather than an afterthought, your backtest engine should provide:

Factor data integration. Factor return series should be treated much like asset return series:

- Stored in the same data infrastructure, with timestamps aligned to the trading calendar.
- Versioned and documented, with clear definitions (for example, "US equity value factor based on book-to-price, rebalanced monthly, dollar-neutral").
- Accessible to the analysis layer but not misused for signal generation unless explicitly intended (to avoid circular reasoning).

Configurable factor models. Users should be able to define factor models as configurations, specifying:

- Which factor series to include.
- The rebalancing or observation frequency (daily, weekly, monthly).
- The estimation window length and step (for rolling regressions).
- Any robust regression or error-estimation options.

Automated rolling attribution. Given a strategy's realized returns and a factor model specification, the engine's analysis layer should:

- Run rolling regressions up to each analysis date, respecting temporal ordering.
- Store time series of factor betas, factor-contributed returns, and residual alpha.
- Make these series available alongside the raw return series for further analysis or visualization.

Standardized reporting. Every performance report for a non-trivial strategy should include, where appropriate:

- A table summarizing average exposures to major factors and their contribution to total return and volatility.
- An estimate of residual alpha, its standard error, and a t-statistic or confidence interval.
- Time-series charts of rolling factor betas, highlighting periods where exposures changed materially.
- Optional decompositions by regime or subperiod (for example, pre- and post-crisis).

By making these attributions standard, the engine encourages a culture in which "alpha" claims are automatically tested against known sources of risk.

Practical Considerations and Pitfalls

While factor models are powerful, they come with caveats that an honest backtest framework must recognize.

Model incompleteness. No factor model captures all relevant risks. If your factor set omits an important driver of returns (for example, a volatility factor for an options strategy), residual alpha may absorb what is really systematic exposure. The remedy is not to abandon factor modeling, but to:

- Choose factor sets that are as comprehensive and relevant as possible for the strategy.
- Interpret residual alpha as "unexplained by this particular model," not as absolute truth.

Data quality and look-ahead. Factor returns themselves must be free of look-ahead bias. If factor portfolios are constructed using information that would not have been known at the time (for example, using future returns to define breakpoints), then alpha attribution becomes circular. Factor construction rules and effective dates should be subject to the same scrutiny as any other dataset in the engine.

Instability over time. Factor relationships are not immutable. A strategy that historically loaded on value and momentum may shift its behavior as its internal logic or the market environment changes. Rolling attribution is essential to detect such changes; a single full-sample regression may average over important shifts.

Overfitting with too many factors. Including an excessive number of factors relative to the length of the estimation window can produce unstable, noisy betas. This is another form of multiple testing: if you search over many factor combinations, some will appear to "explain" returns by chance. Applying the same discipline as in earlier sections—pruning factor sets, controlling for multiple testing when exploring many models—helps avoid spurious attributions.

From Hidden Beta to Transparent Alpha

Incorporating benchmarks and factor risk models into your backtest engine changes the interpretation of almost every strategy:

- A market-neutral equity strategy may turn out to be strongly short volatility and long liquidity, explaining both its attractive returns in calm periods and its sharp losses in crises.
- A seemingly sophisticated multi-factor stock picker may be little more than a leveraged value and momentum tilt relative to a standard style index.
- A macro strategy that appears uncorrelated to equities on average may show significant positive beta in certain regimes, coinciding with its worst drawdowns.

By making such patterns explicit, factor models perform two critical functions in validation:

1. **Risk transparency.** They reveal which systematic risks you are truly taking, enabling better portfolio construction and risk management at the firm level.
2. **Alpha discipline.** They prevent you from attributing to "skill" what is actually compensation for bearing known, and possibly crowded, risks.

In a fully instrumented backtest engine, no serious strategy should make it to production review without a factor-based attribution. When combined with the other tools discussed in this chapter—rigorous temporal validation, bias guardrails, bootstrap-based uncertainty estimates, and multiple testing controls—factor models help transform backtesting from a source of seductive stories into a disciplined framework for understanding where returns truly come from and how fragile they might be.

The final section of this chapter will extend this perspective beyond observed history, using Monte Carlo and scenario simulation to ask not only "What explained past performance?" but also "How might this strategy behave under market conditions we have not yet seen?"

6.6 Scenario & Monte Carlo Simulation

All of the tools introduced so far in this chapter have something in common: they work with what actually happened in the historical record. We slice time carefully, guard against biases, quantify sampling variability, control for multiple testing, and decompose returns into known risk factors—but always within the constraints of observed data.

History, however, is only one realization of what *could* have happened. It may not contain enough stress, or the right kinds of stress, to reveal a strategy's weaknesses. Regimes that dominated the sample may not dominate the future. To understand how a strategy might behave under a wider range of plausible and extreme conditions, we need to go beyond replaying the past.

Scenario analysis and Monte Carlo simulation extend validation from "what happened" to "what could happen." They use controlled random path generation and targeted shocks to expose strategies to many possible futures, while maintaining a clear, reproducible link between assumptions and outcomes. They also bring their own methodological challenges: how to preserve realistic dynamics, how to avoid overfitting models of returns, and how to manage randomness so runs are repeatable and comparable.

In this section we will:

- Describe the role of scenario analysis and Monte Carlo in a backtest engine.
- Contrast simple and richer models for generating synthetic price and return paths.
- Explain how to integrate a path generator into the existing event-driven architecture.
- Discuss stress scenarios as targeted shocks layered on baseline simulations.
- Introduce basic variance-reduction techniques that make Monte Carlo estimates more efficient.

Why We Need Synthetic Paths

Historical backtests suffer from three main limitations that Monte Carlo can help address:

Limited number of crises. Many markets have only a handful of major crises in the available data. If your backtest's evaluation period happens to contain one, estimated risk will look high; if it does not, risk will look low. Monte Carlo can generate many crisis-like paths, giving a richer view of tail risk and drawdowns.

Path dependence. For path-dependent strategies (for example, those with dynamic leverage or stop-loss rules), the exact sequence of returns matters greatly. A single historical path may under- or overrepresent certain sequences, such as multiple moderate drawdowns close together. Synthetic paths explore alternative sequences that are consistent with observed statistics but not literally present in history.

Changing environments. Markets evolve. A strategy calibrated on the recent past may be especially sensitive to a shift in volatility, correlation, or liquidity. Scenario analysis can deliberately perturb these aspects to gauge robustness under different conditions.

Of course, synthetic paths are not "true" in the way history is. They are only as good as the models and assumptions used to generate them. The key is to strike a balance: models rich enough to capture the key dynamics that matter for the strategy, but simple and transparent enough to avoid overfitting and to keep interpretation clear.

Modeling Returns: From Random Walks to Regimes

At the core of Monte Carlo simulation is a model for how returns evolve. There is a wide spectrum of choices:

Simple random walks. The most basic model assumes that returns are independent over time with a fixed mean (drift) and variance (volatility). Each period's return is drawn from the same distribution, often a normal distribution for convenience. Cumulative prices then follow a random walk.

This model is easy to implement and calibrate: you estimate average return and volatility from historical data and reuse them. However, it ignores many empirically important features: fat tails, volatility clustering, and autocorrelation.

Fat-tailed innovations. To better match observed extremes, you can use heavier-tailed distributions for innovations (for example, Student-like behavior) while still keeping returns independent over time. This makes large jumps more likely than under a normal model, improving realism for tail statistics like maximum drawdown and Value-at-Risk.

Stochastic volatility. In reality, volatility changes over time. Models with stochastic or regime-dependent volatility (for example, where volatility itself follows a random process) can reproduce clusters of high and low volatility. For many strategies, particularly those with leverage or options, this is critical: their behavior depends heavily on the timing and persistence of volatility spikes.

Regime-switching processes. Another way to represent changing environments is to define a small number of regimes (for example, "calm," "volatile," "crisis") with different return and volatility characteristics, and then allow the process to switch between regimes according to some probability rules. Regime-switching models can mimic the alternation between bull markets, sideways markets, and drawdown periods that real strategies experience.

Multivariate models. For portfolios spanning several assets or asset classes, you must also model cross-sectional dependence: correlations, co-movements, and joint tail behavior. Simple models assume constant correlations; richer models allow correlations themselves to vary with regimes or volatility.

From an engine-design perspective, you should not hard-code a single model. Instead, build a *path generation interface* with clear responsibilities:

- Accept historical data (returns, volatilities, correlations, factor returns) and configuration parameters.
- Calibrate model parameters in a transparent, logged way.
- Expose functions that, given a random seed, produce one or more synthetic return paths consistent with the model.

Different implementations behind this interface can then be swapped in or out depending on the strategy and the research question.

Calibration Without Overfitting

Calibrating path generators to historical data introduces another opportunity for overfitting. If you tune model parameters too aggressively to match every nuance of the sample, the synthetic paths may understate uncertainty about the future.

A few practical guidelines help maintain discipline:

Use coarser, stable statistics. Focus on matching broad characteristics that are likely to persist, such as:

- Long-run average return and volatility.
- Typical levels of skewness and kurtosis.
- Average correlations across assets or factors.
- Typical lengths and depths of drawdowns.

Do not try to fit every wiggle in the data, or to reproduce every individual event.

Respect validation splits. Apply the same temporal discipline used elsewhere in the chapter. For example:

- Calibrate the model using only the training portion of data.
- Evaluate its ability to reproduce out-of-sample features using the test portion.

This prevents you from inadvertently building a path generator that is tuned specifically to the test period's quirks.

Document assumptions. Calibration choices (such as lookback windows, regime definitions, and volatility models) should be recorded as configuration in the engine. Synthetic results are then interpreted in light of these assumptions, much like factor models in the previous section.

Integrating Path Generation into the Backtest Engine

Once a path generator is available, the next step is to integrate it into the backtest architecture so that the *same strategy logic* can run on both historical and synthetic data.

Conceptually, the engine's event layer should:

- Accept as input either:

- Historical price and return series, or
- Synthetic price and return series generated by a model.

- Generate the same sequence of events: bar arrivals, signal computations, order submissions, fills, and accounting updates.
- Produce portfolio return series and performance reports in the same format irrespective of data source.

To support Monte Carlo simulation, the engine should:

Manage random seeds deterministically. Every simulation run, and each synthetic path within it, should be associated with specific seeds for the path generator and any stochastic components of the strategy (for example, random tie-breakers or stochastic executions). This ensures:

- Reproducibility: rerunning a simulation with the same configuration and seed set yields identical results.
- Comparability: different strategies can be tested on identical sets of synthetic paths by reusing the same path-generator seeds.

Support batched simulations. Monte Carlo work is naturally batched:

- For each synthetic path, run the full backtest and capture relevant outputs (returns, drawdowns, risk metrics).

- Across all paths, aggregate into distributions: for example, the distribution of maximum drawdowns, time to recovery, or worst one-year loss.

The engine should provide infrastructure to schedule and manage these batches, ideally leveraging parallelism across cores or machines.

Stress Scenarios as Targeted Shocks

While Monte Carlo explores a range of typical and moderately extreme outcomes under a given model, risk managers and investors often care about specific "what if" questions, such as:

- What if equity markets drop 30% in a month?
- What if volatility doubles and stays elevated for a year?
- What if correlations across asset classes spike toward one?
- What if liquidity dries up and transaction costs increase abruptly?

Scenario analysis addresses such questions by defining *stress scenarios*: targeted shocks to prices, returns, volatilities, correlations, or market frictions. These shocks can be:

Historical scenarios. Replay an actual crisis period (for example, a past financial crisis or flash crash) but inject the strategy in place as if it had been live then. This is essentially a focused historical backtest over a known stress window.

Historical analogues. Modify or concatenate historical periods to create synthetic crises resembling known ones but with different timing or magnitude. For example, overlay the path of an equity crash onto today's market level.

Hypothetical shocks. Design stylized shocks not seen in history but plausible under your risk understanding. Examples include:

- One-off price jumps of a specified size.

- Persistent changes in volatility or correlation matrices.
- Step changes in bid-ask spreads or trading volumes.

In the engine, these scenarios can be implemented as transformations of the baseline return paths:

- Start with either historical or Monte Carlo-generated paths.
- Overlay shocks at specified times: adjust returns, volatilities, or transaction cost parameters.
- Rerun the strategy under the modified conditions.

Critically, scenarios should be parameterized and stored as part of configuration, not hand-tuned ad hoc. This makes scenario results reproducible and comparable across strategies.

Variance Reduction: Getting More from Each Simulation

Monte Carlo estimates of risk metrics (for example, expected maximum drawdown or probability of a 20% loss) converge slowly as the number of paths increases. Doubling the precision may require many more simulations, which can be computationally expensive.

Variance-reduction techniques aim to improve efficiency: they reduce the noise of estimates without requiring as many simulations. Three basic techniques are particularly relevant for backtest engines.

Antithetic variates. When generating random shocks (for example, daily return innovations), you can:

- Generate a sequence of random draws for one path.
- For a second path, use the "mirror image" of those draws (for example, multiply by -1 in symmetric models, or otherwise reflect them around the mean).

Because these paired paths are negatively correlated, taking averages across them reduces variance in estimated metrics. In practice, this is easy to implement: ensure that for each seed you also generate a paired "antithetic" path.

Control variates. If you know the expected value of some related quantity under your model, and that quantity is correlated with the metric you care about, you can adjust your Monte Carlo estimates using it as a control variate. For example:

- In a simple model where the expected market return is known analytically, you can use the realized average market return in each path as a control variate when estimating strategy return statistics.
- This adjustment effectively subtracts some of the common noise between the market and the strategy.

Implementing general control variates can be more involved, but even modest use (for example, controlling for known factor returns in a factor-based path generator) can stabilize estimates.

Stratified sampling. Rather than drawing all paths from the same overall distribution, you can partition the space of shocks or scenarios into strata and sample a fixed number of paths from each. For instance:

- Ensure that a certain proportion of paths include at least one large downward jump.
- Ensure that some paths represent prolonged low-volatility periods, others represent frequent regime switches.

By deliberately covering different regions of the scenario space, stratified sampling reduces the chance that your Monte Carlo misses important but relatively rare patterns.

For all variance-reduction methods, the engine must manage randomness carefully and record which technique was used in each run, because they affect the interpretation of results and how they can be compared.

Summarizing Monte Carlo Outputs

The raw output of scenario and Monte Carlo simulations is a set of paths: for each path, a time series of returns and equity curves. Turning these into actionable insight requires thoughtful summarization:

Distribution of risk metrics. For each path, compute:

- Maximum drawdown and time to recovery.
- Rolling worst-case loss over fixed horizons (for example, worst 1-month or 1-year loss).
- Sharpe ratio, skewness, and kurtosis.
- Tail measures such as Value-at-Risk or Expected Shortfall at chosen confidence levels.

Across paths, build distributions of these metrics. Report summary statistics (medians, quartiles, tail percentiles) and, where appropriate, compare them to the corresponding historical metrics.

Probability statements. Use the empirical distributions to make statements such as:

- "Under this model, there is a 10% chance that the maximum drawdown over the next three years exceeds 40%."
- "There is a 5% chance that the strategy experiences at least one 25% one-year loss."
- "In 80% of simulated paths, the strategy recovers from its worst drawdown within two years."

These are not predictions; they are conditional on the model and calibration. But they are far more informative for risk management than a single historical drawdown figure.

Comparisons across configurations. Because Monte Carlo simulations can be rerun under different strategy parameters, execution models, or scenario settings, you can:

- Compare risk distributions for different leverage levels.
- Compare vulnerability to shocks under different hedging rules.
- Evaluate how much risk reduction is achieved by adding risk controls (for example, volatility targeting).

The engine's reporting layer should facilitate such comparisons, ideally using consistent seeds and path sets to ensure differences are attributable to configuration changes rather than random variation.

From Historical Backtests to Forward-Looking Risk Views

Scenario and Monte Carlo simulation finalize the transition from backtesting as a backward-looking diagnostic to backtesting as a forward-looking risk tool:

- **Historical backtests** show how the strategy would have behaved if it had existed in the past, under the precise conditions that actually occurred.
- **Factor models** explain which systematic risks drove that historical behavior.
- **Monte Carlo and scenarios** explore how the same logic might play out under other plausible sequences of events, including stresses not seen in history.

For a backtest engine that aims at institutional-grade validation, Monte Carlo should not be a separate, one-off script. It should be deeply integrated:

- Path generation is a configurable, versioned component.
- Seeds and assumptions are logged, making every scenario reproducible.
- Synthetic paths flow through the same event-driven and accounting pipelines as historical data.

- Outputs feed into the same performance and risk reporting system, extended with distributions and scenario summaries.

When this integration is in place, you can ask—and answer—questions such as:

- "How likely is it, under reasonable assumptions, that this strategy suffers a drawdown that the investment committee would consider unacceptable?"
- "How often do we see combinations of factor moves that would cause several of our strategies to lose simultaneously?"
- "If the next decade resembles some rearrangement or amplification of past regimes, where does this strategy sit in our overall risk budget?"

No model-based simulation will ever replace the hard evidence of live trading. But as part of a disciplined validation framework that already includes careful temporal splits, bias guardrails, resampling, multiple-testing adjustments, and factor attribution, Monte Carlo and scenario analysis provide a powerful, structured way to look beyond history and confront the uncomfortable but essential question: *what if the future is worse than the past?*

Chapter 7

Reporting, Monitoring & Governance

Backtests are only as valuable as the questions you can answer from them-and the confidence with which you can defend those answers. This chapter shows how to turn raw PnL streams into interpretable metrics, reproducible reports, and governed processes that can withstand model reviews, compliance scrutiny, and production incidents. You will learn to design a reporting and monitoring layer that not only tells you what happened, but also how, why, and whether it was allowed to happen in the first place.

7.1 Performance Metrics & Attribution

In earlier chapters we focused on how to build a deterministic simulation core: an engine that can replay markets, apply strategies, and generate trades in a reproducible way. We now turn to the question that every researcher, risk manager, and governance committee eventually asks: *What did this strategy actually do?*

Answering that question requires more than a handful of numbers like "Sharpe 1.3" or "max drawdown 18%." We need a coherent *perfor-*

mance object model: a standardized way of representing returns, profit and loss (PnL), exposures, and trading activity so that all subsequent metrics are

- calculated consistently across strategies and runs,
- traceable back to underlying data, and
- reproducible years later, even after code and infrastructure have evolved.

This section develops that model and shows how to derive robust diagnostics for risk, efficiency, and attribution. The theme throughout is discipline: decide once how you represent performance, then compute everything else from that representation in a deterministic way.

A Canonical Performance Object

A backtest run produces a wide variety of outputs: time series of positions, trades, cash flows, exposures, and many other details. If every metric directly re-implements its own view of these objects, you will quickly end up with silent inconsistencies: one metric treating fees differently than another, or one using end-of-bar prices while another uses midpoints.

To avoid that, the reporting layer should work from a *canonical performance object*. Conceptually, this is a structured, time-indexed record of what the strategy did and what it experienced. At a minimum, each time step in the backtest (for example, each bar or each business day) should have:

- **Timestamp:** The exact point in simulated time that this record represents (for example, bar close time or daily close date).
- **Portfolio value:** Total equity, including cash and the market value of all positions, in a well-defined base currency.
- **Period PnL:** The change in portfolio value attributable to:

- market moves (unrealized PnL),

- realized PnL from closing trades,
- explicit costs and fees (commissions, exchange fees, financing, borrow costs),
- any exogenous cash flows that you model explicitly (deposits, withdrawals).

- **Return:** A normalized measure of PnL relative to capital, defined according to a chosen convention (for example, percentage change in portfolio value over the period).
- **Gross and net exposure:** Total long and short dollar exposure, and net exposure (long minus short), expressed relative to equity where applicable (for example, gross exposure 2.5x).
- **Leverage:** A concise measure of balance sheet usage, often identical or closely related to gross exposure.
- **Cash and margin usage:** Cash balance, financing usage, margin utilization, where relevant.
- **Turnover and trading activity:** Dollar traded during the period, broken down by buys/sells, direction, or other useful categories.
- **Risk factor exposures:** If you use a risk model, factor exposures at this time step (for example, market, size, value, momentum, sectors).

In practice, this is implemented as a schema—for example a table or a structured object—with well-documented fields, units, and definitions. The key design decisions are:

- **Single source of truth:** All high-level metrics (Sharpe ratio, drawdown, turnover, capacity, attribution, and so on) must be derived purely from the canonical performance object plus static metadata (such as your chosen risk-free rate).
- **Explicit conventions:** Decide once, and document:

- whether returns are gross or net of costs,

- what time zone timestamps refer to,
- how corporate actions and cash flows are treated,
- how leverage and exposure are defined.

- **Linkage to raw data:** For traceability, each performance point should be reachable from underlying position and trade records, which in turn are tied to specific input market data snapshots and code versions, as discussed in the chapter on provenance.

Once you have this standardized representation, you can think of the metric engine as a pure function: feed in a performance object and metadata, get back a deterministic set of diagnostics. This is what makes cross-strategy and cross-run comparison meaningful.

From PnL to Equity and Returns

Most performance metrics depend on some representation of returns. Before defining specific statistics, we should be precise about how we get from the simulation path to returns:

1. **Construct portfolio value path:** Using simulated positions and prices, compute total portfolio value at each time step, including cash and accrued costs.
2. **Define the return measure:** Common choices include:

- percentage change in portfolio value between consecutive timestamps,
- PnL in dollars divided by a measure of capital (for example, starting equity, average equity over the period).

3. **Adjust for cash flows:** If your backtest models external capital flows (for instance, subscriptions and redemptions), you must distinguish between changes in value due to flows and changes due to market performance. The canonical performance object should record cash flows separately so that returns reflect only investment performance.

4. **Align with the calendar:** Decide whether the primary frequency is daily, intraday bar, or trade-level, and define how you aggregate or sample sub-periods into the reporting frequency.

These steps may seem mundane, but small inconsistencies here will propagate into all higher-level metrics. In regulated environments, you should be able to demonstrate exactly how each return and PnL figure is constructed from the underlying simulation.

Visual Overview: Equity, Rolling Sharpe, and Drawdown

Right after the performance object is defined, it is helpful to show a compact visual summary of how multiple metrics derive from the same underlying PnL and equity curve. Figure gives such an overview.

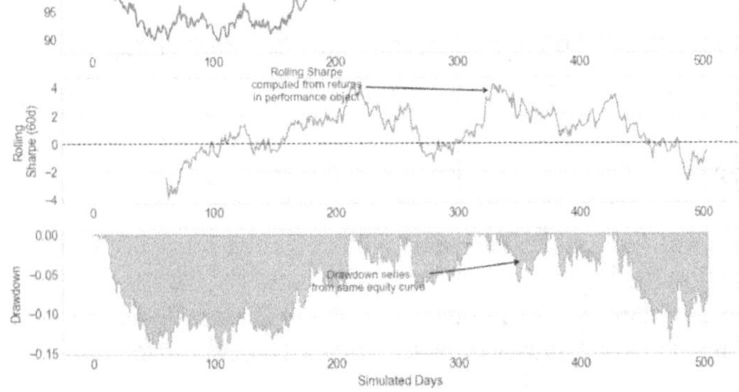

Figure 7.1: Multi-panel summary of a strategy's equity curve, rolling Sharpe, and drawdown, all derived from the same standardized PnL and return stream.

The important lesson from such a figure is not the particular path, but the dependency structure: Sharpe, drawdowns, and many other diagnostics are simply different lenses on the same underlying return and equity series.

Risk and Efficiency Metrics

With returns and equity defined, we can speak in a common language about performance across strategies and time. This language is built from two broad families of metrics: *risk* measures and *efficiency* measures.

Return and Risk Summaries

Every backtest report should start with basic summaries of return and risk:

- **Total and annualized return:** Cumulative growth of the portfolio over the backtest, converted to a standardized annual horizon. The exact formula is less important than being consistent and documenting your choice, especially when the backtest horizon is short or irregular.
- **Volatility:** A measure of typical fluctuation in returns, computed from the return series at your chosen frequency and scaled to an annual number using a documented convention (for example, square-root-of-time scaling).
- **Sharpe ratio:** Average excess return per unit of volatility. You should specify the risk-free rate source (if any) and how it is applied.

- **Sortino ratio:** A variation that penalizes downside volatility only, treating upside moves as harmless. This can be more intuitive for strategies with asymmetric payoff profiles.
- **Information ratio:** If you have a benchmark (for instance, an index or a hedge fund composite), the information ratio compares active returns (strategy minus benchmark) to their volatility. It is particularly useful when governance cares about relative rather than absolute performance.

All of these can be computed at multiple granularities: for example, full-sample, by calendar year, by regime (pre- and post-parameter change), or by scenario (stress window, high-volatility period, and so on). The canonical performance object makes it easy to re-cut the data without re-implementing the underlying logic.

Path-Dependent Risk: Drawdowns and Time Under Water

Point summaries of volatility and Sharpe ignore the *path* by which the strategy got to its final return. Governance bodies, however, care deeply about path-dependent risk: how painful the experience would be for investors.

Common path-dependent measures include:

- **Drawdown series:** At each time step, the percentage decline from the previous peak equity. This reveals not only the worst event but the entire pattern of losses and recoveries.
- **Maximum drawdown:** The single deepest peak-to-trough decline over the backtest. While easy to understand, it is sensitive to sample choice and should be interpreted together with other measures.
- **Average (or median) drawdown:** A more representative notion of what drawdowns "typically" look like.
- **Time under water:** The fraction of time the strategy spends below its previous peak. This metric speaks directly to investor patience requirements.

- **Recovery time:** How long it takes to regain the previous high after a drawdown begins.

All of these measures can be derived purely from the equity curve in the performance object. Crucially, you should define and store parameters such as:

- which frequency is used (daily versus intraday),
- whether drawdowns are computed on gross or net-of-fee equity,
- how you handle gaps in the time series.

By keeping these conventions fixed, you ensure that max drawdown for Strategy A in 2018 is comparable to max drawdown for Strategy B in 2025, and that both can be recomputed if the risk committee later asks for alternative definitions.

Trading Efficiency and Implementability

A strategy can have attractive returns but still be unimplementable in practice if it requires unrealistic turnover, excessive market impact, or violates capacity constraints. The performance object should therefore include trading activity and exposures in enough detail to support implementability metrics such as:

- **Turnover:** How much of the portfolio is traded over a given period. You can define turnover in several ways (for example, one-sided versus two-sided), but you must document your convention and apply it consistently.
- **Average holding period:** A derived measure that tells how long, on average, positions are held before being closed or significantly reduced. This helps categorize strategies as high-frequency, swing, or long-term and informs expectations about costs and slippage.
- **Slippage and transaction costs:** Differences between model prices (for example, midpoints) and executed prices, plus explicit

costs such as commissions and fees. In simulation, these are usually modeled; recording them explicitly in the performance object allows you to evaluate whether assumptions are reasonable.

- **Capacity diagnostics:** Measures of how "crowded" the strategy is relative to market volume. Common diagnostics include average and peak participation rates (volume traded as a share of market volume) and estimates of additional impact under higher capital levels.

These metrics are particularly important for governance because they bridge the gap between backtest and live trading. They also help enforce guardrails discussed in earlier chapters, such as maximum participation limits or borrowing constraints.

Attribution: Explaining Where PnL Came From

While summary metrics tell you *how much* the strategy earned and *how risky* the ride was, they do not explain *why*. Performance attribution fills this gap by decomposing PnL into interpretable components.

A core design principle is that attribution should be mechanically reproducible: for a given performance object and a defined attribution model, the same PnL decomposition should be obtained every time, regardless of when or where it is run.

Allocation and Selection Effects

One classical framework comes from portfolio management: allocation and selection attribution. At a high level:

- The **allocation effect** measures how much value was added (or lost) by choosing to overweight or underweight certain groups (sectors, regions, asset classes) relative to some benchmark.
- The **selection effect** measures the value added by picking better or worse securities within each group than the benchmark did.

To perform this attribution consistently, you need:

- Group definitions (for example, sector classification or strategy sleeve).
- Benchmark weights and returns for each group and, if needed, each security.
- The strategy's own weights and returns for the same groups and securities, as captured in your performance object (or in a linked positions object).

Once these inputs are fixed, you can apply your chosen allocation/selection formulas in a deterministic way. Even if governance debates the "best" formula, the important point is that your engine applies the same rule across all strategies and runs. This allows, for example, a risk committee to compare how much of each strategy's PnL came from asset allocation versus security selection over the same period.

Factor-Based Attribution

In quant strategies, it is common to think in terms of systematic risk factors rather than simple groupings. For example, a long-short equity strategy might be exposed to factors such as market, size, value, momentum, industry sectors, and so on.

Factor-based attribution typically proceeds in two steps:

1. **Measure factor exposures:** Using a risk model, decompose each position (and hence the portfolio at each time) into its exposures to a set of factors. These exposures should be stored in or linked from the performance object at the same frequency as returns.
2. **Combine exposures with factor returns:** Using observed or modeled returns for each factor over time, attribute part of the portfolio's return at each time step to each factor, and the remainder to idiosyncratic or unexplained sources.

The result is a time series of PnL contributions by factor (for example, market, value, momentum) and an idiosyncratic component. From a governance perspective, this allows you to answer questions such as:

- How much of the strategy's performance is explained by standard risk factors versus proprietary signals?
- Did the strategy inadvertently load up on unintended risks (for example, excessive exposure to a single sector or macro theme)?
- Are there periods where factor contributions spike in a way that might violate policy limits?

Because factor returns and exposures are themselves subject to modeling choices, you should version and document:

- which risk model was used (vendor name, version, parameterization),
- the exact factor set and definitions,
- any transformations applied to exposures or returns.

This ensures that attribution results remain interpretable years later, even if the risk model evolves.

Trade-Level and Bucket-Level Attribution

Sometimes committees want to drill down even further: not just "which factor" but "which trades or which clusters of trades drove this PnL?" This is where trade-level or bucket-level attribution becomes useful.

The idea is to group PnL along dimensions meaningful for review, such as:

- symbol or instrument,
- sector or region,
- venue or broker,
- signal or strategy sleeve,
- trade direction (for example, long versus short, opening versus closing).

For each bucket, you can compute:

- total PnL and contribution to total,
- average and distribution of returns,
- cost and slippage characteristics (for example, cost per unit of volume),
- risk-adjusted performance measures.

Because your performance object already ties returns and PnL to positions and trades, bucket-level attribution is simply a matter of grouping and aggregating according to a schema that is itself versioned and documented. For example, if sector definitions changed in your reference data, you would need to know which version was used in a given backtest run.

Reproducible Metric Definitions and Parameterization

All of the metrics and attribution schemes discussed above depend on a set of parameters and conventions:

- frequency and calendar (for example, business days versus all calendar days),
- lookback windows for rolling statistics (for example, 60-day rolling Sharpe),
- definitions of "downside" in Sortino ratios,
- choice of benchmark and risk-free rate,
- groupings and factor sets for attribution.

To make metrics reproducible and comparable:

- **Externalize parameters:** Store metric configurations in explicit configuration objects or files, not hard-coded in the engine. This allows a reporting run to declare which configuration it used.

- **Version them:** Assign version identifiers to metric configurations so that you can say, "this report uses MetricConfig v3.1." If the committee later decides to change, say, the lookback window for rolling Sharpe, that change becomes MetricConfig v3.2. Older reports remain interpretable.
- **Link to performance objects:** Each performance object (or each run) should carry a reference to the metric configuration used to generate its diagnostics. This linkage is essential for audit trails.

Taken together, these practices turn performance metrics from ad hoc calculations into a governed part of the research and production lifecycle. For any given run, you can reconstruct not just the raw PnL path, but precisely how every reported number was derived, with which assumptions and parameters.

Consistency Across Strategies and Runs

The ultimate purpose of this discipline is to make comparisons meaningful. When two strategies are evaluated:

- with performance objects following the same schema,
- with metrics computed by the same engine and configuration, and
- with attribution using the same groupings and factor sets,

then differences in reported metrics are far more likely to reflect true differences in behavior rather than artifacts of the measurement process.

From a governance perspective, this is critical. Strategy approval committees, risk oversight groups, and external regulators are increasingly sensitive to the possibility that backtests might be framed in a way that flatters certain strategies or hides risks. A canonical performance object model, combined with deterministic metric and attribution engines, is your best defense: it enforces a uniform standard and leaves an audit trail that can be re-run at any time.

In the next sections we will build on this foundation by turning metrics into stable, review-friendly dashboards, and by connecting them to the logging and governance machinery that ensures your backtest engine remains not only powerful but also accountable.

7.2 Visualization & Reporting

The previous section established a canonical performance object and a disciplined way to compute risk, efficiency, and attribution metrics from it. We now assume that machinery exists: given a backtest run identifier, the system can produce a rich set of numbers and time series in a consistent way.

The question in this section is different: *How do we present those outputs so that humans can understand them, compare them across runs, and make good decisions?* This is not just a matter of drawing a few charts. Poorly designed reports can obscure important risks, make strategies look better than they are, and waste the time of reviewers. Well-designed reports, by contrast, turn a mass of metrics into a coherent narrative that a risk committee can digest in minutes.

We will proceed in four steps:

- define principles for standardized dashboards and reports;
- design a canonical set of plots and tables for backtests;
- discuss parameterization and templating so that reports are comparable across runs;
- cover report lifecycles and cataloging, so results remain usable months or years later.

Throughout, we assume that reporting consumes the standardized performance object defined earlier and never re-implements calculations. Visualization and reporting are *windows* into the metric engine, not alternative calculators.

Principles of a Good Quant Dashboard

A good quant dashboard is not the flashiest one. It is the one that lets a reviewer answer three questions quickly and reliably:

- What did this strategy do during this period?
- How does that compare to what we expected and to other runs?
- Is there anything here that requires action or further investigation?

To support this, your reporting layer should follow a few basic principles.

Minimal Cognitive Load

Every element on a page competes for attention. If you show twenty charts, none of them will be read carefully. Instead:

- Prioritize a small set of key visuals and tables on the first page: equity curve with drawdowns, headline risk-return metrics, capacity and turnover indicators, and a brief attribution summary.
- Push advanced diagnostics and niche details into secondary tabs or appendices. They should be available, but not in the way of a first pass.
- Use consistent color coding and simple legends. For example, always use the same accent color for the strategy, a neutral gray for benchmarks, and red for losses or breaches.

The goal is that a new reviewer can skim the first page and get a reasonable sense of the strategy before diving into details.

Stable Layout Across Runs

If the layout of a report changes between runs, visual comparison becomes hard. Reviewers end up wasting time looking for where each chart has moved, and subtle layout changes can inadvertently hide unfavorable results. To avoid this:

- Define a fixed layout grid for each report type (for example, single-strategy backtest, cross-strategy comparison, incident review).
- Commit to a stable ordering of sections: overview, risk, efficiency, attribution, governance checks, and so on.
- Reserve space for elements that sometimes do not apply. For example, if a particular strategy has no factor attribution, show an empty or "not applicable" placeholder rather than collapsing the space. This keeps the visual structure stable.

A reviewer should be able to open two reports side by side and see differences in content, not differences in layout.

Explicit Versioning and Traceability

As the metric engine evolves, so will your reports. That evolution must be visible:

- Every report should display, in a prominent but non-distracting place:
  - the backtest run identifier,
  - the code version of the simulation engine and metric engine,
  - the metric configuration version (for example, which Sharpe and drawdown definitions are used),
  - the data snapshot or data version identifier.
- Where appropriate, show the generation timestamp and the user or system that requested the report.

This information is as much a part of the report as the charts themselves. It is what makes the artifact reproducible and auditable.

Clear Mapping from Visuals to Definitions

When you show a chart labeled "Rolling Sharpe," the reader should not have to guess how it was computed. You do not need to print formulas, but you should:

- include concise captions that refer to the metric engine ("60-day rolling Sharpe computed from daily net returns, annualized");
- provide a glossary or appendix where each visual references a named metric definition ("see Metric Definition S1 for details");
- ensure axis labels are unambiguous (for example, "daily net return (percent)" rather than "return").

This practice reduces misunderstanding and allows governance reviewers to ask focused questions: "Why did we change S1 from a 60-day to a 90-day window in this version?"

Canonical Plots and Tables

With these principles in mind, we can outline a canonical set of visuals that most strategy backtests should include. The aim is not to be exhaustive, but to cover the core categories: performance path, distribution of outcomes, exposures, trading behavior, and attribution.

Equity Curves and Drawdowns

The equity curve and drawdown series are the primary visual narrative of a backtest. They should:

- be derived directly from the equity and drawdown series in the performance object;
- appear near the start of the report;
- use a shared time axis to facilitate mental alignment with other time-based charts.

A common design is a stacked layout: equity curve on top, drawdown below. Both are aligned in time so that the reader can see, for example, which drawdown coincides with a volatility spike later shown in another panel.

For multi-strategy or strategy-vs-benchmark comparisons, equity curves can be normalized to a common starting value (such as 100) and plotted together. The report should state clearly whether curves are gross or net of costs and whether they are leverage-adjusted.

Distribution Plots of Returns and Drawdowns

Path plots tell you "what happened when," but they do not summarize the distribution of outcomes. For that, your dashboard should include:

- **Return distribution plots:** Histograms or density plots of daily (or bar-level) returns, possibly split into positive and negative days, or by regime (for example, high- and low-volatility periods).
- **Drawdown distribution plots:** Histograms of drawdown depths and durations, or scatter plots showing depth versus length.

These visuals make tail risks more tangible. For example, a governance committee can see whether the strategy has a small number of extreme losses or many moderate ones. The figures should be annotated with summary statistics from the metric engine (for example, max drawdown, average drawdown, percent of time under water) to tie visuals to numbers.

Turnover, Volume, and Exposure Profiles

Implementability depends heavily on how a strategy trades and where it is exposed. Reporting should therefore make trading intensity and exposure profiles explicit.

Key visuals include:

- **Turnover over time:** A time series of turnover, perhaps smoothed or shown as a rolling average. Spikes are easy to spot and can be cross-referenced with market events or parameter changes.
- **Volume and participation:** For strategies where market impact and capacity matter, plots of daily or intraday participation rates (traded volume divided by estimated market volume) help identify periods of crowding.

- **Gross and net exposure:** Charts showing gross leverage and net exposure over time, possibly broken down by asset class or region. These reveal whether a nominally neutral strategy occasionally takes on large directional bets.

Each of these should be clearly linked to the corresponding fields in the performance object so that reviewers know they reflect exactly the same definitions used elsewhere (for example, exposure in leverage calculations and in risk limits).

Factor Loadings and Risk Contributions

For strategies evaluated within a factor-risk framework, dashboards should visualize how factor exposures and contributions evolve.

Useful elements include:

- **Factor exposure heatmaps:** Time on one axis, factors on the other, color intensity indicating exposure magnitude. This lets you see, for example, that the strategy gradually became more loaded on value and less on momentum over a certain period.
- **Factor contribution bar charts:** For a chosen period (for example, full sample, last year, crisis window), bars showing how much of total PnL is attributed to each factor and to idiosyncratic components.

Exposures and contributions must be computed once by the attribution engine and then simply visualized; the report should never recompute or re-estimate risk model quantities on the fly.

Trade-Level and Bucket-Level Summaries

Lastly, it is often helpful to summarize performance and costs by category. Tables or heatmaps can show:

- PnL by symbol, sector, region, or venue;
- average cost per unit of volume by brokerage or execution venue;
- performance by signal or strategy sleeve (for multi-sleeve systems).

A common pattern is a table sorted by contribution to total PnL, highlighting the top contributors and detractors. Another is a two-dimensional heatmap, for example by sector and holding period, to spot combinations that systematically underperform or incur high cost.

Again, these should be aggregations of precomputed trade- or position-level PnL and cost data, using standardized bucket definitions that are themselves versioned.

Parameterized Reports with Fixed Structure

So far we have sketched what a good report looks like for a single run. In practice, you will want to generate many such reports, varying along several dimensions:

- strategy or model name;
- parameter set (for example, mean-reversion window, leverage cap);
- date range (full history versus specific sub-period);
- scenario (for example, stress dataset, alternative execution cost model).

The challenge is to support this flexibility without sacrificing comparability. The solution is to treat reports as *templates* with parameters, not as ad hoc pages assembled differently for each run.

Separating Template Structure from Data Binding

Conceptually, a report is defined by two separate artifacts:

- a **template**, which specifies:
  - which charts and tables appear, in what layout and order;
  - which metrics or time series each visual consumes (for example, "equity curve from performance.equity");
  - which captions, labels, and glossary references to show.

- a **parameter set**, which specifies:
  - the run identifier;
  - the date range or sub-sampling options;
  - any scenario tags (for example, stress scenario name).

The report generator binds the template to the parameterized data, using the metric engine and performance object as sources. This architectural separation has important consequences:

- Template changes can be governed and versioned independently of data changes.
- The same template can be applied across many runs, making cross-run comparison straightforward.
- It becomes easier to implement regression testing for the reporting layer, since templates are stable and can be fed known inputs.

Keeping Structure Fixed While Content Varies

Even as the user changes strategy, parameter set, or date window, the overall structure of the report should remain fixed. That means:

- The "Risk" section always appears in the same place and always contains volatility, Sharpe, drawdowns, and tail risk metrics, even if some values are "not available" for a particular run.
- The "Attribution" section always has the same sub-panels (for example, allocation/selection, factor attribution, bucket-level), with clear labels indicating where attribution is not applicable.
- If a given report omits a chart because it truly does not apply (for example, no benchmark exists), a placeholder with an explanation should occupy that space.

From a human perspective, this is like reading different issues of the same magazine: the topics change, but the layout and section structure are familiar, making navigation easy.

Scenario and Slice Controls

Reports should explicitly show which slice of data they represent. For example:

- "Full backtest: January 2015 to December 2024."
- "Stress window: March 2020 to June 2020 (COVID shock)."
- "Alternative execution model: high-cost scenario."

Where possible, the report can include a small "control panel" section summarizing:

- date range,
- included instruments or markets,
- scenario name or tag,
- any non-default metric configuration options.

Even if these parameters are chosen programmatically (for example, by a batch job), surfacing them in the report prevents misinterpretation: reviewers know exactly what they are looking at.

Report Generation and Artifact Formats

Although concrete technologies will vary across organizations, there are a few technology-agnostic best practices for generating and storing reports.

Binding Metrics to Templates

The report generator should consume two inputs:

- the canonical performance object (and linked trade/exposure data);
- a metric configuration describing which precomputed metrics to request from the metric engine.

The generator then:

- calls the metric engine to obtain a structured metric object for the chosen run and slice;
- passes that metric object into the template renderer (for example, a LaTeX, HTML, or notebook-based templating system);
- produces a human-readable artifact and, ideally, a machine-readable companion.

The key point is that the template should never compute metrics on its own. It should only format and present the metric engine's outputs. This avoids subtle discrepancies when the same formula is re-implemented in multiple places.

Embedding Provenance Metadata

Every generated report should embed provenance information, both visibly (for readers) and invisibly (for machines). This includes:

- run identifier and date of generation;
- simulation engine and metric engine versions;
- performance object version or schema identifier;
- data snapshot version;
- template identifier and version;
- metric configuration/version identifier.

In human-readable formats like PDF, this can appear on an "About this report" page or in a header/footer. In machine-readable formats like JSON, these fields should live at the top level under a clearly named section such as "provenance."

Export Formats: PDF, HTML, JSON, and Beyond

Different audiences need different report formats:

- **PDF** is well-suited for static distribution to committees, clients, or regulators. It is easy to archive and reproduce, and layout is consistent across viewers.

- **HTML** enables interactive dashboards with tooltips, zooming, and basic controls (for example, switching between sub-periods). It is useful for exploratory analysis by researchers and risk managers.

- **Machine-readable formats** such as JSON or Parquet capture the same metrics and metadata in a form that can be ingested by other systems, such as centralized risk dashboards or automated monitoring tools.

Ideally, all these formats should be generated from the same template and metric objects, not from separate pipelines. That is, the HTML and PDF views are two renderings of a common logical report, not two separate artifacts computed independently.

Report Lifecycles and Cataloging

Even the best-designed report is of limited use if it cannot be found when needed. In a production environment, you will generate large numbers of reports over time: for research experiments, strategy approvals, periodic reviews, incidents, and audits. Managing this flow requires some structure.

Tagging and Indexing

Each report should be tagged with metadata that makes it easy to search and filter later. Common tags include:

- strategy or model name;

- run identifier(s) and date range;

- report type (for example, research experiment, approval pack, periodic review, incident post-mortem);

- approval stage (for example, draft, under review, approved, rejected);

- keywords for notable events (for example, "capacity breach", "drawdown over 20%").

A central index—implemented in a database, document store, or even a version-controlled repository—should expose this metadata and link to the underlying artifacts. Think of it as a catalog of the "story of the strategy" over time.

Summary Dashboards and Comparison Views

Beyond individual reports, it is often useful to have higher-level dashboards that:

- summarize recent backtests across all strategies or within a group;
- highlight runs that triggered governance thresholds (for example, Sharpe below a floor, drawdown above a ceiling);
- allow side-by-side comparison of two or more runs (for example, old versus new parameterization).

These summary dashboards can be built from the same machine-readable metric artifacts that power individual reports. For example, a risk manager might use a comparison view to see how a new execution model affects turnover, costs, and capacity across a family of strategies, using exactly the same definitions and templates as the underlying backtest reports.

Retention and Access Controls

Finally, reporting must align with organizational policies on data retention and access:

- **Retention:** Decide how long different types of reports should be kept (for example, indefinitely for regulatory filings, several years for approval packs, shorter for routine exploratory research), and implement automatic retention policies where possible.
- **Access control:** Restrict access to sensitive reports, especially those that expose proprietary models, parameter ranges, or client-specific information. The reporting catalog should integrate with your authentication and authorization systems so that only authorized users can view or download particular artifacts.

These operational concerns might seem far from visualization design, but they are part of making reporting genuinely useful and safe at scale.

From Metrics to Decisions

Visualization and reporting are the bridge between a technically sound backtest engine and an organization's decision-making processes. A canonical performance object and deterministic metric engine ensure that the numbers are coherent; well-designed dashboards and templated reports ensure that those numbers can be understood, compared, and acted upon.

In the next sections we will connect this reporting layer to logging, audit, and provenance. There we will see how the same discipline—schema-driven design, explicit versioning, and reproducible artifacts—extends from metrics and visuals to the entire execution history of each run, enabling forensic analysis and robust governance.

7.3 Logging, Audit & Run Provenance

Up to this point, we have treated a backtest largely as a black box: given code, data, and configuration, it produces a performance object and a set of metrics and reports. In research mode this can feel sufficient; if the equity curve looks plausible and the diagnostics are reasonable, we move on.

In a governed environment, that is not enough. Risk committees, model validation teams, and sometimes regulators will ask a more demanding question:

> Exactly what did this engine do, with which code and which data, to produce these results?

To answer that question months or years later, you need more than a copy of the final report. You need a *traceable execution record*—a structured way of capturing what happened during a run and how that run relates to code, configuration, and data. This is what we mean by *logging, audit, and run provenance.*

This section develops that idea step by step. We start by distinguishing human-oriented logs from machine-parseable events. We then define a provenance model that ties each run to specific versions of code, configuration, and data. Next we discuss logging design in practice—log levels, schemas, correlation identifiers—and how these feed incident reconstruction. Along the way we introduce a graphical view of provenance that helps both humans and tools navigate this information.

Why Provenance Matters in Backtesting

It helps to begin with two everyday scenarios.

Scenario 1: A suspiciously good backtest.

A strategy shows excellent performance in a backtest run from 2015 to 2024, but when the same code is re-run six months later, results differ noticeably. Perhaps a data vendor revised historical prices, or an execution-cost model changed. Without a clear record of exactly which data and model versions were used originally, you will struggle to explain the discrepancy.

Scenario 2: An incident in live or paper trading.

A live or paper-traded strategy hits an unexpected drawdown. To understand whether the behavior was foreseeable, you want to replay the historical backtest that justified deployment, step through its decisions, and compare the circumstances. Without a detailed execution trace and unambiguous links to the inputs, this replay is guesswork.

Both cases illustrate the same underlying need: you must be able to *reconstruct* what the engine did, not only on a high level, but often at the granularity of individual orders, fills, and risk checks. Provenance provides the scaffolding for that reconstruction.

Human Logs vs Structured Events

Most systems already produce logs of some kind. However, not all logs are equally useful for audit and analysis. It is helpful to distinguish between two broad types:

- **Human-oriented logs:** Free-form text written primarily for developers or operators ("Started backtest run 1234", "WARNING: position limit exceeded for AAPL"). These are easy to produce and useful for quick troubleshooting, but hard for machines to parse reliably.

- **Structured events:** Records with a defined schema—fields such as timestamp, event type, severity, instrument, quantity, order identifier, and so on. These may still be serialized as text, but their structure is rigid and machine-readable.

Both have their place.

Human-oriented logs are good for providing narrative context and ad-hoc diagnostic messages. They function like a running commentary. Structured events, by contrast, are the backbone of any serious provenance system. They support queries such as:

> Show me all order generation events for strategy X between 10:00 and 10:05 on the simulated timeline, along with the risk checks applied and whether they passed or failed.

To enable this, you will want to design your backtest engine around an *event-sourcing mindset.* Rather than thinking of logs as an afterthought, treat important decisions and state changes as events that are first-class citizens:

- order submitted;
- order rejected or amended;
- risk check evaluated (pass/fail and reason);
- position opened, increased, reduced, or closed;
- parameter or regime change triggered;
- simulation clock advanced, and so on.

Each such event is captured with a schema and timestamped against the simulation's notion of time (and if needed, also wall-clock time).

Run Provenance: Linking Code, Config, and Data

While logs and events tell you *what* happened inside a run, provenance connects that run to its environment: which code, configuration, and data snapshots were in effect. Conceptually, you can think of provenance as a graph of artifacts and relationships.

For a given backtest run, the key artifact types are:

- **Run record:** A top-level object that identifies the run (for example, run ID), its type (research, regression test, approval pack), start and end timestamps, and high-level status (success, failed, aborted).
- **Code version:** References to the exact versions of code used, typically in the form of version control system commit hashes (for example, Git SHA) for the simulation engine, strategy logic, and the metric/reporting engines if they are separate.
- **Configuration:** The full configuration used for the run:

- strategy parameters (lookback windows, thresholds, leverage caps);
- engine parameters (execution model choice, latency assumptions);
- reporting and metric configurations (frequency, risk-free rate sources).

- **Data snapshots:** Identifiers for the precise input data set:

- market data snapshot (prices, trades, quotes) with effective dates;
- reference data (symbol master, sector classifications, corporate actions);
- risk model data (factor definitions, loadings, factor returns).

- **Log and event streams:** Pointers to where detailed logs and structured events are stored for this run.

Each of these artifacts should itself be versioned or content-addressed. For example, a configuration file can be hashed so that you can later verify that it has not been modified. A data snapshot can be identified by a human-friendly label ("equities_daily_v2024-01") and a content hash that uniquely represents its contents.

The run record then ties everything together:

- Run 1234 used simulation_engine commit abc123, strategy commit def456.
- It loaded data snapshot equities_daily_v2024-01 and risk model snapshot riskmodel_v5_2023Q4.
- It read configuration file config_meanrev_v2.3.yaml with content hash ....
- Its structured events are stored in log stream run-1234-events, and its human-oriented logs are in run-1234-log.

With this information, you can later reconstruct not only what the engine did, but also with what environment. This is essential for both reproducibility (re-running a backtest exactly) and auditability (demonstrating that results could not have been produced with a different code or data version).

A Graph View of Provenance

A useful mental (and practical) model for provenance is a graph: nodes represent artifacts (runs, code versions, data snapshots, configurations, logs), and edges represent relationships ("uses", "generated by", "configured by").

The following diagram sketches such a graph for a single backtest run.

In a real system, this graph would not be hand-drawn; it would be represented in a database or knowledge store, and tools would query and visualize it. The important idea is structural: every result you see in a report is, in principle, traceable along edges of this graph back to the exact inputs and decisions that produced it.

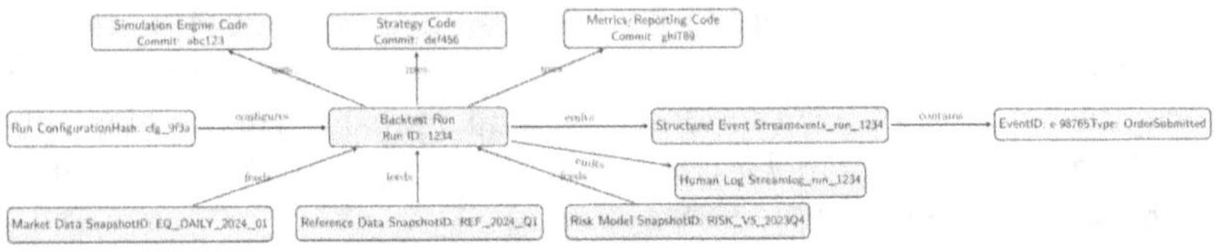

Figure 7.2: End-to-end provenance graph: a backtest run node connected to code commits, configuration, data snapshots, and log streams containing structured events.

Designing Structured Events and Log Schemas

With the provenance framework in mind, we can return to the design of logs and structured events inside the engine.

Event Minimalism vs Log Explosion

There is a natural tension between capturing everything and keeping logs manageable. Logging every tiny detail (for example, every nanosecond of simulated time) can quickly generate unmanageable volumes. Logging too sparsely, on the other hand, leaves gaps that frustrate later analysis.

A pragmatic approach is to log *every significant decision and state change* in structured form, but avoid recording raw data that can be reconstructed from other sources. Examples of events that nearly always deserve structured logging include:

- Before and after a risk check is evaluated, including:

- which check (for example, "max gross leverage 3x"),
- what inputs were used (for example, current exposures),
- whether it passed or failed,
- if it failed, what action was taken.

- When an order is generated, amended, or cancelled, including:

- order identifier, instrument, side, size, and price;
- the decision logic or signal that triggered it;
- any associated correlation identifiers.

- When a position changes materially (for example, crosses zero, doubles, or is force-closed).
- When configuration changes dynamically during a run (for example, a volatility regime change causes leverage to be reduced).
- When serious warnings or errors occur, especially those that affect simulation fidelity (for example, missing data, failed model calls).

Each event type should have a schema that is stable over time, or at least versioned. For example, an "OrderSubmitted" event might include fields like:

- event ID, timestamp (simulation and wall-clock);
- run ID, strategy ID;
- correlation ID (to tie it to upstream signals or downstream fills);
- instrument identifier, side, quantity, limit/market flag;
- originating component (for example, "meanreversion_signal");
- severity level (informational, warning, error).

The exact fields will vary by organization, but the key properties are:

- they are machine-parseable;
- they can be indexed and queried efficiently;
- they carry enough context to reconstruct reasoning in post-mortems.

Correlation Identifiers: Threading Causality

One of the most powerful tools for audit is the *correlation ID*. This is an identifier that threads through a chain of events that belong to the same logical unit of work.

For example:

1. A signal calculation event produces a recommendation to buy 1000 shares of instrument X with correlation ID `c-001`.
2. An order submission event logs the resulting order, also tagged with `c-001`.
3. When the order is filled (possibly in multiple parts), fill events carry the same correlation ID.
4. Subsequent position update and PnL attribution events that refer to this action also carry `c-001`.

Later, when investigating an unusual trade, you can search by the correlation ID and see the full story: which signal triggered it, what risk checks it passed, how it was executed, and how it contributed to PnL.

Correlation IDs can also be used at higher levels—for example, to tie together all events belonging to a given *simulation bar* or *batch* of market data.

Log Storage, Rotation, and Retention

Structured events and logs must be stored somewhere. Common choices include:

- append-only files (for example, one per run or per day);
- centralized logging services or databases optimized for time-series and search;
- object stores with indexing metadata maintained separately.

Whatever the technology, you need clear policies for:

- **Rotation:** How large a log or event file is allowed to grow before a new one is started; how logs are named and organized.

- **Retention:** How long detailed logs are kept for different types of runs (for example, longer for production-related or approval-related runs, shorter for exploratory research).
- **Privacy and sensitivity:** How logs that contain reference data, client identifiers, or proprietary signals are protected; who can access them and under what circumstances.

Good provenance is not only about recording information, but also about managing it responsibly.

From Provenance to Incident Reconstruction

Once you have structured events, run records, and a provenance graph, you can support powerful workflows for incident reconstruction and model review.

Reproducing a Historical Run

Suppose a strategy experienced an incident in 2023 and you want to know whether the backtest run that justified its deployment would have revealed similar behavior.

A robust provenance system allows you to:

1. Retrieve the run record for the original approval backtest (for example, run 1234).
2. Pull the referenced code versions, configuration, and data snapshots.
3. Re-run the backtest in a controlled environment, confirming that you reproduce the original results within expected tolerances.
4. If results differ, use the provenance graph to identify any differences (for example, data vendor corrections, risk model version upgrades).

This process turns what would otherwise be a forensic guessing game into a reproducible scientific exercise.

Explaining Why a Rule Tripped

Imagine a governance rule that caps gross leverage at 3 times equity. In a particular run, this limit is breached and triggers an automated de-risking action.

Using structured events and provenance, you can answer:

- At what simulated times did the rule evaluate as "near limit" and "breach"?
- What exposures and portfolio composition led to those evaluations?
- Which orders or signals pushed the portfolio over the line?
- How did the de-risking orders change positions, and what PnL impact did this have?

The events capture rule evaluations, their input data (for example, exposures from the performance object at that time), and the resulting decisions. The run record ensures that you know which rule configuration and code version were in force.

Demonstrating Integrity to External Stakeholders

Provenance is also a communication tool. When presenting models to external stakeholders, you can:

- show that every reported backtest can be traced to specific, immutable data and code versions;
- demonstrate that key governance rules were active and logged throughout the run;
- prove that reported metrics and charts came from a controlled, versioned metric engine rather than ad hoc analysis.

This builds trust and can significantly smooth interactions with risk committees, clients, and regulators.

Aligning Research and Production Provenance

Finally, provenance is most valuable when it spans the entire lifecycle of a strategy, from early research to live trading. While this chapter focuses on backtests, the same principles should, as far as possible, carry over to paper and live environments:

- Use similar run records for live trading sessions, capturing code versions, configuration, and data feeds.
- Log structured events for orders, fills, and risk checks in a way that is consistent with backtest events, enabling apples-to-apples comparisons.
- Reuse the same correlation ID patterns so that signals can be traced from research through deployment.

When research and production share a provenance model, you can ask powerful questions, such as:

> How often did the live system diverge from the behavior observed in the backtest under similar market conditions, and why?

Answering this requires that the execution record is traceable and comparable across contexts.

Logging, audit, and run provenance turn a backtest engine from a black box into a transparent, inspectable system. By:

- distinguishing human-oriented logs from structured events,
- designing a provenance model that connects runs to code, configuration, and data,
- threading correlation identifiers through event streams, and
- managing log storage and retention carefully,

you create an execution record that can support rigorous analysis, incident reconstruction, and credible communication with stakeholders.

In the next section we will build directly on this foundation, showing how governance and compliance controls can be expressed as rules that operate on the same metrics and events, and how their status is surfaced in dashboards and reports. Together, these pieces form a coherent framework for designing backtest engines that are not only powerful and flexible, but also accountable.

7.4 Governance & Compliance Controls

The previous sections equipped us with three essential capabilities:

1. a canonical performance object and metric engine that produce consistent diagnostics;
2. standardized visualization and templated reports that present those diagnostics clearly;
3. detailed logging and provenance that record exactly what each run did and with which inputs.

We now put these ingredients to work in service of governance and compliance.

From the perspective of a risk committee or regulator, the key questions are no longer just "How did the strategy perform?" or "Can you reproduce this result?" They also include:

- Did the strategy respect our risk limits during the backtest?
- Were prohibited instruments, markets, or data sources avoided?
- Are approvals and sign-offs for this strategy properly documented?
- If a rule was breached, can we see when, why, and what the system did about it?

To answer these questions convincingly, controls cannot be bolted on as an afterthought. They must be embedded directly into the reporting and monitoring layer, tied to the same standardized metrics and provenance structures that underpin the rest of the system. This section lays out how to do that.

Control Objectives for Quant Simulation

Before designing controls, you need a clear list of what you are trying to control. Typical objectives in a quant simulation setting include:

- **Risk limits:** Ensuring simulated portfolios do not exceed bounds on leverage, concentration, liquidity usage, or other risk metrics that would be unacceptable in live trading.
- **Instrument and market restrictions:** Preventing strategies from trading prohibited instruments (for example, certain derivatives, restricted securities) or markets (for example, jurisdictions where the firm is not authorized).
- **Data usage policies:** Enforcing rules about which datasets may be used, and in what way (for example, no use of restricted client data in research; careful handling of alternative data that may contain personal information).
- **Separation of environments:** Maintaining clear boundaries between research, paper trading, and production, including who can run what, on which data, with which parameters.
- **Approval and change control:** Ensuring that strategies, parameters, and model changes go through defined approval workflows before being used in higher-stakes contexts (for example, client portfolios or firm capital).

These objectives must be translated into machine-checkable rules that operate on the kinds of objects we already have: performance metrics, exposures, event logs, and provenance records. Once encoded, the rules should surface into dashboards and reports in a way that is:

- **visible** (violations and near-misses are easy to see),

- **explainable** (reviewers can understand why a rule was tripped),
- **enforceable** (the system can take or demand action when a violation occurs).

From Policies to Machine-Checkable Rules

Organizational policies are often written in natural language: "gross leverage must not exceed three times equity," or "no single issuer exposure over 10% of NAV." The first technical step is to map each policy to:

1. a specific metric or measurable quantity;
2. a threshold or boundary;
3. a scope in time and space (when and where it applies);
4. an associated action or workflow when the boundary is approached or crossed.

Examples of Metric-Based Rules

Using the standardized performance object and attribution outputs, you can define rules such as:

- **Leverage limit:** At any time, gross exposure divided by equity must not exceed a specified multiple. This uses the same exposure and equity fields that feed risk metrics.
- **Concentration limit:** For each issuer or sector, the share of total portfolio value must remain below a specified percentage. This uses grouped position or exposure data.
- **Liquidity and capacity constraints:** The simulated position in each instrument must not exceed a certain fraction of average daily volume; daily traded volume must stay below a participation cap. These use the same volume and turnover diagnostics used for implementability analysis.

- **Risk factor limits:** Factor exposures (for example, to market, value, or momentum) must remain within pre-agreed bands; sudden jumps trigger alerts.

Note that each rule can be expressed entirely in terms of the performance object, trade data, or risk model outputs already available to the metric engine. There is no need to build a parallel measurement system.

Pre-Trade, In-Run, and Post-Trade Checks

Controls operate at different stages of the simulation:

- **Pre-trade constraints:** Before a simulated order is accepted, the engine evaluates whether executing it would violate a rule. If so, the order may be scaled back, rejected, or queued for review.
- **In-run monitoring:** During the run, the engine periodically checks risk metrics (for example, once per simulation bar or per day) to detect emerging issues—approaching a leverage cap, a concentration building up, or liquidity usage creeping higher.
- **Post-trade and end-of-run checks:** After the run completes, a summary evaluation confirms whether any rules were breached at any point, and how often. This feeds directly into the governance view of the backtest.

Embedding these checks into the engine means they are captured in the same structured event logs we discussed earlier. Every time a rule is evaluated, an event records the inputs, the result, and any action taken.

Surfacing Controls in Dashboards and Reports

Controls are only useful if decision-makers can see and interpret their status. A common failure mode is to implement checks that merely set internal flags or populate obscure log lines, leaving reviewers to infer that "no news is good news." A more robust approach is to treat control status as a first-class element of the reporting layer.

Limit Utilization Visuals

For each key limit, the report should display:

- the limit value (for example, max gross leverage 3.0);
- the range of observed values over the run (min, max, typical);
- a visualization of how close the strategy came to the limit over time.

A practical representation is a bar or gauge for each limit, showing maximum utilization as a percentage of the allowed value, with color-coding:

- green for comfortable distance (for example, below 70%);
- amber for approaching thresholds (for example, 70–90%);
- red for violations (above 100%).

Alongside, a simple time series chart can show when the limit was most stressed. This lets a reviewer answer quickly: "Does this strategy routinely live near its risk limits, or only occasionally—and under what conditions?"

Rule Violation Timelines

When rules are breached or strongly approached, the report should show:

- a timeline marking each breach or near-breach;
- the type of rule involved (for example, leverage, concentration, liquidity);
- whether the system took an automatic action (for example, scaling down positions) or simply logged the event.

This can be implemented as a simple event strip over the equity or drawdown chart: small markers indicating limit events at the corresponding times. Clicking or drilling down (in an interactive setting) or turning to an appendix (in a static report) reveals details sourced from the structured event logs:

- the exact metric value,
- the threshold,
- the instruments or positions driving the breach,
- the de-risking or remedial actions taken.

This direct link from rules to visuals makes violations both visible and explainable.

Exception Summaries for Committees

Governance committees rarely have time to read every chart in detail. They need concise summaries of what went wrong, what was done about it, and whether it is acceptable.

The reporting layer can generate an "exceptions page" that lists, for the backtest period:

- all rule violations, grouped by rule type and severity;
- the number of occurrences and total time spent in breach;
- the aggregate PnL impact of any automatic de-risking actions;
- flags for potential false positives (for example, minor limit oversteps due to rounding or stale data).

Each exception entry should be linked (logically and, in interactive settings, via hyperlinks) back to the underlying events and to the full rule definition. This maintains traceability while giving committees a high-level narrative: "We breached the liquidity participation cap twice during the March 2020 stress window; both times the engine scaled down orders, and the total foregone PnL was X."

Operational Controls: Kill Switches and Access Management

Risk and policy rules are about *what* the strategy is allowed to do. Operational controls are about *who* can do what, and how the system responds when something looks wrong.

Kill-Switch Design for Simulations and Live Trading

A *kill switch* is a mechanism that can halt a run—or an entire class of runs—when anomalies are detected. In a simulation environment, kill switches are particularly valuable when:

- a bug causes runaway trading behavior that would be unacceptable in live markets;
- a new configuration leads to extreme leverage or concentration;
- an upstream data or model feed is clearly corrupt.

Design principles include:

- **Clear triggers:** Tied to rule evaluations (for example, leverage above twice the allowed maximum) or to health checks (for example, data completeness failures).
- **Deterministic behavior:** On trigger, the system either gracefully stops the simulation, or transitions to a safe mode (for example, no new positions, only closing trades).
- **Recorded decisions:** The activation of a kill switch is itself logged as a high-severity event, with reasons and context, and surfaced in reports.

In live trading, kill switches must integrate with order management and actual trading systems, but the conceptual architecture can mirror the simulation environment. Sharing rule definitions and monitoring logic across both contexts strengthens governance.

Role-Based Access Control (RBAC)

Not everyone should have the same power to run or modify backtests. Role-based access control is the standard approach:

- **Researchers** may be allowed to run exploratory backtests with fewer constraints, but not to produce official approval packs or alter governance rules.
- **Portfolio managers** may request approval runs and see sensitive reports, but not change core engine code or risk limit definitions.
- **Risk and compliance staff** may approve or reject strategy proposals and modify certain risk parameters, but not alter strategy code.
- **Administrators** manage the system itself, including user permissions.

Access control should be enforced at several layers:

- who can launch which type of run (for example, approval versus exploratory);
- who can access particular datasets (for example, restricted alternative data);
- who can view or download certain reports (for example, client-specific material).

Crucially, access decisions and changes to permissions should be logged and linked to provenance, so that later reviews can answer: "Who was allowed to do what at the time this backtest was produced?"

Approval Workflows and Lifecycle Governance

Controls do not exist in a vacuum. Strategies and models move through a lifecycle: idea, research, pre-approval, pilot, production, and retirement. Governance controls should align with these stages and be visible in reporting.

Approval States and Promotion Paths

Each strategy (and, in many organizations, each configuration variant) should have an approval state, such as:

- "Research only";
- "Submitted for review";
- "Approved for paper trading";
- "Approved for limited capital";
- "Fully approved";
- "Suspended" or "Retired."

The reporting system should:

- display the current approval state in every report;
- record which backtest runs formed the basis for each promotion decision;
- ensure that promotion steps themselves require sign-offs (for example, risk, portfolio management, compliance) that are recorded and auditable.

Promotion rules can also be made partially machine-checkable. For example, a strategy cannot move from "research only" to "submitted for review" unless certain minimum backtesting conditions are met (for example, minimum history length, no unresolved rule violations).

Embedding Governance Metadata in Reports

A governance-aware report does more than show performance and risk; it also signals its own status within the approval process. Typical metadata elements include:

- the intended use of the report (for example, initial review, periodic review, incident investigation);

- the approval state of the strategy at the time of generation;
- pending actions or decisions requested from reviewers (for example, "Risk sign-off required to proceed to paper trading");
- references to prior reports and decisions (for context).

This turns each report into a chapter in the strategy's documented history, not a standalone artifact.

Aligning Simulation Governance with Production Controls

Finally, a key goal of embedding controls into the reporting and monitoring layer is to minimize the gap between "what we test" and "how we trade." If a backtest is allowed to operate under looser or different rules than the live system, it becomes harder to defend the relevance of backtest results.

To align simulation governance with production:

- Use the same or closely related risk metrics and limit definitions in both environments (for example, same leverage and concentration metrics).
- Share rule engines or at least rule specifications, so that a limit check has the same semantics in simulation and in live trading.
- Include in backtest reports a summary of the live controls that would apply, and highlight any mismatches (for example, "Backtest used a max leverage of 4x, but production policy allows only 3x").
- After deployment, periodically compare live rule utilization and violations with those observed in backtests, to validate that behavior is consistent.

When these pieces are in place, a statement like "This strategy passed governance" has real substance: it means that, under production-like controls and policies, the strategy has been evaluated, exceptions have been documented and accepted, and the entire chain from code to results is traceable.

Closing Remarks

Governance and compliance controls are sometimes perceived as constraints that slow down research. In a well-designed backtest ecosystem, the opposite is often true. By embedding policy, risk, and access controls into the same reporting and monitoring machinery that researchers already rely on, you gain:

- faster, more focused reviews (because violations and near-misses are clearly surfaced);
- fewer surprises at the approval stage (because strategies are evaluated under realistic constraints from the start);
- stronger external credibility (because you can demonstrate not only results, but also the discipline with which they were obtained).

The key is integration: controls should not be a separate world, but a natural extension of the performance metrics, visualizations, and provenance structures that this chapter has developed. Together, they turn a backtest engine into a platform for reproducible, accountable quantitative research and trading.

www.ingramcontent.com/pod-product-compliance
Lightning Source LLC
LaVergne TN
LVHW052019200926
848481LV00005B/1526

9798896652250